Creating New Knowledge in Management

Creating New Knowledge in Management

Appropriating the Field's Lost Foundations

Ellen S. O'Connor

STANFORD BUSINESS BOOKS
An Imprint of Stanford University Press
Stanford, California

Stanford University Press
Stanford, California
©2012 by the Board of Trustees of the Leland Stanford Junior University.
All rights reserved.

Special discounts for bulk quantities of Stanford Business Books are available to corporations, professional associations, and other organizations. For details and discount information, contact the special sales department of Stanford University Press. Tel: (650) 736-1782, Fax: (650) 736-1784
Printed in the United States of America on acid-free, archival-quality paper
Library of Congress Cataloging-in-Publication Data
O'Connor, Ellen S., author.
Creating new knowledge in management : appropriating the field's lost foundations / Ellen S. O'Connor.
pages cm
Includes bibliographical references and index.
ISBN 978-0-8047-7075-0 (cloth : alk. paper)
1. Management—Study and teaching—United States. 2. Business schools—United States. I. Title.
HD30.42.U5O25 2011
650.071—dc22
2011015038
Typeset by Bruce Lundquist in 10/12 Sabon

To Richard

Can a mind that irresponsibly contemplates the situation be sufficiently caught up into it to move with it?

Mary Parker Follett, 1924

Contents

Contents

Tables

Preface

This book is based on my forty years in higher education, and particularly my thirty years in higher business education, where I worked on integrating business and the humanities. For a long time, I conceived of my work as interdisciplinary. After more research, I realized that, in fact, the two fields had once been linked and that the rupture between them was only a few generations old. Understanding this rupture became my central focus. I took a genealogical approach (Part I), which led to the view presented in this book: for centuries, humankind has pursued knowledge for governance, including self-governance, and institutions that preserve, create, and disseminate this knowledge, for individual *and* collective flourishing. However, also for centuries, this idea was interwoven with ideas about and institutions associated with class, exclusivity, and continuity.

This combination fell apart in the twentieth century. Institutions organized under a new logic that valued the new per se and that linked new knowledge to new wealth and status. Reliable paths developed for individuals and organizations to exploit this synergy for themselves. In particular, science institutionalized in the research university as "basic science" in the disciplines and "applied science" in the professional schools. Together, they created far more value than either could do alone. The academy, the professions, and industry thus developed and thrived as a whole. The United States became a leader in all three domains and in the overarching idea of opportunity—what Mary Parker Follett called "dynamic society" and the chance for individuals to grow it and grow themselves in it. Both she and Chester I. Barnard envisioned a new knowledge field that would understand and master this mutually creative process.

At the same time, then, the possibility of a science of and for society emerged. But this science was not easy to distinguish from the old knowledge for governance. Also, the logic of separation and specialization, rather than integration, prevailed in science and industry because it generated knowledge, wealth, and status immediately. For these reasons, the idea of integrating science with the old knowledge for governance to form a science of and for society was not pursued.

My experience, research, and inquiry over many years have convinced me that today the subject of management and the graduate school of business come closest to realizing this idea. However, as explained in Part I, there is still no discipline of management; more accurately, the discipline of management, because of its subjective nature, grew in the individual realm; and the business school, following professional science, grew institutionally and separated its formal knowledge from the individual's experiential knowledge. For Follett and Barnard, this move denied the creative, and therefore subjective, work of science. Moreover, it could not begin to comprehend the most elementary processes of human value(s) creation at the heart of cooperative endeavor, not just in science but in all fields.

For the opportunity to reintroduce the idea of knowledge for governance and interpret it today, I am grateful beyond words. It has been and continues to be the chance of a lifetime.

Margo Beth Crouppen of Stanford University Press, in contracting to publish this book, showed that she believed me capable of articulating this idea. She saw its expression through the most awkward stages, which certainly tested my own confidence and perhaps hers as well. Armand Hatchuel was my most vital interlocutor. Our many discussions over three years helped me understand the relationship between the history of the business school and the institution's inability to integrate the ideas of Mary Parker Follett and Chester Barnard. When the first critiques of the manuscript came in, he helped me approach them constructively with no loss of morale or energy. With his claims that seemed too bold—that management lacked a foundation, that Follett was a creative genius—he kept pushing my vision further even as I stayed close to the facts, which always proved his argument in the end. If the management field ever advances substantively, Armand will have had much to do with that progress, whether the historical record shows it or not.

By inviting me to give seminars at his institution, the Center of Management Science, MINES ParisTech, and at the International Federation of Scholarly Associations of Management (IFSAM), Armand also provided valuable opportunities to discuss my arguments and findings with many interested scholars, particularly his close colleagues Pierre Guillet de Monthoux, Romain Laufer, Pascal Le Masson, Blanche Segrestin, and Benoît Weil. Others who provided such occasions were Nicolas Berland, Jean-François Chanlat, and Anne Pezet of the University of Paris

Dauphine; and Chris Steyaert of the University of St. Gallen. The Haniel Foundation supported my seminar at the University of St. Gallen.

Many individuals critiqued the research at every stage. Charlotte Fillol commented on the first formal presentation of what became Part I. André Delbecq, Paul Godfrey, Joe Mahoney, Joel Podolny, André Spicer, and Ken Starkey offered helpful comments on drafts, including the original proposal, the first draft, and two revisions. I have incorporated their suggestions to the best of my ability. Even more valuable than the comments was their encouragement, which gave me the wherewithal to complete the task despite adversities.

My formal education and temporary lectureships have always left me feeling peripheral to the management academy. Without James G. March's many invitations to keep joining and rejoining the circle, this book would not have been written because I would have left the field. Whether it was to present a paper, contribute to a book, or visit with a distinguished colleague, Jim welcomed me in, time and time again, and moved others to do likewise through his example and his recommendations. If integration is the heart of management, then Jim has built the field through his practice as well as his theory—or as Chester Barnard would say, nonlogically as well as logically—more than anyone I know. I am also grateful to Jim for introducing me to Arjay Miller, the dean of Stanford Graduate School of Business from 1969 to 1979, who led the school to the top rank it holds today. My conversation with Arjay shed important light on how the business school integrated responsibility, adulthood, and higher education.

Over the years, many other colleagues extended invitations that brought me into and kept me in the fold. In particular, I thank Magnus Aronsson, Dominique Besson, Barbara Czarniawska, Jane Dutton, Jeffrey Ford, Bill Gartner, Slimane Haddadj, Daniel Hjorth, Sharon Livesey, Ian Mitroff, Mette Monsted, Milorad Novicevic, Woody Powell, Pushkala and Anshu Prasad, Zur Shapira, Chris Steyaert, Lucy Suchman, Valérie-Inès de la Ville, Karl Weick, and Mayer Zald.

This book has benefited greatly from the contributions of practitioners. Max Périé, my co-author on Chapter 8, worked steadfastly and patiently with me for three years. He brought executive experience and more important, the desire to codify this experience in terms meaningful to researchers as well as to his peers. Max cares about good scholarship, and his example gave me faith in the emerging institution of the executive-scholar and the possibilities for its development. Max's colleague Corinne Chamarande candidly shared her experience of working with Max. She provided a perspective that usually stays buried in the organizational hierarchy. This perspective lends rare insight into the executive's relationship with the larger whole of which he is a part, albeit a formative one. I am especially grateful to Corinne and Max for their willingness to put their names on this research. This gesture indicates the genuine possibilities for accessing managerial knowledge, a necessarily personal knowledge as shown in Parts II and III.

I am deeply grateful to my students, particularly the group that provided the occasion to write Chapter 9, and most particularly to Olivier Hug, who gave permission to include his work in this book. I also thank the students in my course "Human Resource Management and the Management of Human Beings" in the Executive MBA program at the University of Paris Dauphine. Showing special appreciation for the teachings of Barnard, they named their graduating class in his honor. This proved his contemporary worth and validated this study unreservedly.

The book follows on crucial foundational work done by others—particularly Joan Tonn's biography of Follett, which provides a rigorously documented and complete picture of Follett the theorist, scientist, and institution-builder; and the late William Wolf's research on Barnard. Bill passed away in June of 2009, one month before Stanford University Press and I signed the contract for this book. More than any other scholar, Bill appreciated Barnard's contribution and dedicated his professional life to keeping it at center stage. He gave the field the only extensive interview that it has of Barnard, obtained only months before his death in 1961. Recognizing the difficulty of Barnard's original text, Bill issued numerous "translations" that rendered Barnard's prose more accessible without compromising its meaning. He oversaw the publication of many important rare texts that help give a complete picture of Barnard the scientist and Barnard the executive. In our last conversation, Bill emphasized that my book must capture "Barnard the man." I promised him I would do my best. If I have met that goal, it is due to Bill's generosity in sharing his scholarly knowledge and his personal experience of Barnard the man.

Research and administrative personnel at the libraries of the City of Boston (Rare Books and Manuscripts Department, especially Roberta Zonghi), Carnegie Mellon University, Harvard University, Stanford University, the University of Chicago, and the University of Pennsylvania (especially Nancy R. Miller), provided invaluable assistance. I am especially grateful to Alice Schreyer and her staff at the University of Chicago Library and to Mary Munill of the Stanford University Libraries. In the former case, I gathered that my large scope and limited timeframe tested the system's limits. Despite that, every demand was met punctually and perfectly. As for Mary, she proved repeatedly that if the document existed it could be located and obtained in a matter of days.

Judith Hibbard, coordinating with the many different parts of Stanford University Press, saw the book safely through all stages of production. Janet Mowery read every line and made suggestions that improved the book's substance as well as its readability. I am also grateful to the many others at the Press, whom I do not know, who supported the idea and making of this book.

I could neither have started nor completed this work without the unflagging support of a close circle, in particular my mother, Mary Swanberg; my sisters, Ann Swanberg and Mary Lambeth; my stepson, Neil O'Connor, and his wife, Shannon O'Connor; my son, Alex O'Connor; and my dear friend Rosanne Kramer. They listened to arguments, read drafts, and put up with a mind that was always on this book.

Finally, the deepest thanks of all must go to my husband, Richard, who made this book possible in every conceivable way. Our twenty-five years together have proven the true foundation—visible and invisible—of this work.

Abbreviations Used in the Text

BRB   Business Research Bureau
CIT   Carnegie Institute of Technology
CSB   collegiate school of business
GSB   graduate school of business
EMBA   Executive Master of Business Administration
HBS   Harvard Business School
HLS   Harvard Law School
MRM   Municipal Reform Movement
NYUC   New York University School of Commerce, Accounts and Finance
PSB   professional school of business
SHM   Settlement House Movement
SOO   School of Opportunity
SCM   School Center Movement
USO   United Service Organizations
WCM   Women's Club Movement
WMLB   Women's Municipal League of Boston
WSFE   Wharton School of Finance and Economy
VEM   Vocational Education Movement
VGM   Vocational Guidance Movement
VSB   vocational school of business

Creating New Knowledge in Management

CHAPTER I

Introduction and Problem

No Institution of Management Knowledge

☾

Society needs institutions dedicated to developing the science and profession of management. But those charged with this task, the business school and the management academy, do not do so and have not organized themselves to do so. Mary Parker Follett (1868–1933) and Chester I. Barnard (1886–1961) established foundations of a science of management in the early twentieth century. The institutions never integrated their work, however, and it remains largely unrecognized and unutilized. This book recaptures these lost foundations and explores how to build on them.

The project to develop a basic and applied science and an applied art of management has in fact gone deferred since the founding of collegiate schools of business (CSBs) in the mid-1800s. Facing intense demand for practical higher education and elevated business practice, educators did not pursue a new field. They did not even go so far as to reach a common understanding of management. Instead, they shrank new ideas to fit old institutions. Today, the so-called management curriculum and academy consist of many different disciplines whose sole tie is a bearing on "organizations" (Augier et al., 2005).

But management is not a smattering of many disciplines; nor does it resemble any existing discipline. It is not a specialist field because it pertains to many fields. Also, it differs from specialist fields because it entails responsibility that exceeds disciplinary boundaries. In fact, specialists flock to MBA programs precisely to transcend specialization and learn management. But once there, they find only more specialist training. Among the academic subjects encompassed by the management curriculum are economics, psychology, sociology, political science, statistics, and computer science. The technical subjects include accounting, finance, marketing, human resources, operations, and management information systems. These subjects presumably *add up to* the content of management.

This situation dates from the business school's earliest formation in the mid-1800s. The fledgling school did not find a home in mainstream higher education. Using a peripheral institution, University Extension, occupational specialists controlled business education through the mid-twentieth century. The vocational school of business (VSB) was organized to satisfy popular demand. It brought a new and large population of working adults into higher education. It also brought in a new revenue source, the corporation, which used the business school for training and recruiting. Academics deemed the school unscholarly and a threat to the entire university. In a mainstreaming arrangement, academic specialists in the behavioral and quantitative sciences took control of the "basic sciences" in the business school; and occupational specialists retained control of the technical disciplines as "applied sciences." This move won consensus in the academy and in industry. It also instituted the MBA degree and the elite MBA program in the elite research university. Finally, it set up a selective admissions standard for which a new candidate, aspiring to leadership of the highest status, cultivated himself. This candidate had already demonstrated success in responsible positions and entered business school as part of executing this responsibility and reaching this status. The management academy, following norms of professional science, did not see that this candidate brought vital new knowledge and knowledge-creating methods.

Follett and Barnard, like this candidate, took management seriously because they lived it. Follett led the transformation of "her" city, Boston, from a static to a dynamic society that integrated new populations and enterprises into what she called a functional whole. Barnard led the transformation of "his" organization, Bell Telephone, from a local to a statewide entity when local logics dominated the state. Studying these developments and their personal stakes in them, Follett proposed a science of "dynamic relating," and Barnard an "applied social science." They worked separately but had a common purpose: to develop self-government and knowledge of self-government at increasing levels of scale. Beginning in adolescence, they built this project systematically for the rest of their lives.

But the management academy did not use their work because it did not fit into any academic or technical specialty. It also contradicted mainstream science, which distanced itself from lay activities and cultivated separate, specialist enclaves within itself. Professional science especially prized the natural and physical sciences and the idea of discovering their laws. Follett's and Barnard's science, on the other hand, ran with the premise that knowledge is consciously created and that it grows in a value system that prizes human creativity. In particular, they focused on the synergy between individual and collective creativity. This approach to knowledge and knowledge creation imposes new burdens of responsibility: so-called findings have to do with the exercise of personal responsibility by actors who understand that "findings" follow from and act back on them. In particular, Follett and Barnard explored the implications of this logic in a dynamic society: as one studied, he or she actually "made" the object of study—the city in Follett's case; the organization in Barnard's. Furthermore, while professional science organized around values of neutrality and detachment, Follett and Barnard assigned personal stakes and normative significance to science: as one made the life that one desired to have, one made the society in which one desired to live. And as one made the society in which one desired to live, one made the life that one desired to have.

Follett's and Barnard's science coincided with the explosion of adult education generally and the research university specifically. By affiliating with institutionalized science in the university, one could elevate his or her social status from the occupational to the professional level. University Extension made this affiliation and elevation available to the general public. It offered a new, reliable path to new, well-paying jobs in emerging specialist fields. Follett's and Barnard's science also related to the large, formal organization and the job of manager. Follett and Barnard observed that the managerial position created value in accordance with the manager's ability to integrate diverse specialist elements into the organization. They traced this ability to the manager's subjective experience of a mutually creative relation between himself and larger wholes. They isolated the lever of this relation in the conscious decision to *organize oneself* in accordance with this idea and its value-creating possibilities.

Thus Follett and Barnard are best understood not only as building a new discipline but also as reforming the classical tradition of knowledge for governance, or paideia/humanitas (Jaeger, 1963a [1944], 1963b [1943], 1962 [1939]; Hoskin, 2006). Previously, U.S. society bundled knowledge for governance into two institutions: the rite of initiation performed through college residency and graduation, and inculcation in theological doctrine and in the sacred texts of Western civilization as administered in the core curriculum. Governance and knowledge were treated as a static inheritance to be claimed. College professors did not create knowledge. They preserved it and passed it on from biological and clerical fathers to sons. With the rise of science and the fall of the clergy's monopoly of higher education and the professions, the idea of fixed knowledge and passive inheritance proved untenable. In a dynamic society, governance had to cultivate new knowledge (science), new industry (applied science), and a new synergy between science and industry (knowledge for governance). Thus Frederick Taylor proposed his scientific management (1911) and Henri Fayol his general administration (1916) because they found that the old knowledge institutions did not support dynamic industry.

Follett and Barnard went the furthest in this regard because they did not seek a one-time adjustment for the new conditions but rather a science of adjustment or integration for *continuously new conditions*. In a nutshell, they integrated the institution of science into classical paideia/ humanitas and remade it for dynamic society. This move entailed a conscious transfer of responsibility from institutions—the college, residency, the core—to the self-governing individual acting interdependently with larger self-governing units. Henceforth, knowledge for governance was no longer a thing. Rather, "it" inhered in ways of relating that were oriented toward creating new value and values, again and again, in ever-new circumstances.

But the logic of specialization prevailed. To an unprecedented extent, it created new knowledge, wealth, and status rapidly and reliably. But by continuously separating knowledge into finer units, experts became masters of smaller domains. More important, they could not envision and pursue the greater uses of their knowledge. Follett and Barnard thus posited an integrative knowledge of equal sophistication to reap the full harvest of specialization.

Although this idea of management remains virtually forgotten, the need for it is clearer than ever. The publication of this book coincides with an economic crisis that lends new urgency to longstanding discussions of key aspects of management education such as ethics, research, and curriculum. Yet these discussions have also long ignored the elephant in the room: the appearance but missing substance of management. This is the true economic, scientific, and leadership crisis at hand.

ETHICS

In his pioneering study of management education, Rakesh Khurana (2007) argued that the business school helped legitimize management and transform it into a profession. However, he did not see how the business school developed to serve the professional and academic specialties. To professionalize management further, Khurana and his colleagues at the Harvard Business School (HBS) instituted an ethics vow analogous to medicine's Hippocratic oath. In 2009, 55 percent of the HBS graduating class signed the oath (the figure stayed the same in 2010), as did over 1,000 other graduating MBAs worldwide. But to have force, such a vow must be taken before a community that finds or makes it meaningful. In this sense, HBS's vow might have impact for the HBS community but not for a community of professional managers, because such a thing does not exist.

As stated at the outset, there is no professional community that takes responsibility for management knowledge. Moreover, concerning vow-taking specifically and ethics generally, Follett and Barnard go deeper. They ground ethics in the project of institution-building, which they further ground in the project of self-government. In this context, ethics is more than a matter of professing and keeping one's word. Self-government entails subordination, a form of action of the self on the self, which further entails integrity in the Latin sense, meaning "whole." For Follett, one subordinates oneself to creative principles that support human flourishing. For Barnard, if the executive does not subordinate himself to the moral codes he creates in relating to himself, others, and the larger whole, then he loses the respect of the organization's members and they withhold the necessary contributions. More deeply, they refrain from making the necessary attributions such that the organization acts back on the executive and makes him a leader, so the organization dies.

RESEARCH

A longstanding debate in business schools concerns the balance of influence between the business school's "parents," academicians and practitioners. This debate is framed in many ways: rigor versus relevance, abstraction versus concreteness, theory versus application. Entire issues of the *Academy of Management Journal*—August, October, and December of 2007—have addressed this topic. However, this debate ignores the missing discipline of management and even capitalizes on the business school's bipolar parentage. For example, Andrew Van de Ven (2007) posited four forms of "engaged scholarship": informed basic research, collaborative research, design/policy evaluation research, and action/intervention research. In fact, these forms align with one side or the other and reinforce the bipolarity. Van de Ven thus pursues not a unified enterprise but a synergy between complementary but distinct communities. He does not take up the prospect of academics and practitioners collaborating in the common purpose to build a discipline of management, which would turn both parties into institution-builders and collapse the divide altogether.

Professional groups in accounting, finance, and other fields use the business school to build their disciplines by affiliating with basic science in the academy. Academic specialists in economics, psychology, and other fields do the same by affiliating with applied science in industry. By recalibrating their location on the academe-practice continuum—that is, by aligning more or less with the scientific or technical specialists—business schools differentiate themselves and compete with one another. They also undergo regime changes and differentiate their new incarnations from their old ones. Finally, they interact with broad trends: for example, Henry Mintzberg reacts to the dominant graduate school of business (GSB) model (Mintzberg, 2004: Chap. 4). In other words, the academe-research bipolarity may address the science-lay divide, but its integrative logic conforms to disciplinary limits.

TEACHING

George Leland Bach, a leading reformer in management education, found a bipolarity between "people-oriented" and "analytically oriented" business curricula (see discussion in Chapter 4). Writing in the mid-1980s, he called this the most serious problem facing management education. He made no reference to history, but his statement recalled the field's simultaneous origins in engineering, with Frederick Taylor and Henri Fayol, and in psychology, with Elmer Southard and Elton Mayo (Wrege, 1979; O'Connor, 1999a).

Fayol collapsed the bipolarity between engineering and psychology by claiming that workers respect managers with scientific knowledge of all kinds (1962 [1916]: 112). Mayo collapsed the bipolarity by conceiving of his work as an extension of Taylor's (Mayo, 1924: 258), which had called for "scientific investigation . . . [into] the motives which influence men" (Taylor, 1911: 129–30). But as the business school became recognized as the quintessential institution linking wealth creation and knowledge, various disciplines competed to lead it. In doing so, they exaggerated their differences with one another and reinforced bipolarities, such as scientific versus lay knowledge and scientific versus humanistic knowledge.

Business schools also try to correct a bipolarity passed on from college: the gap in education between what the "poet" (or liberal arts–educated student) learns, and what the "quant" (engineering student) learns. They aspire to correct the imbalance of the previous education and make a more complete individual.

All of these bipolarities only distract from the root problem. Lacking a foundation or core around which to orient themselves, institutions calibrate and recalibrate along a continuum. The vital question remains unasked and forgotten: What are the foundational principles of management—that is, the bases on which the field may build a creative synergy between theory and application as in the more established professions?

The stakes have been raised as the elite business school has become the heir-apparent to the tradition of knowledge for governance. It claims to teach leadership and has won broad acceptance as doing so. Leadership research draws from the academic specialties of social and cognitive psychology, among other disciplines. However, no science examines the integration of scholarship, institution-building, and self-government. Yet as Follett and Barnard show, substantive knowledge of governance must comprehend these dynamics.

RESEARCH CONTRIBUTIONS

This book offers three new contributions: a pre-history of the university-based business school that encompasses its mutual institutionalization with the professions and the research university (Part I); an interpretation, based on unpublished and rare documents, of Follett's and Barnard's management science (Part II); and the results of experiments in applying their science in contemporary teaching and research (Part III). Part II also presents theory that explains how the foundations were ignored in the first place. Together, the three parts fulfill the promise of this book's title: they recover and use the lost foundations of management.

Part I assembles references that have not previously been connected. It plots the business school in the trajectory of the research university understood as a means to exploit the wealth-creating dynamic between basic and applied science. In this context, "applied science" means not only applications of science, such as to technology, but also further applications such as job training and even organization itself. I reviewed histories of business schools (Broehl, 1999; Cruikshank, 1987; Gitlow, 1995; Gleeson, 1997; Gleeson et al., 1993; Gleeson & Schlossman, 1995; 1992; Hotchkiss, 1941, 1913; Marshall, 1913; McCrea, 1913; Person, 1913; Phillips, 1964; Sass, 1982; Scott, 1913; Schlossman & Sedlak, 1985; Schlossman et al., 1998; 1989a, b; Sedlak & Schlossman, 1991; Sedlak & Williamson, 1983; Van Metre, 1954) as well as histories of universities that include studies of their business schools (Cleeton, 1965; Baldridge, 1971; Cheyney, 1940; Dyer, 1966; McGrane, 1963; New York University, 1956; Pollard 1952; Solberg, 1968; Tarbell, 1937; Townsend, 1996; Yates, 1992) and histories of business education (Daniel, 1998; Haynes & Jackson, 1935;

Khurana, 2007; Marshall, 1928; Ruml, 1928; Schlossman & Sedlak, 1988). This research showed how the collegiate business school related to large-scale reforms in education and industry.

Understanding the research university itself became a central focus of this work. Studies of the nation's oldest universities and how they changed over time were particularly useful, such as Edward Potts Cheyney's history of the University of Pennsylvania (1940), as were histories of institutions that started out as technical institutes, for example, and gradually became universities (Cleeton, 1965; Mann, 1918; McGivern, 1960; Rezneck, 1968; Stratton & Mannix, 2005; Tarbell, 1937). Sources examining the founding and conversion processes generally were also helpful (Brubacher & Rudy, 1997; Geiger, 1986; Hall, 2000; Hawkins, 1979; Herbst, 1982; Hofstadter & Hardy, 1952; Hofstadter & Metzger, 1955; Hofstadter & Smith, 1961; Veysey, 1965). This research defined the university as integrating formerly external, loosely coupled, or even entirely unrelated parts: (1) the college (Allmendinger, 1975; Bailyn, 1960; Boroff, 1961; Burke, 1982; Church & Sedlak, 1997; Geiger, 2000; Geiger with Bubolz, 2000; Guralnick, 1975; Leslie, 1992; Levine, 1986; Meyer, 1972; Peterson, 1964; Rudolph, 1981); (2) the scientific and graduate school (Cordasco, 1973; Chittenden, 1928; Mann, 1918; McGivern, 1960; Storr, 1953; Ryan, 1939; Turner & Bernard, 2000); (3) the professional schools, i.e. (a) the theological seminary (Gambrell, 1937; Scott, 1978; Williams, 1941; Woods, 1884); (b) the law school (Johnson, 1978; LaPiana, 1994; Stevens, 1983; Warren, 1908); and (c) the medical school (Kaufman, 1976; Kett, 1968; Rothstein, 1987); and (4) popular education in various forms, such as the lyceum, the public lecture, the learning society, and even self-education (Kett, 1994; Kohlstedt, 1976; Sinclair, 1974).

The study also examined how the early business school interacted with the classical college. Content-wise, the college-based business school had two parents: political economy, a reform of moral philosophy (Bryson, 1932a, 1932b; O'Connor, 1994); and accounting (Haskins, 1904; Lockwood, 1938; Wildman, 1926). The two parents, one based in theological doctrine and in the classics (see Table 1; all tables are in the Appendix), and the other in mastery-apprenticeship (Table 2), were on a collision course and suffered a schism at the turn of the century. A major reform in the mid-twentieth century resolved the rupture. Political economy became positive economics following the institution of professional science (Bannister, 1987; Fox, 1967; Furner, 1975; Oberschall, 1972; Ross, 1991; Sass, 1982); and accounting, as well as the other occupational specialties, became an applied science. The two parents divided labor according to the research university's governing logic, which simultaneously differentiated and pursued synergies between basic and applied science.

Part II reintroduces Follett and Barnard as the founders of management science. It draws from unpublished and rare sources, as well as secondary sources. The chapter on Follett draws extensively from biographical data (Tonn, 2003). Because Follett's society and her way of relating to society differ significantly from contemporary social science and social work, the chapter presents generous background data on the woman's club, settlement house, municipal reform, and vocational education movements. It also discusses related initiatives such as education for citizenship and for democracy—in fact, reforms of classical paideia/humanitas—that Follett followed and led. It is difficult to convey the unity that Follett found and created in her theory and practice, her research and life. I thus aim to capture the conditions that established the need for systematic knowledge of dynamic relating *in her experience.* I draw extensively from her unpublished and rare texts, particularly those on management training, to show her in action, publically interpreting these conditions with and for others. For Barnard, I draw even more extensively from unpublished correspondence and drafts because no biography of him exists. This material shows the extent to which Barnard used himself as a scientific subject in the new experimental condition that he called "the executive in formal organization." After his World War II experience, Barnard understood organization itself and all of its members as being in this condition, which he further understood as an evolutionary opportunity for humankind. Part II also traces the management academy's lineage to Barnard, showing how the tie was, and still remains, broken.

Part III is based on my own original field research exploring how to build on Follett and Barnard today. The first experiment, a three-year collaboration with an executive, focuses on how Follett's and Barnard's ideas inform management practice and how management practice clarifies their ideas. The second experiment uses Follett's and Barnard's ideas and their experiential methods in Master's-level teaching.

HOW THIS BOOK IS DIFFERENT FROM OTHERS

This book presents, for the first time, a history of *institutionalized and uninstitutionalized* management knowledge. This enables capturing the content and methods that flourished outside the academy. It also shows how institutionalization set limits on new knowledge creation in management. Other works, Khurana's (2007) most recently, have taken the university-based business school as a given. This move obscures the extent to which the business school became the instrument of professionalization in the academy and in the occupations.

This book also differs from works that focus on Follett and Barnard, notably those by Joan Tonn (2003) and William B. Wolf (1974, 1973), which do not use Follett and Barnard, respectively, as foundations for new knowledge. Finally, where scholars have pointed out the need for a discipline of management, notably Armand Hatchuel (2009, 2005, 2000), this book lends substance to that claim by showing the historical conditions that blocked foundational work altogether and by recovering this work in Follett and Barnard.

In contrast to books on the reform of management education, here I explain the dynamics that hold the field in specialist logic, both academically and occupationally. The originality of the ideas comes from addressing the root problem. Thus, whereas leaders in individual academic fields increasingly call for closer engagement with the humanities (March, 2008: 434–53; Bennis & O'Toole, 2005: 104), they fail to see that this simply adds more specialist fields to the current array dominated by the behavioral and quantitative sciences.

PLAN OF THE BOOK

Part I explicates the lack of a discipline of management despite the existence of business schools of solid repute, as well as the conditions that still prevent its emergence. Part II rediscovers the lost foundations of management in the life and works of Follett and Barnard. Part III builds on their work and suggests future directions.

Following this introduction, Chapter 2 examines the research university in which the business school became embedded. The research university was a twentieth-century invention. In particular, it established the research profession and professoriate. It integrated the values of professional science into higher education and in industry, and it established a strong academic community that operationalized these values. The business school would become the laggard in these respects (Chapter 3). It was initially included in the college to reform the classical curriculum for contemporary conditions. However, the college did not accept reform, and it had declined so far that not even the new curriculum could invigorate it. The business school took off under a new model, a partnership with specialist-practitioners. It drew massive new populations to the university and effectively put the university in the business of job training at the lowest (entry) levels. Academic entrepreneurs at elite and elite-oriented institutions, such as Wallace Donham of Harvard and George Leland Bach of the Carnegie Institute of Technology, organized for the high end (see Chapter 4). They recast the business school as graduate professional education, following medicine and law. Despite Donham's efforts to discover the principles underlying a science of management, his project succumbed to specialist logic. In fact, Donham reinforced vocationalism by giving it pedagogical content and the Harvard name. Bach and his colleagues moved more expeditiously. Instead of finding or creating a core of management, they defined management as a hybrid discipline with scientific foundations in the academic specialties. In a well-organized campaign, elite business schools secured status and won consensus for this idea.

Part II (Chapters 5–7) recovers the lost work of Follett and Barnard. Because their ideas remain unutilized for theory-building and research, I provide generous introductions to their biographies and contributions. Chapter 5, on Follett, aims to overcome the bias that she was a "social worker" as that phrase is understood today. Rather, Follett conceptualized social work as the work entailed in building the self, society, and knowledge together. Moreover, whereas the tendency is to separate her life into two parts, with her social work in her early career and her management work at the end, the more accurate view is that Follett worked continuously on the core problem of how individuals could *organize themselves* to create value for themselves and for larger wholes. Here, "value" does not mean profit; nor does it mean any one thing. Rather, it refers to the full array of individually meaningful values that each person associates with his or her contribution and with the whole.

Chapters 6 and 7 take up Barnard. Chapter 6 departs from the tendency to focus on his classic work, *The Functions of the Executive*. The book is important, but it is just the tip of the iceberg. The chapter shows that Barnard never stopped working on *The Functions*. Throughout his life he modified his ideas; but his executive work took precedence and he did not issue formal announcements of his changes in thinking. Furthermore, Barnard began working on *The Functions* at least ten years before its publication. Beginning with his first managerial positions, he considered himself in a new experimental condition—the executive in a formal organization. He recognized that this condition entailed individual contributions on a new scale and of a new quality. He explicated this condition based on his experience and offered it for further testing by others. Chapter 7 explains the epistemological reasons why the institutionalizing management academy did not, and could not, integrate Follett and Barnard. Their methods privileged experience, and more specifically, experience consciously directed to creative ends. Chapter 7 also examines the "organic applied social science" that Barnard's book exemplified.

Building on Chapter 7, Chapters 8–10 take the ideas of Follett and Barnard as the management field's core and propose ways to build on them. Chapter 8 focuses on research collaborations with practitioners based on the explicit, shared goal to develop a discipline of management. It demonstrates that Follett and Barnard have resonance today. It also shows how state-of-the-art technologies help operationalize their ideas.

Chapter 9 uses my own classroom experience as an opportunity to develop self-government and personal responsibility. It also examines the microprocesses entailed in dynamic relating. Chapter 10 proposes research that the status quo could readily accommodate. More ambitiously, it proposes an institutional reform that would create new knowledge by integrating executive-scholars into the management academy.

PART I

Institutional Fault Lines in and around the Business School

The business school became institutionalized in the research university, a twentieth-century invention that led, and was led by, a new knowledge and social order. The classical order had bundled clerical and aristocratic ownership, theological and classical content, and values of preservation and conservatism. It supported and was supported by the idea of a stable status quo in the social order and in knowledge. The new order bundled scientific and secular ownership, scientific and applied-scientific content, and values of wealth creation. It supported and was supported by an interacting social and knowledge order. Mary Parker Follett and Chester I. Barnard would see great personal, social, and scientific stakes in this change and develop a new science to realize them.

The business school began as a reform of the classical college, designed to adjust it to this new order and logic. For centuries, the college had occupied the top of the knowledge-status order. However, it was an institution in decline, along with its associated institutions, the clergy and the aristocracy. At the turn of the twentieth century, the business school severed ties with the college and grew at the university's periphery, in University Extension. The business school made the university popular; but at the same time, the school fell out of step with the professionalizing academy. With its large and growing enrollments, the Extension-based business school threatened the academic legitimacy of the entire university. After World War II, reformers integrated the business school into the professionalizing academy. This move required a synergy between basic and applied science—that is, between professional research in the academy and professional practice in industry. Since both the academy and Extension had institutionalized through specialization, a convenient solution was to make the academic specialties into the foundations of business and the technical specialties into the applications of business. Adopted by business schools in elite research universities and aided by generous foundation funding, this model became the national and international standard. It also brought an end to any serious thought of a discipline of management.

CHAPTER 2

The Institutionalizing
Research University

Rise of the Scientific Tradition

☽

The business school came into being relative to another new institution, the research university. The university took over and elevated amateur science and occupational training, institutions that had developed outside the college for centuries. In and through the research university, these two institutions acquired professional status sufficient to exceed that of the previous sole profession, the ministry. They, and the research university as a whole, organized under the value of specialization and the value-creating synergy between basic and applied science. That is, professional or basic science developed, and practitioners became professional by associating with it. The research university exploited synergies among basic research, applied research, and further applications of applied research (training and certification). In this process, the college fell from the top to the bottom of the new knowledge order and became "undergraduate" or pre-professional school. While the academy and research professionalized, the university also popularized its offerings. Occupational groups used a new institution, University Extension, to achieve professional status, and corporations used it for recruitment and training. The distance between the university's center and periphery, and between its high and low ranks, became more pronounced. Developing and flourishing at the university's periphery and in its lowest ranks, the business school became a rogue actor in the university.

The research university added two new values and purposes—knowledge discovery and occupational training—to the university's traditional function of cultural preservation (Shils, 1981; Kimball, 1996). In the nineteenth century, two new institutions, the graduate school and the professional school, were born and operationalized these values. They also established an order between themselves: the graduate school became a professional school for the professoriate, which provided basic scientific or "foundational" content that the medical or healing arts, for example, "applied" to rise from occupational to professional status. The requirement that candidates for professional school have earned a Bachelor's degree, which was established in the early twentieth century, was also a factor in achieving professional status.

These developments led, and were led by, formal and substantive changes in higher education and in the social order and ordering process to which it was attached. The clergy's monopoly of higher education and of society's sole profession, the ministry, ended. Secular institutions took control of higher education and of the new professions. These professions quickly attained status equal or superior to the ministry. As the sciences separated and specialized, other occupations claimed a similar basic–applied logic and professional status; and the university—Extension and business in particular—accommodated them.

The research university was a new institution, made in new ways. This is evident when one compares it with its models: the British college, the German university, and the French *polytechnique*.

THE CLASSICAL COLLEGE

Through the end of the nineteenth century, the most advanced institution of higher education was the classical college, following Oxford and Cambridge (Bailyn, 1986). The Bachelor of Arts degree was the credential for the lifetime "occupation" of gentleman, except for the relative few who went on to the theological seminary. The classical college facilitated integration into the social order and ordering process (see Table 1). In the United States, Harvard College set the gold standard among classical colleges, and it was imitated even by those who claimed to reform it. Although the country never had a national college, Harvard assumed this function informally beginning in the colonial era (Townsend, 1996: 15).

Contrary to its current private status, Harvard College "was created as a public institution" and "governed as such for almost two hundred years." The state of Massachusetts supported it "well into the nineteenth century" (Bailyn, 1986: 11–12); in the colonial period, it gave Harvard over $500,000 (Burke, 1982: 41). State and local governments, as well as a private board of trustees, had stakes in Harvard's governance.

Shortly after Harvard was founded in 1636, the British Parliament began annulling the colonies' charters, which halted the formation of new colleges. Harvard thus benefited from its timing. Yale, the second college, explicitly organized to escape attention. It called itself a "collegiate school" rather than a college; its head was not a "president" as at Harvard but a "rector." Yale never caught up with Harvard in many respects. Its first president took office in 1899, seventy years after Harvard's. Yale abolished required chapel attendance in 1926; Harvard did so in 1886. Harvard dropped Greek as an entrance requirement in 1884; Yale did so in 1903. Yale's elective system was not as liberal as Harvard's throughout the nineteenth century. Harvard had $13 million in its endowment by 1900; Yale had $5 million (Townsend, 1996: 29). Yale finally beat Harvard by twelve years in one key respect when it bestowed the United States' first Ph.D. degree in 1861. However, this degree was not granted by Yale College or Yale University but by Yale's Sheffield Scientific School, an institution with its own governing board and policies separate from the college.

Harvard was imitated locally in New England and throughout the westward expansion, which involved not only settling new territories but also establishing outposts where the fracturing Protestant sects could grow and stand up against one another (Allmendinger, 1975: 65). That is, the college was integral to settlement in the first place and to educational and cultural flourishing. It attracted settlers; local communities actually bid for colleges (Church & Sedlak, 1997: 142).

Education reform gained momentum in the nineteenth century, through sea changes such as the Morrill Act of 1862, which brought federal and state governments, and public constituencies, into higher education. The Morrill legislation targeted this education to the "industrial classes" who would receive "training in the mechanical and agricultural arts" (Cross, 1999; R. Williams, 1991). Following the interest in "useful knowledge" (Kett, 1994), reformers also developed technical institutes such as Rensselaer Polytechnic Institute (1824). However, despite their having been modeled after France's prestigious Ecole Polytechnique for nation-building in the civil-engineering sense (Artz, 1966), even these institutions used the classical college as a key reference. Also, Morrill funds often went to classical colleges because they were considered the leaders in higher education (Kett, 1994: 226). In other words, the status institution in France did not translate to a status institution in the United States.

Reform institutions organized themselves not necessarily to take over first-class status but certainly not to accept second-class status. For example, Henry Morton, the first president of the Stevens Institute of Technology, from 1871 to 1902, planned a department of "Belles-Lettres" to "furnish the means of acquiring that culturation of literary taste and facility in the graceful use of language, both in speaking and in writing, which is desirable in the engineer and men of science as in the classical student" (McGivern, 1960: 104). In allocating professorships at a land-grant institution, Ohio State University, trustees gave "modern and ancient languages" one position. However, they argued over this professorship, favoring either modern or ancient languages, or both. Because these discussions reveal much about the cultural and pedagogical stakes at the time, they merit full citation.

One trustee argued that one who "wishes to keep thoroughly posted in Agriculture as a science, or with the constant progress in the Mechanic Arts, Chemistry, and other sciences, will need to read as many books and memoirs in French and German, as he will in English." Concerning the ancient languages, he stated:

Whatever may be said in these modern days about utilitarianism and the practical, it is an indisputable fact that the leading minds in all civilized nations have for many centuries been trained and developed in classical studies, and it may be fairly concluded they have not lost all efficacy . . . The mere fact that agriculture or mechanics are to be taught in our school will not secure it success, which will depend more upon being a good school . . . Trained and educated minds ever have, and ever will take precedence over ignorance and limited knowledge, in all the affairs of life, and it is a mistaken notion that a narrow and technical education is all that is required in the industrial pursuits of men . . . while the Board of Trustees . . . will make the principles of Agriculture and the Mechanic Arts "leading objects" in their institution, they do not desire to educate those confided to them simply as Farmers or Mechanics, but as men, fitted by education and attainments for the greatest usefulness and highest duties of citizenship . . . Not until the liberal is added to the practical in education will those great departments of human industry, Agriculture and the Mechanic Arts, the creators of wealth in all countries, attain to that elevated social position they are so justly entitled to occupy. (Pollard, 1952: 18, quoting Sullivant)

Since the colonial era, reformers had attacked the college, especially its forced curriculum, and for requiring "dead" or "useless" Latin and Greek for entrance and exit. Among them were Benjamin Franklin and Thomas Jefferson, who helped found the University of Pennsylvania (1749) and the University of Virginia (1819), respectively. In 1749, Franklin proposed a higher-education curriculum to teach "the keeping of accounts, the history of commerce, and the principles of mechanics as well as arithmetic, English, and geography" to fit students for "any Business, Calling, or Profession" (Kett, 1994: 7). Jefferson considered a two-tier system, one for the working class and one for the privileged class, in proposing an evening school for "mariners, carpenters, ship-wrights, pumpmakers, clockmakers, machinists, opticians, metallurgists, founders, cutlers, druggists, brewers, distillers, dyers, painters, bleachers, soapmakers, tanners, powdermakers, saltmakers, and glassmakers" to study "technical philosophy" or "geometry, mechanics, statics, hydro-statics, hydraulics, hydrodynamics, navigation, astronomy, geography, optics, pneumatics, physics, chemistry, natural history, botany, mineral-ogy and pharmacy." Jefferson eventually abandoned this populist idea and chose instead to educate southern leaders to oppose the Federalist influence in New England colleges (Kett, 1994: 8).

Franklin was more persistent; and Philadelphia, a scientific and ex-perimental center, provided a hospitable environment (Bridenbaugh & Bridenbaugh, 1942). He desired "instruction that trained not for limited goals . . . but for the broadest possible range of enterprise. He had no ar-gument with the classics as such. What he objected to was their monopoly of the higher branches of education which denied the breadth of prepara-tion needed for the open world he saw." Formal higher education had to allow that "one's role in life had not been fully cast, that the immediate inheritance did not set the final limits" (Bailyn, 1960: 35–36). Franklin's reforms advanced at the University of Pennsylvania; but by the late 1870s the institution's "completely spelled-out curriculum" differed little from that of the classical college (Sass, 1982: 30; Cheyney, 1940: 259).

The classical college maintained coherence both internally and exter-nally. Externally, it fit into a longstanding social and moral order led by the clergy and the aristocracy, the local pillars. The college president, a clergyman, led both the college and the community. At and around Harvard, the so-called Brahmins constituted this community (Baltzell, 1979; Story, 1980).

Internally, the prescribed curriculum remained fairly stable from generation to generation; clerical and biological fathers literally passed it down to their pastoral and biological sons. The consistency ensured "cultural cohesion" (Geiger with Bubolz, 2000: 89). This cohesive con-tent was administered particularly in the moral philosophy course. Based on theological doctrine, it was taught by the college president (Peterson, 1964: 37). This "feel" of the college was captured in the image of the latter's "discussing with graduating seniors any subject under the sun and exploring the lessons students could draw from it for their ethical conduct as gentlemen-scholars" (Herbst, 1982: 203–4). Latin and Greek were the other cohesive elements. They were not arbitrary requirements, useless (as reformers so often alleged), or mere mental gymnastics. On the contrary, they substantiated the claim of knowledge for governance because they afforded direct access to the original sacred texts of the great Western civilizations. Thus, on this basis, defenders attacked the elective system for "exalt[ing] the individual and loosen[ing] the bonds of social organization" (Peterson, 1964: 50–51).

In the late nineteenth century, the new "social scientist" or "sociologist" began to replace the clergyman. Henceforth, knowledge for governance would have a scientific basis. Professional scientists would dispense information to occupational-becoming-professional specialists (Herbst, 1982: 204). Science now occupies the highest rung of the knowledge-status order. However, it had humble beginnings, evident in today's hobbyist, tinkerer, and amateur.

THE SCIENTIFIC SCHOOL

The scientific school is the precursor of today's graduate schools. From the outset, it aspired to replicate the German university, "philosophical faculty," laboratory, and seminar. It also embraced the values of *Lernfreiheit* and *Wissenschaft* (Brubacher & Rudy, 1997: 174–97; Chittenden, 1928: 52). The German university was connected to humanist and idealist traditions. Jurgen Herbst described how German-trained U.S. scholars preserved the spirit of their training. Gathering in seminars, parties, and bars, they "exclaim[ed] as did the German humanist Ulrich von Hutten: 'O Jahrhundert! Die Geister erwachen. Die Studien blühen. Es ist eine Lust zu leben.'" [Oh, century! Minds are awakening. The studies are flourishing. What a pleasure it is to be alive] (Herbst, 1962: 247). In the United States, the scientific school most fully embodied and transmitted this romance with science (see Table 2).

The scientific school formed outside the college, which of course did not take Germany as a model. However, the college had mechanisms that accommodated new knowledge: the elective system, "special" (non-degree) students, and "lecturer" (non-permanent) faculty. The latter were paid on a pro rata basis according to the number of students they enrolled. The college also drew from full-time faculty at the occupational schools with which it affiliated. With the founding of the University of Pennsylvania's medical school in 1765, colleges began affiliating with or acquiring proprietary law and medical schools. These relationships established the legal concept of the university as joining the college with these schools (Burke, 1982: 268). The first such outsourced elective was chemistry, a basic science, which the practical arts applied. Thus chemists from the medical school taught future engineers. The elective was readily scaled up from a single course to a series and then to a "school" (Guralnick, 1975: 20, 51, 130).

Colleges used the elective to varying degrees, in accordance with the views of the president, faculty, trustees, and benefactors. On the conservative end of the spectrum, Noah Porter of Yale, for example, advocated a prescribed curriculum with no exceptions. Charles Eliot of Harvard, credited with promoting the elective system during his 1869–1909 tenure, represents the other extreme. For Eliot, the decision to offer electives touched on moral, developmental and even political questions: the "freedom to choose was in itself an educational experience, forcing the student to take stock of himself." Eliot deemed academic choice "more appropriate for students in a democratic society than compulsion" (Herbst, 1982: 204).

The scientific school developed as colleges exhausted their capacity to accommodate science electives. Typically, reformers accumulated the necessary wealth, and governing boards and faculty organized free of the college's restraints. Thus Yale established the Sheffield Scientific School; Harvard, the Lawrence Scientific School; Dartmouth, the Chandler Scientific School; Princeton, the Green Scientific School; and the University of Pennsylvania, the Towne Scientific School.

The scientific school worked according to logics that differed significantly from those of the college. It did not require Latin or Greek. It did not stigmatize students who wanted to take only one course or a series of courses. Russell Chittenden, in his history of Sheffield, captures the cultural and intellectual differences. Students arrived "with earnestness of purpose and [with an] . . . enthusiasm which kept the laboratory a beehive of activity." Compared to the college, there were "few or no rules and regulations." Most of the men were:

mature, or if young in years they were wise in experience and they came to work, young and old alike. Freedom was the rule of the house, but the laboratory, poor though it was, was sufficiently attractive to hold the men through all the working hours of the day and sometimes into the night. There were no compulsory morning prayers, no compulsory church service, no compulsory study hours prescribed by higher authority, but each man was more or less a law unto himself and his one object was work. The time-honored traditions of college were not for them, and as a rule they had no interests outside the special field of their activities.

The school also departed significantly from the college's teaching methods:

It was mainly personal contact in the laboratory, where students worked out for themselves chemical reactions, studied the behavior of acids, bases, and salts, applied analytical methods for determining the composition of unknown compounds, and in various ways gained first-hand knowledge of the facts and principles upon which chemical laws are based. In a sense, each man was an investigator, feeling his way carefully along paths which were unfamiliar . . . and acquiring habits of self-reliance and the power of drawing sane and safe deductions from observed facts. The professor and his assistant were there to guide and to advise

. . . and hence there was engendered a freedom of thought and action conducive to mental independence. (Chittenden, 1928: 48–49)

At the outset, Sheffield had two distinct populations: college graduates who wanted more scientific knowledge and students preparing for jobs in mining, engineering, agriculture, and manufacturing (Chittenden, 1928: 67). Gradually, however, these groups separated into two: those studying basic science and those studying applied science. The former organized around the Ph.D. degree, the latter around the professional-graduate degree or Master's.

The Ph.D.

As noted earlier, the first Ph.D. awarded in the United States was in chemistry, at Yale's Sheffield School of Science, affectionately called "Sheff," in 1861 (Chittenden, 1928). Throughout the nineteenth century, the United States outsourced its Ph.D. education to Germany. From 1815 to the onset of World War I, over 10,000 U.S. students pursued advanced study there, initially in the natural sciences and later, as the century came to a close, in the social sciences (Brubacher & Rudy, 1997: 175; Geiger, 2000: 352). The college did not consider the German university a competitive threat. For example, in 1870, the president of Columbia College (later Columbia University) expressed concern over the "exodus" of students to Germany. But owing to "opposition from an 'old guard' which feared diminution of the interests of Columbia College," fourteen years elapsed before Columbia established its own Ph.D. program (Brubacher & Rudy, 1997: 183, 485). The few institutions that did attempt to match Germany suffered economic setbacks. Johns Hopkins University, often cited as the United States' first serious competitor with Germany, paid a heavy price when its eponymous donor insisted that the institution hold his Baltimore & Ohio Railroad stock. The university's total endowment consisted of 15,000 shares of that one stock, whose value crashed in 1887. Likewise, Stanley Hall's vision of a graduate school at Clark University in Massachusetts dissolved when its founder withdrew his financial support (Hefferlin, 1969: 43). However, the University of Chicago capitalized on these failures by raiding the struggling universities' faculty (see below) and enjoyed first-mover advantage from the turn of the century until mid-century.

The impetus grew to replicate and surpass Germany. Presidents of five elite institutions informally organized the so-called Ph.D. trust (Hawkins, 1992: 15): Nicolas Murray Butler of Columbia, Charles Eliot of Harvard (who did graduate work in chemistry in Germany), Daniel Coit Gilman of Johns Hopkins (co-founder of Sheffield), Benjamin Ide Wheeler of the University of California at Berkeley (Ph.D., University of

Heidelberg), and William Rainey Harper of the University of Chicago (Ph.D., Yale Sheffield School). They aspired to stop depending on Germany and build the domestic Ph.D. (Geiger, 2000: 270, 315). They also stopped colleges from awarding honorary Ph.D.'s to their own faculty. This gratuitous practice had convinced German universities that all U.S. Ph.D.-granting institutions were diploma mills.

Graduate students in particular organized to protect and advance their status (Kohler, 1996: 110–14). They turned to the Ph.D. trust, which added fourteen more members and organized formally as the Association of American Universities (AAU) (Hawkins, 1992: 10–15). The trust and the graduate students eventually distinguished a German-equivalent U.S. Ph.D. (Brubacher & Rudy, 1997: 195; Selden, 1960: 68). In 1904, the University of Berlin formally recognized AAU members as the standard of U.S. graduate-school education, and the AAU became the de facto accrediting agency for the U.S. Ph.D. degree (Selden, 1960: 69–70). The AAU set up a committee to oversee accreditation. It ranked colleges according to their graduates' success in graduate school. (In doing so, it not only took away the colleges' self-authorization to grant Ph.D.'s but also undermined the college's broader authority: using students' performance in graduate school to evaluate the college implied the college could not evaluate itself, much less Ph.D. candidates, and that undergraduate education had only instrumental, not intrinsic value.) As a result, colleges exited the Ph.D. business (Geiger, 2000: 351).

In professionalizing, basic and applied scientists formed a hierarchy, with the former based in the graduate division and the latter in the professional schools. However, they also defined each another. Basic science needed applied science, and vice versa. This dynamic merits discussion because of the greater complications in the institutionalization of social science than in natural science.

In the early 1870s, Charles Eliot began his extensive reform of Harvard College. He conceived of the university as integrating previously separate parts (Wert, 1952; James, 1930). At that time, Harvard University included the college, a law school, a medical school, and the Lawrence Scientific School. In an unprecedented action, Eliot took control of the law school, a previously autonomous institution with its own board (James, 1930: 268). Eliot also resolved the problematic coexistence of the Lawrence Scientific School and Harvard College, which he thought compromised the academic integrity of the whole institution. Distinguishing between technology and fundamental science, he separated the former into two parts. He placed "general science" in the college and gave the "necessary and separate function"—"merely to train engineers"—to Lawrence. He then began negotiations to spin off the latter to the Massachusetts Institute of Technology (MIT). At the same time, he socially integrated Lawrence and Harvard College by allowing Lawrence students to live in the college dormitories (James, 1930: 293–95).

Eliot's actions followed the emerging movement to professionalize science, embodied in a scholarly circle known as the Lazzaroni (Kohlstedt, 1976: 156–68). Harvard had a Lazzaroni champion on its faculty, Louis Agassiz. The Lazzaroni sought to elevate science from the second-class scientific school and the even lowlier popular domain (Sinclair, 1974). The Lazzaroni particularly resented the itinerant lecturer and the entertainer-lecturer ("Professor Marvel") associated with the college and lyceum (Kohlstedt, 1976: 19). In addition to Harvard, this circle prevailed at the Franklin Institute, which organized around the idea of pure science (Sinclair, 1974; McMahon & Morris, 1977). The Lazzaroni held that science could advance only when separated from the mechanical and industrial arts and, more radically, from teaching. They insisted on exclusive devotion to research (Sinclair, 1974: 152–54). The Lazzaroni organized the United States' first elite science movement, following Britain's Royal Society (Kohlstedt, 1976: 156). Their campaign advanced with the U.S. government's establishment of the National Academy of Sciences in 1863—the very same Congress that passed the Morrill Act (Stratton & Mannix, 2005: 288–89). Ironically, the eclectic Benjamin Franklin gave birth to both the popular and the elite scientific traditions: in Philadelphia, he founded the philosopher-mechanics societies; and his grandson, Alexander Dallas Bache, was a Lazzaroni who oversaw the Franklin Institute's transition from a working man's club in the popular-science tradition to the most elite scientific organization of its day (Sinclair, 1974).

The pure–applied bipolarity explains the coexistence of Harvard and MIT. Agassiz dominated the former; William Barton Rogers, MIT's founder, had a more "eclectic" vision that combined cultural, pure-scientific, and applied-scientific subjects (Stratton & Mannix, 2005: 288–89). Harvard, a traditional institution, did not quickly embrace the values of science and applied science (Baltzell, 1979: 44). Colonial life associated vocational education with education for the poor (Mann, 1918). Localities taxed populations to "educate" poor children to earn a living instead of depending on the public treasury. "Manual" education was thus stigmatized. However, it gradually became associated with wealth creation instead of relief from impoverishment. This evolution shows in the definition of science given by Nathan Bailey, an English lexicographer, as early as 1730. Bailey defined science as "a formed system of any Branch of Knowledge, comprehending the Doctrine, Reasons, or Theory of the Thing, without any immediate Application of it to any Uses or Offices of Life." He associated technology with "Arts, especially Mechanical Ones"—that is, "such arts wherein the Hand and Body are more concerned than the Mind, and which are generally cultivated for the sake of the Gain or Profit that accrues from them" (Stratton & Mannix, 2005: 99). The definition shows the change in values and practices from the colonial to the industrial era; that is, the embrace of gainful values and practices was both a condition and a consequence of the knowledge-status reorganization in the research university and in society.

The scientific school and professional science remained fledgling institutions throughout the nineteenth century. Their founders and leaders moved quickly, however, on another front—the synergy between occupational training and science and the university's gaining of the authority to confer professional status.

THE OCCUPATIONAL-BECOMING-PROFESSIONAL SCHOOL

The university grew not only by transforming science from amateur to professional status but also by taking over job training from the guilds (see Table 3). It initially appropriated legal and medical training (Stevens, 1983: 37; Kaufman, 1976: 117).

As noted previously, colleges had affiliated with law and medical schools. At Harvard, although the schools were formally "departments of the university" in 1848 (Warren, 1908: 371), Eliot fully activated this relationship. By making college a prerequisite for law and medicine, he coordinated the parts of the university to make a new whole (Wert, 1952). This radically changed the occupations' culture, or, according to Eliot, their lack of culture and even their barbarism.

In an influential 1869 article in the widely circulating *Atlantic Monthly*, Eliot stated that he could only speak "sarcastically" of law and medicine as "learned professions" (Hofstadter & Smith, 1961, quoting Eliot, 1869: 635). Theology could prepare "young men of scanty education" to be "successful pulpit exhorts" in eighteen months. But the fact that "only a very small proportion of lawyers and doctors" had earned Bachelor of Arts degrees was scandalous. Eliot singled out the University of Michigan as an example. Its catalogue for 1867–68 listed 387 law students,

not one of whom appears to have possessed . . . any degree whatever . . . To enter the school, a young man must be eighteen years of age, and he must present a certificate of good moral character. Nothing else is required. To obtain a degree he must follow certain courses of lectures through two terms of six months each. Nothing else is required.

The same catalogue listed 411 medical students, nineteen of whom possessed a Bachelor of Arts degree. "The school is established in the small town of Ann Arbor, quite remote from large hospitals. Poor humanity shudders at the spectacle of so large a crop of such doctors" (Hofstadter & Smith, 1961, quoting Eliot, 1869: 635).

Historians of legal education (Stevens, 1983; LaPiana, 1994; Johnson, 1978) and medical education (Rothstein, 1987; Kaufman, 1976) describe the long and complicated process by which universities, beginning with an elite group that included Harvard (as in the case of the Ph.D. trust), took control of occupational training. Stevens (1983) and Johnson (1978) note that in legal education this move eliminated proprietary evening schools, established the Bachelor's degree as a prerequisite, and set a residency norm of three years. If dated to Eliot's presidency of Harvard, this process transpired from the 1870s to the 1940s. A milestone event occurred in the mid-1920s, when the medical profession (Kaufman, 1976: 178), legal profession (Stevens, 1983: 193), and the university agreed on a prerequisite of four years of high school and two years of college (Kaufman, 1976: 178). A second milestone occurred in the 1940s, when the standard of four years of college plus three years' residency was widely established for law school (Stevens, 1983: 207). This process involved protracted negotiation among the professional communities, the universities, and the states, which regulated the guilds. It initially took hold in elite schools and devolved to a middle tier; then it eliminated the lower tier of part-time and night schools. Highly restricting access, this move also established these two professions at the top of the professional hierarchy and set the gold standard that other aspiring professionals, such as engineers and accountants, would follow (see Chapter 3).

The basic–applied conversion, fairly smooth in medicine, was problematic in law. The field recalibrated from a basis in divine order to secular order and principles (LaPiana, 1994). At Harvard Law School, Dean Christopher Langdell (1870–95) pursued a legal science by systematically identifying influential legal decisions and determining the principles governing these decisions (LaPiana, 1994). Eliot and Langdell also sought to advance the status of legal education by devaluing apprenticeship and night schools. They met with a serious problem because legal education did not have a professional professoriate but only moonlighting practitioners (Johnson, 1978: 102–5). Harvard pioneered in this respect by hiring James Barr Ames, the first law school faculty member with no experience practicing law. Harvard celebrated this milestone in professional legal education. With Langdell's approach, Harvard built a reputation as the nation's premier educator of law school faculty (Johnson, 1978: 114).

For over three decades, then, beginning in the early 1870s, Eliot and Langdell labored to raise the status of law schools—not just Harvard, but all law schools—as graduate institutions. Consensus took time because each state issued its own bar exam and license, and each had its own legislative group and process. In 1900, Langdell's successor, professor James Bradley Thayer, joined with colleagues of other elite institutions to form the Association of American Law Schools (AALS). They targeted the evening proprietary schools owned by practitioners, a holdover from the apprenticeship system, and depicted them as diploma mills. Robert Stevens (1983: 74) argued that the move also targeted immigrant, minority, and working-class groups. If this is so, then the business school's institutionalization in University Extension (see Chapter 3) proves its singular importance in the School of Opportunity (Kett, 1994).

Eliot and his colleagues fully transformed legal education. They established it as graduate education, with content based on science—or at least professional research understood as pursuing legal science. More important, they established a new knowledge hierarchy: Law professors, not practicing attorneys, developed and dispensed this knowledge. The new law professoriate/legal scientist was crucial to the university's appropriation of legal education. At the same time, this category brought an end to the unprofessional educator and the occupational practitioner. Henceforth, the professional scientist trained the professional practitioner. Also, the new student was strictly a full-time and pre-qualified student. These requirements raised the financial stakes of legal and medical education not only because the schools charged tuition, but more important, because students had to forgo earning income for an unprecedented length of time. Wallace Donham would draw from Harvard's success in reforming legal education to develop Harvard's professional model of the business school in the early twentieth century (see Chapter 3).

EXTENSION: THE UNIVERSITY APPROPRIATES THE SCHOOL OF OPPORTUNITY

As law and medical schools raised their requirements, University Extension welcomed everyone, particularly a new population of working adults in the School of Opportunity (SOO) tradition (Kett, 1994), which turned the university into a social elevator: virtually anyone could become a professional by affiliating, however loosely, with the research university.

In the colonial era, those excluded from or uninterested in the classical college pursued their education through alternative means—informally, alone and/or in small groups, following "do-it-yourself" logic (see Table 4). Anne Hutchinson started a Bible study group in her home. Benjamin Franklin organized the Junto study group and the philosopher-mechanics societies (Sinclair, 1974). Women organized clubs around religious, charitable, and eventually political causes (Blair, 1980). Correspondence schools thrived for women, rural populations, working persons, and those of modest means. Itinerant scholars conducted traveling lecture shows. Ralph Waldo Emerson, Henry David Thoreau, Horace Greeley—even Louis Agassiz—were "veterans of the lyceum platforms" and thus the "perennial and peripatetic schoolmasters of America" (Tyler, 1944: 263). In the late nineteenth century, a particularly strong SOO developed in the United States. Eldon Snyder traced this success to the adult education movement based at Chautauqua, in New York, and the lyceum or lecture series, which served "the common men and women in villages and farming communities" (Snyder, 1985: 79). Community organizations such as the Young Men's Christian Association (YMCA) served this population in more organized forms (Lee, 2010). In 1860, four YMCAs offered classes. Most prepared students for the ministry. However, in the 1880s, YMCAs began to offer evening classes "in commercial subjects." In the 1920s, about twenty YMCAs housed evening law schools, and about seventy-five had evening schools for auto mechanics (Kett, 1994: 243). The SOO secured broad consensus that education led to, and should lead to, good jobs and higher status (Kett 1994: 234).

Universities entered the SOO through Extension. The "Extension movement" began in Great Britain (Kett, 1994: 183–84). In the United States, it incorporated the lecture series, the correspondence school, and the summer school. It also maintained close ties to local communities. In contrast to the more conservative and privately oriented eastern institutions, midwestern universities used Extension to win enrollments, revenue, and popularity. Extension's itinerant lecturers enjoyed the local hospitality. "The local mainstays of Extension were the teachers and church and social clubs whose members made house-to-house ticket sales and opened their homes to the teachers" (Kett, 1994: 186, quoting Rosenstreter).

In the top institution of higher education in the Midwest, the University of Chicago, Extension enjoyed exceptionally high regard. The founding president of the university, William Rainey Harper, had taught Hebrew and held a formal administrative position at Chautauqua. When Harper took the helm at Chicago, "his idea was to make the new University the greatest center in the country for adult education" (Reeves et al., 1933: 3) and he pursued this idea throughout his tenure (Ryan, 1939: 136). Before Harper's presidency, adult education had not figured much in conversations about the emerging U.S. university (Storr, 1966: 61).

Harper offered four adult-education programs: public lectures, evening courses at a downtown location for full-time working adults, correspondence school, and "special courses in a scientific study of the Bible in its original languages and in translation" (Storr, 1966: 61). He also gave library borrowing privileges to students in all programs. Chautauqua offered summer programs for teachers, and Harper repeated this practice at Chicago.

For Harper, Extension fulfilled the university's highest aspiration. Harper held that science could not flourish "except in a community in which interest in a higher education is widespread." The university met a demand for knowledge; more important, it engaged in the "more difficult and important work of creating in the community at large that demand for the best of everything in the intellectual, aesthetic, and moral world which is at once the evidence of, and the surest means toward, the higher civic life" (Storr, 1966: 197). Harper also emphasized reciprocal learning between students and teachers. Extension would bring the University "into direct contact with human life and activity" (Storr, 1966: 197). For faculty, Extension teaching would "promote wider appreciation of the viewpoints and interests of non-academic people and should also stimulate faculty members to carry over into their classroom work the vitality and interest that are necessary for success in the public-lecture field" (Reeves et al., 1933: 83).

Harper's enterprise flourished: "The gospel of culture and enlightened citizenship touched the lives of persons in 368 centers in 21 states. The number of courses was 1,326 and of traveling libraries 715. A total of 272,967 seats were taken for lecture courses . . . the number of admissions to the individual lectures was 1,637,802" (Storr, 1966: 204). Furthermore, Harper wanted to raise Extension's standards from the "cultural entertainment" of one-time lectures to steady attendance and to degrees. But as the university became more scholarly, Extension became less scholarly. Gradually, two different faculties—one traveling, one resident—formed. Municipal, city, and community colleges offered courses locally and better served local demand by being exclusively local institutions. At the University of Chicago, Extension became a peripheral, and eventually an inferior, part of the research institution. However, more than any other part of the university, the business school would fulfill Harper's vision through a new institution, that of the executive-scholar (see Chapter 4).

DE NOVO INSTITUTIONS:
LEADING IN BASIC AND APPLIED SCIENCE

The above exposition has focused on the Harvard case and that of a college integrating its loosely affiliated parts to form a university. But pure and applied science advanced with greater ease in new institutions that did not orbit around the college. At Chicago, Harper's "underlying purpose" was "to free the University from the handicaps of the traditional college and thereby stimulate scholarship and research." Harper did not temper his criticism of the college: He said that it had "actually destroyed the intellectual growth of thousands of strong and able men" (Ryan, 1939: 140).

Science was professionalized in the technical institute and the graduate school. The following section takes the Carnegie Institute of Technology (CIT) and the University of Chicago (Chicago), respectively, as exemplars in this regard.

The Carnegie Institute of Technology (CIT)

CIT began as a vocational school in 1903. As early as 1880, Andrew Carnegie had shown interest in "technical rather than classical education, in the practical instead of the liberal arts," by funding the Lauder Technical School in his birthplace of Dunfermline, Scotland. "More . . . than any one man, Lauder and his solutions of mechanical problems as they arose demonstrated to Carnegie the value of a technically trained mind." In 1878, a young metallurgist told Carnegie that some material he tossed out contained more pure oxide of iron for his blast furnaces than what he was shipping in from outside the area for nine dollars per ton. Carnegie ordered the metallurgist to develop the idea in secret. He succeeded, and the secret was kept for two years. During that time, Carnegie reaped "an enormous saving." As Carnegie wrote, "Chemistry was the agency, above all others, most needful in the manufacture of iron and steel . . . we trod upon sure ground with the chemist as our guide" (Tarbell, 1937: 14–15).

CIT's director (later given the title of president), was Arthur Arton Hamerschlag, a former trade-school principal. He was educated at the Hebrew Institute, "one of the few places in the entire City of New York where a poor lad could, in the evenings, learn the rudiments of the trade he wished to enter." He taught mechanical drawing at an elementary school and organized evening classes at a "boys' club." By 1902, he was considered a leader in industrial education (Tarbell, 1937: 28–29).

But CIT suffered because it did not hold collegiate status. Ironically, it could not even benefit from the Carnegie Foundation's pension program for teachers. State legislation required that teachers have a college degree, so CIT's graduates could not teach in the public schools. CIT decided to raise its status. It briefly separated into two parts, a trade school and an engineering college, which created "vexatious" problems in campus social and extracurricular life. By 1920, though, CIT had transitioned from a "sub-collegiate trade school" to "an engineering school doing full collegiate work" (Tarbell, 1937: 90–95).

In 1909, CIT established a Division of Applied Psychology. Hamerschlag featured the news in his 1916 annual report. He emphasized the opportunity for "the study of important problems which confront commercial and manufacturing enterprises, and the relationship of education to those interests." With his "characteristic zeal when fostering innovations," Hamerschlag established six bureaus of "human engineering." Tarbell captures this zeal: "Disavowing the traditional theory of the Declaration of Independence, of Greek civilization, and of modern labor unions as to the equality of man, and proceeding on the premise that all men are not equal, that there are enormous fundamental differences in individuals and that these differences can be tabulated to a workable degree by a rating scale," the researchers developed psychological tests to fit the man to the job—in sales, supervisory, and clerical work. Thirty major corporations sponsored the research. The bureau also worked on "industrial education, employment management, analysis of jobs, and the trade testing of workingmen." Walter Dill Scott, who had developed the field of industrial psychology at Northwestern University, became professor of applied psychology at CIT; Tarbell calls this the first such appointment (1937: 61). When the United States entered World War I, "the Carnegie bureaus stood out . . . as the only group of experts doing work of this description in civilian life." By 1917, Carnegie's rating scale became "the official system used by the Government for promoting, demoting, and transferring the 150,000 officers in the U.S. Army." The group's tests were used to classify 2 million enlisted men. "It was not long before the entire military personnel system was administered by The Committee on Classification of Personnel in the Army," whose heads, CIT professors, now bore colonels' commissions. General Pershing cabled orders that every officer be rated before arriving in France (Tarbell, 1937: 64).

CIT's experiment with its applied science put the institution in a new league, far from its beginnings as a vocational school for immigrant youths. Although the Applied Psychology Division was gradually eliminated from 1919 to 1924, President Robert Doherty, trained in Yale's (Sheffield's) scientific tradition, revived the research agenda in the mid-1930s. He attached research laboratories to the teaching departments. With research labs in molecular physics, applied chemistry, metals research, and coal research, CIT now specialized in the hard sciences. This success established the infrastructure for CIT to conduct nuclear research for the U.S. government in the mid-1940s and to win confidence in a new, engineering-based business school model, the Graduate

School of Industrial Administration (GSIA). Ultimately, CIT secured elite status in applied science and set the bar for other institutions in this regard.

The University of Chicago

Some reformers, giving up on the college, pursued a "university proper," devoted exclusively to graduate work (Ryan, 1939: 96). The University of Chicago was founded by the Baptists, who desired their own high-status educational institution. Augustus Strong, a Baptist leader who had presided over the congregation attended by John D. Rockefeller when he was "a rising young business man" in Cleveland (Ryan, 1939: 92–93), lamented to Rockefeller in 1887:

[W]e Baptists, with two millions and a half of members and ten millions of constituency, are so unspeakably behindhand in matters of education, are making so insufficient provision for the future, are letting other smaller bodies of Christians go so far ahead of us, are losing day by day so many of our best and brightest men because we have no proper facilities for their education. We have no theological seminary that has a quarter of the strength of the Union Seminary in New York. We have no college that has a tenth of the influence or equipment of Harvard or Yale. So our young men go to Harvard and Yale and Princeton, and—leave the Baptist ranks . . . We need an institution which shall be truly a university, where, as at Johns Hopkins, there shall be a large number of fellowships, where research shall be endowed, where the brightest men shall be attracted and helped through their studies, where the institution itself shall furnish a real society of people distinguished in science and art. (Ryan, 1939: 95–96)

The key decisions concerned the location and the leadership of the new institution. Rockefeller oscillated between Chicago and New York; but he definitely decided on William Rainey Harper as founding president. Frederick Gates, secretary of the American Baptist Education Society (and later, overseer of all Rockefeller's philanthropic endeavors), urged Rockefeller to choose Chicago. He gave a paper before the Baptist Ministers' Conference, convening in Chicago, entitled "A New University in Chicago: A Denominational Necessity." Gates shifted the discussion from a denominational to a regional level. Alluding to the liaison between agrarian populism and higher education, he underscored the need "to counteract the western tendency to a merely superficial and utilitarian education." The city of Chicago, he asserted, was "the most commanding social, financial, literary, and religious eminence in the West . . . Chicago is the heart of the West, the fountain of western life . . . All roads lead to Chicago. All cities, all rural homes face Chicago . . . Nothing great or worthy can be achieved or attempted for education in the

West until this thing is done" (Ryan, 1936: 100). Although Rockefeller had originally envisioned founding a college, Harper "had never had in mind anything less than a real university, with colleges and graduate departments." When Rockefeller agreed to the proposal, Harper turned his back on Yale, where he had accepted a position. One of his colleagues chastised him:

You "draw" well, undoubtedly. But, my dear fellow, back of you and of all of us here is the one great power that lends to us more effectiveness than we contribute to it. It is "Yale" that draws. While you are in your prime few men will care for a Ph.D. or even a B.A. from your new university, who can manage to get a similar degree from an institution like this. (Ryan, 1939: 106)

Beyond Rockefeller's initial contribution, Harper convinced him to donate another 1 million dollars "for the express purpose of establishing graduate work." Harper did not delegate the job of hiring faculty, following the principle that "it is men and nothing but men that make education." One of Harper's deans, Marion Talbot, commented that Harper "scoured the academic world for great scholars who would dare exchange comfortable and safe positions for the hazards and excitement of a new undertaking." Harper enjoyed a "heaven sent" opportunity when Clark University began to fail. The "migration" from Clark gave Harper "a group of the best-equipped men to be had anywhere in America, already selected and trained to do, in graduate work especially, the very things Harper wanted the University of Chicago to undertake" (Ryan, 1939: 119).

Chicago's next visionary leader, Robert Hutchins, commented in 1929, "If the first faculty of the University of Chicago had met in a tent, this would still have been a great university" (Ryan, 1939: 117). In 1934, Hutchins could boast that the American Council on Education ranked the university as distinguished in twenty-one out of twenty-six fields:

The University has the largest number of starred scientists in American Men of Science in proportion to the size of its faculty. A study of the Association of American Colleges shows that the University leads all other institutions in training teachers of distinction. The University, by all the tests we can apply, is appealing to better and better students. ("The Excellence of the University," 1934, SCRC-UCL, RMHP, B385: F10)

More difficult to describe was the "intellectual intensity" among faculty and graduate students, which two researchers associated with Chicago's "geographic isolation (both from the centers of American higher education on the east coast and from the urban center of the city of Chicago itself)" (Emmett & Kovacek, 2009: 5). CIT and Chicago would become key actors in raising the business school's academic status (see Chapter 4).

Chicago and CIT pioneered in securing elite status and in providing institutional models for doing so in basic and applied science. As science took on more rarified status, the business school pioneered on the opposite end of the spectrum: it popularized the university and higher education to the point of threatening this status. Mainstreaming the rogue business school would become a central preoccupation of the twentieth-century research university, and arguably its greatest business opportunity.

CHAPTER 3

The Nineteenth-Century Business School

Fall of the Classical and Rise of the Vocational and School of Opportunity Traditions

☽

Even as the old order, which was based in the college, clergy, and aristocracy, declined, business education first developed in the classical college because of its high status. The founders of the collegiate school of business (CSB) sought to remake the gentleman for industrial life. This chapter uses the Wharton School of Finance and Economy (WSFE) at the University of Pennsylvania as the exemplar of the CSB. After a half-century of experimentation, however, the business school did not integrate with the college. Students used it not to earn a degree but to take short courses and earn certificates that would allow them to obtain jobs and promotions in the near term. Also, although the business school's practitioner faculty did not value or pursue the Ph.D., they nevertheless resented their secondary status in academe. They were particularly offended by the political economists aligned with the Social Gospel movement, whom they accused of using the CSB for political advocacy. The WSFE accounting faculty therefore spun off a new institution, which I call the vocational school of business (VSB); it broke with the college and partnered with Extension and the SOO. The VSB grew knowledge and jobs by fragmenting into finer-grained specialties and by codifying the newest practices in each specialty. It attracted students by linking education to employment and by popularizing the path whereby law and medicine had risen from occupations to professions—that is, by affiliating with the research university. The VSB attracted a large and entirely new population to the university, but it also created a legitimacy crisis in the professionalizing academy.

THE COLLEGIATE SCHOOL OF BUSINESS

The CSB was an experiment in elevating business training and in making higher education practical. It was predicated on the college's high status in society and education and on an aspiring gentleman seeking a Bachelor's degree and completing a four-year residency/initiation. However, the CSB also incubated a very different constituency that eventually took over the institution and used it to further specialist interests in sufficiently massive numbers, and with sufficient variety, to make the business school and the research university as a whole into a popular institution.

Historians often call the WSFE (today, The Wharton School) the nation's oldest business school; but this statement ignores institutions whose short lives reflect the CSB's fledgling nature. If one defines "business school" as a place where full-time faculty members teach a subject called "business" in a college, then the University of Louisiana opened the United States' first business school in 1851. However, the school closed in 1857. Likewise, Illinois Industrial University (now the University of Illinois) established its School of Commerce in 1870 but terminated it in 1880: the transformation of a mere "business college" (a reference to the then-dominant form, commercial education) into a "University School of Commerce" had failed. "The school had done little more than prepare clerks and bookkeepers. It had not been realized that the function of a university school of commerce was to prepare for future leadership in economic enterprise, not for clerkships" (Lockwood, 1938: 132). The program was restarted in 1902 just as the VSB began to dominate business education.

Consistent with the logic of the classical college, the CSB changed business from a proprietary school for clerks to an institution providing higher education for gentlemen. Thus it offered not only clerical instruction in "the forms and details of business" but also taught "the principles of commerce, economy, trade and mercantile law." The point merits emphasis: the business school did not attach itself to the college, as law and medicine had done, but was located *within* the college. The CSB went to the heart, literally, of higher education. Gentlemen prepared for business while still obtaining "scientific and literary culture" (Ruml, 1928: 54).

Reformers justified higher business education in two ways: they maintained that the classical college, through its required political economy course, already taught business, so the old category absorbed the new "applied economics"; and they held that accounting, having theory and principles that bookkeeping applied, constituted the higher learning of business. Absorbing business into political economy kept the reforms in the college's control and minimized disruption: even the most conservative faculty could teach the old political economy under the new name of business, hire a local practitioner to teach an accounting elective, and call itself a business school.

Joseph Wharton attempted a more ambitious overhaul (Wharton, 1881); however, the college's economics faculty gradually subsumed it financially and administratively (Sass, 1982: 44–45; Cheyney, 1940: 365). Wharton lost interest in the institution and severed it from his will in 1906. Similarly, the University of Chicago, usually regarded as the second or third business school to be established, after WSFE and the University of California at Berkeley, founded its school as "a group of existing courses within the existing organization" and foresaw its future accordingly (Marshall, 1913: 99, 109–10). The school did not have administrative autonomy—for example, the ability to grant Bachelors' and advanced degrees—until 1916 ("Business Training and Research," 1930, SCRC-UCL, RMHP, B56: F8). Harvard founded its business school in 1908; but it did not establish administrative autonomy until 1913 (Morison, 1930: 538). It achieved financial autonomy, such as the authorization to solicit its own funds, in the early 1920s. A large donation in 1924 gave the school physical autonomy—its own buildings (Morison, 1930: 546–47).

In fact, colleges had difficulty accepting "a business major in an arts [classical] college" (Marshall, 1913: 41). The first Master's degree in business, at Dartmouth's Tuck School in 1900, posed no threat to the college faculty because they ran it. The college trustees "wished to guard jealously the established policy that the college is an institution of the arts, humanities, and sciences" (Ruml, 1928: 58) and did not introduce new courses into the curriculum. The college's economics faculty controlled admission to Tuck. The Master's and Bachelor's degrees were integrated, so that the men earned both in five years. Initially, though, the trustees went so far as to refuse to give Tuck students a degree. They found no "existing degree" that "adequately expresses the character of the work done." Instead, they gave a certificate, which they deemed would "prove more acceptable than an academic degree to the business community" (Broehl, 1999: 42). The proprietary schools had also offered certificates, so Dartmouth was acknowledging comparability with them while also affirming that graduates earned academic status through their Dartmouth diploma.

The fate of the University of Illinois "Commerce Department" epitomized the business school's difficulties with the college. In the late 1870s, the Commerce Department "became an embarrassment" when its head offered a second year of bookkeeping consisting of simulating banking operations using a fictitious currency (Solberg, 1968: 160). The university's president held that this "fatuous play-acting" violated the public service principles of the Morrill Act.

The CSB brought the college's paternalism into relief. Although the institution was perceived as moving young men along to their inheritance of property and status, "college men" had a reputation for indolence and irresponsibility (Kanigel, 1997: 129). Through the nineteenth century, boys as young as 14 could attend college (Bailyn et al., 1986: 51), which in some cases hardly differed from an "academy" (today's secondary school). In this way, the college's pedagogical purpose (from the Greek, "child") and its other familial values and customs ("in loco parentis"; "alma mater") took on literal meanings. Clergymen teachers and administrators reared the young men, checking that they attended chapel and punishing them corporally for offenses.

Joseph Wharton set the bar higher. He aimed to create an institution that would create a "vigorous" gentleman for the industrial age.

The Wharton School of Finance and Economy

Joseph Wharton distinguished himself from other reformers through careful planning and execution. His project also benefited from the interest in science and experimentation in Philadelphia (Bridenbaugh & Bridenbaugh, 1942) and particularly at the University of Pennsylvania under Provost William Pepper (Cheyney, 1940).

Wharton's WSFE made the college into a strategic economic institution. It cultivated a gentleman oriented to policymaking for wealth creation. It also linked individual, regional, and national wealth creation. These synergies were not new; the classical college had grown hand in glove with economic and cultural institutions (Charlton, 1986: 7). However, in New England, this process had occurred organically, the exemplar being Harvard's co-institutionalization with the Boston Brahmins and the Massachusetts commonwealth (Baltzell, 1979; Story, 1980). The WSFE worked more deliberately: Wharton used the WSFE as an instrument in his protracted campaign to extend the tariff on industrial metals.

The tariff advanced U.S. interests—northern interests particularly (Bensel, 2000), Pennsylvania's industrial over New England's mercantile interests more particularly (Hartz, 1948: 15), and Wharton's own financial interests most particularly. Pennsylvania possessed great natural resources. The new science of applied chemistry enabled extraction and manufacturing of precious metals and their conversion to arms and machines. Wharton deemed that new industry needed new policy. The college had long held to theological and classical-economic doctrine, but it did not advocate concrete action on legislation. Wharton thus went to new lengths in applying "applied moral philosophy," or underlying protectionist principles (Rudolph, 1981: 177), to pro-tariff policy specifically.

Traditionally, New England's economic philosophy emphasized free trade as opposed to Southern "republicanism," following Jeffersonian and mid-Atlantic "protectionism" (O'Connor, 1994). Wharton helped found a school of protectionist philosophy in Philadelphia, led by Henry Carey. Until then, protectionism did not enjoy intellectual prestige (O'Connor, 1994: 284) although the University of Pennsylvania had taught a mild form of protectionism since the early 1860s (Sass, 1982: 32–33).

When he founded the WSFE, Wharton had worked on his tariff campaign for over fifteen years, having begun it to extend the tariff after the Civil War ended. He redefined the purpose of the tariff from war-funding to nation-building. (The United States had no income tax until 1913.) Wharton led a group of fellow industrialists to draft legislation and win congressional approval. He also wrote, published, and distributed protectionist literature, including an 1875 textbook that he had placed in libraries nationwide (Sass, 1982: 15).

The classical college's courses in moral and political philosophy, or political economy, inculcated values grounded in theological doctrine (Bryson, 1932a, 1932b). In the nineteenth century, political economy became the disciplinary base for the emerging "science of society" (Guralnick, 1975: 31), particularly the idea of replicating natural science's advances in the social realm. As the moral philosophy course became the political-economy course (Bryson, 1932a, 1932b), economic-philosophical content, such as Bentham's dictum of action for the greatest good to the greatest numbers, replaced theological content (O'Connor, 1994). Wharton took this logic a step further by adding direct advocacy.

Political economy teaching began integrating concrete action by shifting from indoctrination to discussion of "various social institutions and relations, abstracted and considered as fields for the application" of theological as well as economic principles (Bryson, 1932a: 306). Francis Wayland's textbook, extensively used in New England colleges, shows the difficulties associated with this change (O'Connor, 1994: 281–82). In the traditional logic, divine principles elucidated economic principles, which in turn elucidated action principles. Wayland did not derive tariff policy in this way. Rather, he insisted that students should know both sides and have evidence to reason the matter for themselves (Wayland, 1859 [1837]).

Wharton, for all his progressiveness, would have none of this exchange of ideas. Laissez-faire ideology, to Wharton, was "a fungus . . . which healthy political organisms can hardly afford to tolerate" (Sass, 1982: 21). Its teaching would compromise "the necessity of bold inculcation" of protectionism.

In terms of wealth and knowledge both, Wharton was in a unique position to reform the classical college and the gentleman. He founded the WSFE with a fortune he had already made four times: by discovering and perfecting a new process for manufacturing zinc, which gave him a 420 percent return on his investment from 1855 to 1862; by rebuilding a bankrupt nickel mine and refinery and combining with other manufacturers to dictate the price of Bismarck's new coin, which gave him a 300 percent return on his investment from 1868 to 1871; by investing in iron with perfect timing to exploit demand from the transcontinental railroad; and by leading the formerly Quaker and traditionally pacifist Bethlehem Iron Company (later Bethlehem Steel) into the lucrative arms business (Sass, 1982).

Wharton's family had given him an excellent education, beginning with highly reputed private elementary schools and tutoring from one of their headmasters (Sass, 1982: 4). He excelled in chemistry and studied in local chemists' laboratories. Scientific pursuits were taken more seriously in Philadelphia than anywhere else in the United States, including Boston (Baltzell, 1979; Bridenbaugh & Bridenbaugh, 1942). Wharton also apprenticed in accounting with a local merchant and learned bookkeeping, insurance, foreign exchange, and contracts. He was self-taught in metallurgy as well as in the administrative and legal aspects of his industrial metals businesses.

Wharton's entry into education reform merits attention because of the care he took in preparing and executing his move. He began in 1879 by researching the history of higher education and particularly the "vocationally oriented university" (Sass, 1982: 35). Two years later, he submitted his proposal to the University of Pennsylvania trustees. It specified the number of faculty and the names, order, and content of courses. The trustees referred Wharton's proposal to a subcommittee chaired by the vice-provost, a professor of moral philosophy. Three other professors—of political economy, mathematics, and Latin—also served on the committee (Sass, 1982: 38). The committee and the faculty agreed to a two-year trial.

Wharton wrote a strategic plan for the WSFE (1881), which has been published only in excerpts (Sass, 1982). In this document, Wharton exposed the failures of both the higher education provided by the classical college and the lower education provided by the apprenticeship system. His exposition, and his specifications for operationalizing his vision in the WSFE, demonstrate that Wharton understood business as a new type of knowledge for governance and the CSB as the means to deliver it. (Note: in the following section, all quotations are from Wharton, 1881.)

Wharton's Strategic Plan for the Strategic CSB

Wharton held that the college failed miserably in preparing students for "the actual duties of life" outside the ministry, law, and medicine. However, he took inspiration from the new technical and scientific schools, which disproved the "general conviction" that college could not accomplish such a broader and better preparation. By basing their instruction "upon the broad principles deduced from all human knowledge," and grounded "in science, as well as in art," these new schools accomplished far more than the institution of apprenticeship, which only perpetuated the "narrow, various, and empirical routines of certain shops." Pupils were thus fit "both to practice what they have learned and to become themselves teachers and discoverers." The world of commerce, however, with the exception of houses "of the first rank for magnitude and intelligence," neglected the institution of apprenticeship, which fell apart with the decline of the "counting-houses of the old-time merchants." Nor did the proprietary schools suffice "to fit a young man for the struggle of commercial life, for wise management of a private estate, or for efficient public service." In short, the conditions of business practice afforded little to no opportunity for the proper learning. The "over-worked heads" of business establishments could not instruct novices, who learned mostly from other employees. Moreover, to whatever extent learning took place, it did so in narrow bounds and according to routine. Novices did not learn "the various branches" but rather remained in areas where they had proven aptitude or "where [their] service was most needed." Furthermore, "ordinary prudence requires that many things indispensable to mastery of the business should be kept secret from these novices" (8–9).

Wharton also noted a clash between the college and apprenticeship. Upon completing college, young men were "too old to be desirable beginners in a counting-house, or to descend readily to its drudgery." However, these young men possessed a great material, intellectual, and cultural inheritance and the potential to use it for the greater good. By "inheritance, wealth, keenness of intellect, and latent power of command or organization," they possessed "wealth and capacity." But they lacked "that fundamental knowledge" that would enable them to use this inheritance "with advantage to themselves and to the community." Possessing such knowledge would also bring "tastes and self-reliance." Not possessing it would increase the "speedy ruin to great estate" and "indolent waste of great powers for good." This cost the nation greatly in the short and the long term.

Nor can any country long afford to have its laws made and its government administered by men who lack such training as would suffice to rid their minds of fallacies and qualify them for the solution of the social problems incident to our civilization. Evidently a great boon would be bestowed upon the nation if its young men of inherited intellect, means, and refinement could be more generally led so to manage their property as [sic], while husbanding it to benefit the community, or could be drawn into careers of unselfish legislation and administration.

Such a "class of men" would likely "become most useful members of society, whether in public or in private life." In other words, the business school was an "opportunity for good" comparable to the changes effected by the technical and scientific schools, but in the domain of service rather than matter—the husbandry of tangible and intangible inheritances "to benefit the community" and to build "careers of unselfish legislation and administration" (9–10).

Wharton described this knowledge generally as "the principles underlying successful business management and civil government." He provided further details in an attachment entitled "The Project." His purpose was to

provide for young men special means of training and of correct instruction in the knowledge and in the arts of modern Finance and Economy, both public and private, in order that, being well informed, and free from delusions upon these important subjects, they may either serve the community skillfully as well as faithfully in offices of trusts, or, remaining in private life, may prudently manage their own affairs and aid in maintaining sound financial morality: in short, to establish means for imparting a liberal education in all matters concerning Finance and Economy. (11)

Wharton thus proposed his "Liberal Education in All Matters Concerning Finance and Economy." He specified five faculty members and their curricula. He began with the accounting position, which would teach "the simplest and most practical forms" of private and commercial book-keeping and "the routine of business between a bank and a customer." The next three positions show how Wharton redefined the classical political economy so it could no longer be taught by theologians. He broke it into finer elements fitting the logic of specializing industry; and consistent with the college's cultural function, he also set forth the appropriate values to be inculcated in each specialty.

The professor or instructor of "Money and Currency" would teach:

[the] meaning, history, and functions of money and currency, showing particularly the necessity of permanent uniformity or integrity in the coin upon which the

money system of a nation is based; how an essential attribute of money is that it should be hard to get . . . the advantages of an adequate precious-metal fund for settling international balances as well as for regulating and checking by redemption the paper money and credits of a modern commercial nation; how such metallic hoards are amassed and defended; the extent to which paper money may be advantageously employed . . . the uses and abuses of credit, both private and public; the uses and abuses of bills of exchange, letters of credit, and promissory notes . . . the advantages and dangers of banks of issue, banks of deposit, and savings banks . . . the phenomena and causes of panics and money crises. (12–13)

The professor of "Taxation" would teach:

the history and practice of modern taxation as distinguished from the plunder, tribute, or personal service which it for the most part replaces; the proper objects and rates of taxation for municipal, State, or National purposes; the public ends for which money may properly be raised by taxation . . . the influences exercised upon the morality and prosperity of a community or nation by the various modes and extents of taxation; the effects upon taxation of wars and of standing armies; the extent to which corporations should be encouraged by the State, and to what extent they should be taxed as compared with individuals engaged in similar pursuits. (13)

Wharton devoted the longest discussion to the professor or instructor of "Industry, Commerce, and Transportation," whose subject would cover:

how industries advance in excellence, or decline, and shift from place to place; how by intelligent industry nations or communities thrive; how by superior skill and diligence some nations grow rich and powerful and how by idleness or ill-directed industry others become rude and poor; how a great nation should be as far as possible self-sufficient, maintaining a proper balance between agriculture, mining, and manufactures, and supplying its own wants; how mutual advantage results from the reciprocal exchange of commodities natural to one land for the diverse commodities natural to another, but how by craft in commerce one nation may take the substance of a rival and maintain for itself virtual monopoly of the most profitable and civilizing industries; how by suitable tariff legislation a nation may thwart such designs, may keep its productive industry active, cheapen the cost of commodities, and oblige foreigners to sell to it at low prices while contributing largely toward defraying the expenses of its government; also, the nature and origin of money wages; the necessity, for modern industry, of organizing under single leaders or employers great amounts of capital and great numbers of laborers, and of maintaining discipline among the latter; the proper division of the fruits of organized labor between capitalist, leader, and workman; the nature and prevention of "strikes"; the importance of educating men to combine their energies for the accomplishment of any desirable object, and the principles upon which such combinations should be effected. (13)

Like "Accounting," the course "Elementary and Mercantile Law" would teach current local, state, national, and international law pertaining to commercial transactions. However, Wharton added that in addition to teaching "the history and present status" of this legislation, the course should also teach "the directions in which improvements may be hoped and striven for" particularly with regard to "harmonizing or unifying under United States laws, the diverse legislation of the several States of this Nation" (13–14).

Finally, Wharton insisted on the need for classical liberal arts training in "clear, forcible, and unembarrassed utterance before an audience of whatever [students] may have to say" and athletic exercise to promote "vigor and self-reliance." He called for courses in Latin, German, French, mathematics, geography, history, and "other branches of an ordinary good education." He did not elaborate on these, taking their definition for granted in proposing a "liberal education." Instructional methods had to be "clear, sharp, and didactic; not uncertain nor languid." Students were to be "taught and drilled, not lectured to without care whether or not attention is paid." The WSFE had to "inculcate and impress upon the students" seven points:

The immorality and practical inexpediency of seeking to acquire wealth by winning it from another rather than by earning it through some sort of service to one's fellow-men. The necessity of system and accuracy in accounts, of thoroughness in whatever is undertaken, and of strict fidelity in trusts. Caution in contracting private debt or by endorsement, and in incurring obligation of any kind; punctuality in payment of debt and in performance of engagements. Abhorrence of repudiation of debt by communities, and commensurate abhorrence of lavish or inconsiderate incurring of public debt. The deep comfort and healthfulness of pecuniary independence, whether the scale of affairs be small or great. The consequent necessity of careful scrutiny of income and outgo, whether private or public, and of such management as will cause the first to exceed, even if but slightly the second. In national affairs, this applies not only to the public treasury, but also to the mass of the nation, as shown by the balance of trade. The necessity of rigorously punishing by legal penalties and by social exclusion those persons who commit frauds, betray trusts, or steal public funds, directly or indirectly. The fatal consequences to a community of any weak toleration of such offences must be most distinctly pointed out and enforced. The fundamental fact that the United States is a nation, composed of populations wedded together for life, with full power to enforce internal obedience, and not a loose bundle of incoherent communities living together temporarily without other bond than the humor of the moment. The necessity for each nation to care for its own, and to maintain by all suitable means its industrial and financial independence; no apologetic or merely defensive style of instruction must be tolerated upon this point, but the right and duty of national self-protection must be firmly asserted and demonstrated. (14–15)

Throughout the trial period, University of Pennsylvania college faculty taught WSFE courses. Then the school recruited its own "genuine" faculty (Cheyney, 1940: 289). However, from 1881 to 1884, the terminal degree depended on the college department in which the student had completed his first two years of study. Beginning in 1894, all WSFE graduates received a Bachelor of Science degree in economics (Cheyney, 1940: 291). As noted previously, despite Wharton's demand that the business school have financial autonomy, the college took control of its finances (Sass, 1982: 44–45). Wharton did not sue, but the move contributed to the increasing rift between himself and the university. In the meantime, the WSFE cultivated other alliances.

Implementing the Plan: Unintended Consequences

The college used Wharton's money to raise its prestige by recruiting the academic gold standard of the day—professors who had earned German Ph.D.'s. German "academic economics" was particularly strong; two-thirds of the annual economics literature was in German (Locke, 1984: 109). The German school followed cameralism and aligned with state institutions and administration (Clark, 2006: 223). More specifically, the WSFE faculty affiliated with the Verein für Sozialpolitik, an academic and professional community that rejected classical economics (the "Manchester School") and advocated statist policy and reform (Gide & Rist, 1948). The newly hired WSFE economics Ph.D.'s brought this school of thought to Philadelphia. There they aligned with social movements such as the Municipal Reform Movement and the Social Gospel, a Protestant revival movement (Oberschall, 1972; Schafer, 2000). Initially, their academic prestige and their shared interests with Philadelphia high society commanded respect. However, as public opinion coalesced for industrial reform and as the federal government began to take regulation (of interstate commerce, for example) seriously (see Berk, 1994), university trustees, who increasingly aligned with Pennsylvania industrialists, deemed the WSFE faculty's activism too radical.

The case of WSFE faculty member Scott Nearing marks a turning point at the WSFE and in academia because it led to the institution of tenure. Nearing, who advocated against child labor, commented in class about the abusive industrial practices of a WSFE student's father. Nearing was summarily dismissed. Trustees, administrators, and funders had long purged faculty for political reasons, particularly socialistic sympathies (Hofstadter & Metzger, 1955). The Nearing case, however, accelerated momentum for professors to organize. They formed the American Association of University Professors and won the institution of lifetime tenure, established to protect academic freedom (Hofstadter & Metzger, 1955).

A similar incident occurred at Dartmouth. However, the economics faculty member—who not only served under a president active in the Social Gospel movement (Tucker, 1919) but also had married into his family—was not censured (Broehl, 1999: 59–68). In addition, Dartmouth's president was close to Edward Tuck, the business school's founder, and their friendship softened the controversy.

Accusations of partisan politics created and perpetuated a bipolarity in the CSB between the political economists and the technical specialists. As noted earlier, the business school curriculum had two parts—political economy, outsourced from the college, and accounting, outsourced from practitioners. On the academic side, the clergymen and sociologist sons of clergymen used the college to make the church relevant and more socially legitimate and to develop a reform-oriented applied social science, essentially a new kind of "hands-on" knowledge for governance. On the practitioner side, the accountants who affiliated with a CSB enjoyed higher status and built up their practices. The two sides eventually took separate paths and formed the school of social work and the VSB, respectively.

The School of Social Work Breakaway

WSFE graduates formed in the Verein/Christian Socialist/social-reform tradition did not go into industry. They developed a new profession, social work (Fox, 1967: 95), and a new institution, the charity organization society (COS), the precursor of the school of social work. These students took the idea of applied social science to a level of professionalism and specialization that the college did not accommodate (Morgan, 1969). This new science and profession would work to solve poverty and other social problems.

Edward Devine, a WSFE graduate, helped found the COS of New York (later, the New York School of Philanthropy) in 1898. The first COS was established in Britain in 1869. It pursued effective, efficient administration of relief, without duplication of effort. The first COS in the United States was founded in 1877, "with the specific goal of avoiding waste of funds and of becoming a center of intercommunication between the various charities" (Reid, 1981: 50). In New York, Devine instituted formal training in this work. Following his mentor at WSFE, Simon Patten, he experimented with a new approach. Whereas the earliest COS movement held to a "traditional religious belief" that poverty was "a fortunate necessity that led the poor into paths of industry and the rich into acts of charity," Patten asserted that "America was a land of plenty" and poverty was unnecessary (Reid, 1981: 51). Patten held that scientifically informed action could end poverty. The new profession of "social workers" would implement the "age of abundance." Fox speculated that Patten coined the term "social work." Devine credited Patten with developing social work as a field and profession (Fox, 1967: 95, 96–97). Devine, in turn, formulated a program of "conscious social action" that transformed charity into "a type of anticipatory justice which deals not only with individuals who suffer but with social conditions that tend to perpetuate crime, pauperism and degeneracy" (Reid, 1981: 51).

Harvard also had a social work program, but it was grounded in Harvard's divinity school tradition rather than in political economy. Harvard established its Department of Social Ethics in 1904 in partnership with Simmons College (Morison, 1930: 225–26). A Social Gospeler, Francis Greenwood Peabody, initially led the department. He retired in 1913 and Richard Cabot assumed the directorship. In Harvard's Social Ethics program, students examined "case records of social service agencies . . . with a view to discovering ethical principles which should underlie professional technique" (Morison, 1930: 227). Harvard's president believed that the Social Ethics Department belonged in the Divinity School (Potts, 1965: 120). Pitirim Sorokin's arrival at Harvard and assumption of the sociology chairmanship was interpreted as a threat to the department (Potts, 1965: 124). Within two years, Social Ethics was dismantled despite Gordon Allport's efforts to "inform Sorokin on the Peabody tradition in social ethics and convince him that training students 'for an intelligent participation in public and private social enterprises' was a worthy academic endeavor'" (Potts, 1965: 126).

In sum, the WSFE's efforts in applied social science succeeded as professional social work but not as a business school. As the latter, it failed, quite literally, to attract and retain students (Kett, 1994: 270). Two-thirds of the students dropped out (Sass, 1982: 137). This academic failure also explains the seventeen-year gap between WSFE and the next CSBs. However, the WSFE did contain a germ of the new institution whereby business became "a veritable craze" (Marshall, 1928: 4)—the VSB.

The VSB Breakaway

CSB students followed their own, not the college's, requirements and constructed their education on an ad hoc basis (Kett, 1994: 273). In this sense, what the WSFE called a "drop-out rate" actually reflected students' choice to use the institution as they wished—typically, to improve short-term job prospects (Sedlak & Williamson, 1983: 30). The VSB would capitalize on this desire and purposely organize to serve popular demand. The University of Wisconsin, for example, set its business school curriculum based on students' elective choices.

Wisconsin's dean of business stated that half of the students entered with no intention to complete four years of education, but to stay the minimum time "to get a rudimentary training for business" (McCrea, 1913: 114). Students and employers utilized particular courses to remedy "specific defects in themselves and in their employees" (Scott, 1913: 128). Accommodating popular demand was the business school's very organizing principle: Wisconsin "backed in" to its curriculum by following the elective choices of "a large and troublesome group" of "special" students who were "picking and choosing for themselves and constantly hammering away at the artificial regulations they found in their way" (Scott, 1913: 129). These students "never intended to be engineers, lawyers, or farmers" but selected courses from law, engineering, agriculture, and liberal arts departments and schools "because of the courses in them which had a more or less direct relation to business training." Their numbers increased "until it was finally irresistible"; and by 1900, the university held "an untenable position" in business education. Eventually, a revised four-year program compromised between the college's traditional requirements and the new responsiveness to popular demand: students spent their first two years in general studies. Even so, students begged to "reverse the curriculum" and take business courses first and general education last. The business school dean noted that about 70 percent of students left after two years to enter business. He stated that the school took the students' appeal seriously (Scott, 1913: 134).

Reviewing the WSFE's experience in 1913, its dean assessed its "sociological and socio-economic courses" as having evolved "more or less accidentally" and opined that such courses would better "grow within one of the more general departments of a university, preferably in the college and graduate schools" (McCrea, 1913: 115). Instead, he aspired to offer "increasingly specialized vocational work" in the four-year business program (McCrea, 1913: 116). The WSFE had already long cultivated this growth principle, however. In addition to WSFE's five Verein-trained faculty, local businessmen lectured in "appearances which flattered prominent Philadelphians" (Sass, 1982: 132). The courses met student demand for new content and linked students and employers. These exchanges also provided financial support for the business school as local businessmen funded courses for their industries and companies. At the national level, this occurred in railroading. A railroad president and Harvard alumnus submitted one of the earliest proposals to Harvard, in 1895, for a school of "railroad science" (Cruikshank, 1987: 7–9). When railroad executive James Hill wrote textbooks on railroad management, business school founder Edward Tuck of Dartmouth appealed to the school's president to use this new content (Broehl, 1999: 60). The shoe industry figured prominently in Harvard's business courses, as did meatpacking in Chicago's. Thus the unprecedented variety of business instruction in the early twentieth century (Daniel, 1998) had to do with business education's propensity to grow in tandem with local economies.

This organic model was incubated at WSFE. As new business specialties emerged or were created, senior faculty assigned them to junior faculty, who developed new content for their courses and consultancies (Sass, 1982: 140). This procedure not only built new subfields but also faculty careers. Sass, for example, called Emory Johnson WSFE's first full-time "business specialist." At first, Johnson taught many courses that did not interest him. He turned over his geography and "general commerce" courses to his doctoral students. He specialized in railroads, then waterways. He published textbooks on railroad traffic and rates and earned a national reputation in this domain. The same trustee who had fought to fire Nearing named Johnson to a statewide railroad commission at about the same time (Sass, 1982: 143). After World War I, Johnson mediated in disputes among industrialists and built consensus with labor groups through the transition from government to private ownership (Sass, 1982: 144).

Johnson and his students continuously parsed subjects into finer degrees of specialization (Sass, 1982: 145–47). In 1890–91, WSFE offered 28 courses. By 1930, it offered 118; New York University's business school, however, led the way with 213—"an extreme example of a general national trend" (Kett, 1994: 276). Some junior faculty and doctoral students earned degrees matching their specialization; for example, one candidate sought a "doctor in economics in transportation." The university instead awarded a "doctor in economics in economics" (Sass, 1982: 146).

The case of Solomon Huebner, one of Johnson's doctoral students, is also illustrative. Huebner noticed that newspapers devoted attention to insurance, a field absent at WSFE. In 1904, Huebner, who also sold insurance and encouraged his students to do so, offered the first university-based instruction in insurance, and he was promoted shortly thereafter (Sass, 1982: 147). Affiliating with the CSB helped the entire insurance industry change negative beliefs about insurance, such as that it was a bet with God.

Edward Mead's career provides a further example of the business school's parallel development with corporate specialties. Johnson had delegated accounting and finance to Mead and to his colleague, Frederick Cleveland. They specialized in the emerging field of "corporation finance" and investment banking (Sass, 1982: 150–51). Mead's true innovation, however, was in academic entrepreneurship. In 1904, he founded a school within the WSFE: "Mead's Evening School of Accounts and Finance." From 1904 to 1913, the school expanded to four Pennsylvania cities and offered "most of the business courses" offered at WSFE. Mead established his school in the same year that the University of Pennsylvania established its first summer school (Cheyney, 1940: 346–47).

In essence, the VSB incorporated the SOO tradition into the university through Extension. It served those with little formal education and/or those of a social status not typically associated with the college. It was oriented to short-term goals, particularly training and certification for technical specialists.

The VSB had strong formal ties to the SOO tradition. WSFE's first dean, Edward Janes James, left WSFE for the University of Chicago—not to build its business school but to lead University Extension. He then went to Northwestern, which organized in the night school model (Sedlak & Williamson, 1983). Columbia University's first business school dean had previously directed Extension (Van Metre, 1954: 24). Columbia formed its business school out of its Extension program, which had begun in 1910, and which offered one course in elementary economics and one course in banking (Van Metre, 1954: 15). Columbia reorganized Extension into a business school in 1916. It faced the problem of "virtual transformation of University Extension into a degree-granting institution" (Van Metre, 1954: 105–6). Almost every aspect of Extension—open admissions, certificates, short courses, moonlighting practitioner-faculty, and full-time employed students—raised academic suspicion. Ultimately, the college exploited the fact that business attracted students to the college: It controlled the first two years of the students' undergraduate education. Business thus enabled the college to prosper, but it also packed it with disinterested students.

From 1894 to 1914, the WSFE served three different student groups. About one-third used the institution to prepare for law school. Another third, a group of "well-connected students" who were "well-satisfied with the old historical and social science curriculum," used WSFE as a classical college. The last third—"students who had to make their own way in the business world, without the aid of family connections" and who, furthermore, represented "a relatively new and rapidly expanding group," pursued "expertise in some functional area" (Sass, 1982: 137). This group dominated the VSB, the leading example of which was the New York University School of Commerce, Accounts, and Finance (NYUC), founded in 1900.

The New York University School of Commerce, Accounts, and Finance

Charles Haskins and Elijah Watt Sells led the movement to professionalize accountancy in the United States, specifically to establish the Certified Professional Accountant (CPA). They established their reputations when the U.S. government hired them to revise its accounting system in 1893. They then revised the accounting system of the city of Chicago. Their work converged with nationwide municipal and citizens' movements to fight corruption and bossism (Stewart, 1950). Haskins also campaigned for a new model of business education that would counter WSFE's "applied social science." Other WSFE finance and accounting faculty—notably, Frederick Cleveland and Edward Mead—left within two years to join Haskins. This move reified the break that established the CSB in the first place: the outsourcing of political economy from the college and the outsourcing of the accounting elective from practitioners.

Haskins and Sells advocated a model of education based on specialization. However, they also argued for the primacy of accounting because of its consolidated view of the enterprise, which they deemed superior even to Frederick Taylor's scientific management. Cleveland explained this in introducing Haskins's book:

No longer could the manager of enterprise come in direct contact with every detail of the business—for his information he must rely on his books and records of financial results. Mr. Haskins was inspired with the idea of reducing financial records to a scientific basis of classification and to be in a position to give professional advice to those who were made responsible for the safe conduct of large affairs. (Cleveland, 1904: 10)

An "accounting science" would "kee[p] track of wealth, of determining the financial condition of affairs." Haskins emphasized the long history of accounting as well as its basis in established principles (Haskins, 1904: 138–217).

Haskins and Cleveland took direct aim at the WSFE-Verein school. They attacked the "old-time treatises on political economy," which had "little in common with the experience of business men." "The method of Political Economy . . . has been partisan—its literary and rhetorical form in the nature of special pleading directed towards legal and social reform" (Cleveland, 1904: v). Cleveland argued that political economy had become identified with "scientific business literature" although its political leanings rendered it unscientific. However, the general impression was that political economy was business science. This ruined the credibility of business education (Cleveland, 1904: v–xii) and the possibility that business could be considered scientific. Thus Haskins distinguished his institution as "in no way to be confounded with or substituted for the course of liberal culture in a College of Arts and Science" (Gitlow, 1995: 3).

The accountants argued that their work represented "the most advanced thought . . . on the subject of business training and on the possibility of raising high professional standards in . . . business specialties"

(Cleveland, 1904: vii). Their announcement for NYUC began by stating an affiliation with "the professional accountants of the State of New York." The CPA examination required an "educational basis" to "insure to the profession of certified public accountancy the confidence and respect of the commercial and financial world." This required "a new institution for professional instruction."

They also noted that, because of "the multiplying exigencies of modern business," an important new "calling" known as the profession of administration, was emerging. This profession was

represented by men of affairs whose bent of mind and whose studies and experience fit them to grasp, in all its fullness and in all its parts and ramifications, any enterprise, of whatsoever kind, in the world of trade and commerce, and to take full charge of the venture and carry it forward to a successful issue. The administrator, the man of signal executive ability, handles the reins of a multifarious business on comprehensive principles; principles which are to him of more importance than the knowledge of technical details possessed by his subordinates, however valuable this knowledge may also be to him as accessory to his administrative capacity. From these leaders of affairs in the world of commerce and finance—for themselves as proprietors and managers, and for their assistants who are to succeed them in control of business—has come the present universal appeal to professional educators for university instruction in the sciences immediately connected with practical life. (New York University, 1900: 291–92)

The announcement proclaimed this "twofold demand" for "higher commercial education" and for "a school or college of accountancy." The catalogue listed courses in accounting, commerce, finance, law, and administration. The latter category contained no offerings, however—only a disclaimer that the School, being a pioneer, could not borrow experience from others, that professors of administration would study the "comparative needs of the various departments" and then prepare appropriate descriptions (New York University, 1900: 291–92, 298). Seven years later, the course catalogue listed no entries under "Administration"; in fact, the category had disappeared.

Accountants and finance professionals financed, governed, and ran NYUC. It functioned "mainly to train bookkeepers and other office workers for the new examinations." In 1912, NYUC established an undergraduate commerce college that offered even more occupational specialties, but more importantly gave business students access to a less exigent college degree (see below). Of all business schools, NYUC went to the greatest extremes in this regard (Kett, 1994: 272, 275, 276).

Initially, university administrators feared that NYUC would fail, so they required it to sustain itself financially (Gitlow, 1995: 18–19). This new institution indeed differed from "the several schools of finance and commerce established by prominent universities in America" because "its entire instruction" was "professional in character" (Haskins, 1904: 78); that is, its faculty were "professional scientists" (Cleveland, 1904: viii). NYUC adopted accounting's "scientific" principle of separating into corporation finance, investment, taxation, and insurance and applied it to other specialties. As its founders anticipated, this "separate, highly specialized science" of business would afford "still more minute subdivision for scientific research." Just as "General Surgery has profited from Eye-and-Ear surgery, Oral Surgery, Nasal Surgery, Abdominal Surgery, etc.," so would "practice" benefit from "scientific specialized research" (Haskins, 1904: 37). Eventually, NYUC offered twenty-four "certificate programs" for specific occupations. The 1948–49 catalogue listed twenty-nine major fields of business, including brokerage, real estate, and retailing. All courses were taught by businessmen, with the exception of business law, which was taught by law school faculty (Gitlow, 1995: 4).

Enrollments rose and the school introduced late-afternoon and morning courses. Day courses attracted newly graduated high school students, and they began attending full time (Gitlow, 1995: 9). The business school became a "cash cow" and "power center." Because of its part-time faculty, the school's costs were lower than other departments'. "Advertising men" in particular taught for no salary because they used the school for referrals. NYUC more than kept its promise to the university that it would never be a financial drain. In fact, the university subsidized its financially strapped parts with NYUC's surpluses (Gitlow, 1995: 19). An indication of the tenor of this relationship shows in an exchange between John Madden, NYUC's dean from 1925 to 1948, and the Arts and Sciences dean. The latter accused Madden of "presiding over a school that prostituted higher education"; Madden replied that a more despicable practice was to "be the pimp living off her earnings." A "substantial part of the Arts and Sciences [faculty] shared the sentiment that undergraduate professional education for business was inferior and tolerated only because it generated large tuition revenues for the university" (Gitlow 1995: 18–19). However, one NYUC professor asserted that "the whole University lived off [NYUC's] money" (Gitlow, 1995: 52). The relationship grew worse as the business school began to replicate the college under its own roof—business math, business English, business foreign languages. It also offered "cultural courses" in a "General Course" department and assembled a "mini Arts and Sciences faculty" under its control. Regular college faculty and students regarded this institution, and NYUC generally, as "inferior intellectually and academically." Opined Gitlow: "they had a convenient query to support such bias . . . if

[NYUC] students were of equal quality, then why did they not take the cultural course work in the College?" (Gitlow, 1995: 33).

In 1920, over half of NYUC's faculty consisted of part-timers, drawn from business firms, government, and even a local commercial high school. The dean encouraged other faculty to "maintain some business connections so that they could enrich their lectures with the fruit of their practical experience." In recruiting faculty, he favored teaching ability over academic accomplishments (Gitlow, 1995: 16–17). The quality of NYUC declined to that of an "educational factory" focused solely on jobs for graduates and employers' short-term needs (Gitlow, 1995: 20). Hitting academic bottom, NYUC began to change its status (Baldridge, 1971). It raised entrance and graduation requirements. The reinvention gained momentum in the early 1960s, when NYU received a Ford Foundation grant of $25 million in connection with a nationwide initiative to strengthen private education. The grant enabled NYUC's and NYU's transition to "academic superiority" among "leading schools and colleges" (Gitlow, 1995: 46, 47).

The VSB model, however, now dominated business education. Groups such as the local Chambers of Commerce, bankers' associations, and accountants guaranteed the financial stability of programs; but they also used the institution for their particular interests. In Louisiana, for example, 104 businessmen partnered to fund business education at Tulane University beginning in 1914; the local Association of Commerce provided classrooms (Levine, 1986: 56). Northwestern University followed this model (Sedlak & Williamson, 1983: 167–68). Northwestern's business enrollments grew from 255 in 1908–09 to over 1,000 by 1917; and it did for the Chicago area what NYUC did for New York.

The VSB brought the university into the business of occupational training at the low end, with entry-level jobs, further down the food chain from basic science, and more attached to immediate commercial use. The VSB succeeded with the public but made the business school a rogue actor in the research university. The next business school model would sidestep the problem of integrating with the college by organizing as a graduate professional school. However, as described in Chapter 4, it actually perpetuated the vocationalist logic in the business school and its rogue status in the academy.

The Twentieth-Century
Business School

Integrating the Vocational and Scientific Traditions

Twentieth-century reforms elevated business education to graduate-professional status and delivered the research university's requisite synergy between basic and applied science. The first reform, at Harvard Business School (HBS), established a professional school of business (PSB) (see Table 5) following Harvard Law School (HLS). HLS established that law professors and the university, instead of master-practitioners and the apprenticeship system, controlled legal education. The law professor made law into an applied science: he discovered and taught underlying decision principles from the corpus of documented legal opinions, which professionally trained practitioners applied. Similarly, HBS's "case method" proposed that business faculty would discover the underlying principles of administration that their students could apply in decision-making. However, business did not have the law's tradition of opinion-writing and of decision based on precedent. In addition, the business school had already organized according to the logic of specialization. HBS never discovered the principles of administration, and specialists used the case method to specialize even further.

The business school still lacked the basic applied logic to substantiate its status as a professional school. The graduate school of business (GSB) put the business school's foundations in the behavioral and quantitative sciences. It also fit the vocational school of business (VSB) into to this logic by interpreting the technical specialties as applications of these sciences. The model won consensus in the academy and in industry, and it devolved to lower-tier institutions. It grew readily in any VSB attached to a research university. In the postwar economy particularly, business schools were turnkey operations. Administrators hired Ph.D.'s from "the disciplines" to meet the demand of World

War II veterans, who funded their higher education under the GI Bill. More than any other part of the university, the business school accommodated veterans. Whereas law and medical students typically entered graduate school straight from college, the business school rewarded work and life experience. Elite business schools, attached to elite research universities, attracted a new student: the executive-scholar.

HARVARD BUSINESS SCHOOL

HBS elevated higher business education above the VSB fray. It established itself as a professional school of business (PSB) following law and medicine. In parallel, it sought to establish a basic science and applied art of administration. It did this in two ways: through the "case method," which accountants had long used for "problem solving" (Wildman, 1926) and which HLS had successfully used to establish the legal professoriate; and by proposing psychology as a foundation to supplement economics.

As noted in Chapter 3, Harvard founded its PSB just as the Harvard Law School (HLS) and its peer group of elite schools achieved nationwide consensus on the Bachelor's degree as a prerequisite and on a three-year, full-time residency. Also, their long campaign to close the evening and proprietary law schools succeeded, and the reign of the apprenticeship and School of Opportunity traditions in the law came to an end. At about the same time, medical schools also reached consensus on the Bachelor's degree as a prerequisite. Thus law and medicine achieved the same status that the ministry had held exclusively through the nineteenth century: the most demanding in residency, tuition, and forgone income.

While law and medicine raised their requirements, the VSB accommodated virtually everyone. HBS positioned itself far above the VSB, as education for the future executive. In keeping with Harvard's status and traditions, it updated Wharton's "vigorous gentleman" to executive-statesman. Under its dean, Wallace B. Donham, HBS took on the most pressing economic, political, and social problems of the day. As Wharton's new gentleman would create wealth in the new industrial economy, Harvard's new leader would overcome class divisions and resolve contradictions between democracy and capitalism (O'Connor, 1999a).

Donham faced enormous challenges: to raise money for a new, unproven institution; to develop a new basic science and an applied art derived from it; and to develop pedagogy for teaching this art. More fundamentally, he had to overcome strong negative biases in both industry and the academy. Many businessmen believed that business could not be taught; and some thought that, by attending college, young men showed passivity rather than responsibility. In 1901, for example, R. T. Crane, a Chicago CEO, charged that college administrators deceived young men and their families by taking their money and giving "nothing in return but useless knowledge" (Cruikshank, 1987: 26). Frederick Taylor, despite occasionally lecturing in collegiate schools of business, also attacked the institution. In a 1908 lecture, he told the New York chapter of the Harvard Engineering Society that he had "ceased to hire any young college graduates until they [had] been 'dehorned' by some other employer" (Cruikshank, 1987: 56). Academics, on the other hand, believed that business could not be a profession. Some of them—and many among the general public—believed that businessmen, particularly those associated with massive new wealth, were corrupt. Thus, contrary to the claim that HBS won immediate legitimacy for the business school and for business (Daniel, 1998: 39), Donham labored for years to change these negative attitudes on both ends of the spectrum.

Before taking the deanship in 1919, Donham had lectured at HBS on a part-time basis, in banking. He had served as vice president and chief legal officer at Old Colony Trust Company in Boston. He established his professional reputation as a court-appointed receiver for a troubled railway company from 1917 to 1919. He "kept several thousand disgruntled streetcar workers on the job" in World War I (Cruikshank, 1987: 92). He also distinguished himself as a fundraiser for Harvard College.

Donham also knew that HBS had already met with severe critique in the academy and at Harvard particularly. In 1918, the economist Thorstein Veblen attacked the rise of "pecuniary standards" in higher education. Universities substituted "the pursuit of gain and expenditure in the place of the pursuit of knowledge, as the focus of interest and the objective end in the modern intellectual life." Veblen also condemned the increasingly "habitual inclination . . . among academic men to value all academic work in terms of livelihood or of earning capacity" (Veblen, 1965 [1918]: 203). At that time, HBS had on its faculty Harvard's first professor to be hired without a Bachelor's degree (Cruikshank, 1987: 42).

As HBS gained notoriety, critics targeted it. Abraham Flexner, whose 1910 report on medical education led to extensive reforms in that field, blamed business schools generally, and HBS particularly, for falling standards in higher education. The Donham papers at Harvard contain a typed copy of a 1931 speech given by Flexner, with annotations that appear to be in Donham's handwriting. Donham, text in hand, may have added to it as, or after, Flexner made further comments. The notes indicate that Flexner "singled out" business schools "because they threaten to be a malign influence in American life." Universities "should bend their energies towards bringing into intellectual activities the most promising brains of the nation," but instead "we are a business nation bent on getting along and making money" (O'Connor, 1999a, quoting Donham: 121). Flexner condemned HBS: No "genuine scientist would give the name of 'research'" to its "researches in advertising: 'What Effect does the Summer Time have on Listening In,' 'How Long can a Radio Campaign be Run Before it Begins to Wear Out,' which received Award." Donham's handwritten notes conclude, "How much more powerful our colleges would be if these irrelevancies were dropped and men could devote themselves to the increase of knowledge and the education of scholars."

To counter the ongoing attacks, Donham built alliances with pedigreed disciplines, beginning with history and philosophy. In 1927, he hired a Harvard-trained historian, Norman S. B. Gras, to study management. Gras had worked with Edwin Gay, HBS's first dean, who recommended Gras. In 1926, Donham had written to Harvard's president, Abbott Lawrence Lowell: "The School is subject to the most severe criticism at the present time because it is organized to present nothing but contemporary conditions" (O'Connor, 1999a, quoting Donham: 121). Thanks to a gift from the retailer Gordon Selfridge, Donham purchased two centuries of Renaissance business documents concerning the Medici family. Selfridge personally intervened with Mussolini to resolve controversy in Italy surrounding the loss of the documents. Donham also engaged the eminent British philosopher Alfred North Whitehead to lecture at HBS. Then chemistry professor Lawrence Henderson helped Donham bring psychologist Elton Mayo, who subsequently recruited the philosopher's son, T. N. Whitehead, to HBS.

Donham arguably added to his burden by rejecting legitimating ties that business had formed with the university. He did not consider business a subfield of economics; nor did he view it as a grouping of specialties. Donham believed that business was its own discipline, but he had no substance to back up this belief. Collaborating with Elton Mayo, Donham pursued a crucial element of management that economics could not supply: "human relations" and "leadership"—that is, a scientific foundation of psychology to address pressing problems in the economy generally and in corporations particularly. Donham assembled a circle of scientists, funders, and executives: researcher Mayo; funder Beardsley Ruml of the Laura Spelman Rockefeller Memorial (LSRM) foundation; and leading CEOs, organized by Owen Young (General Electric) and his "little industrial group," consisting of those "particularly interested in the human aspects of the industrial problem"—the CEOs of Standard Oil of New Jersey, Goodyear, U.S. Rubber, AT&T, International Harvester, DuPont, Bethlehem Steel, Westinghouse, and General Motors (O'Connor, 1999a: 123). The "industrial problem" included threats to the political order (socialism, Marxism, Bolshevism); social order (class conflict, violence, sabotage), and economic order ("capital versus labor" specifically, but also the economic effects of the political and social-order threats combined; O'Connor, 1999a).

The "human relations school," led by Mayo and Donham, involved securing workers' cooperation with, and favorable public opinion of, the policies and practices of corporations, particularly anti-unionism on the part of CEOs (O'Connor, 1999a). It also aimed to help individual executives with their leadership and reputations in this regard. For example, in 1914, the so-called Ludlow massacre, in which strikers and members of their families (two women and ten children; Chernow, 1998: 578) were killed, ended a months-long strike at a Rockefeller-owned coal mine in Colorado. Helen Keller—a respected public figure and a beneficiary of Rockefeller philanthropy—reacted to the tragedy by calling John D. Rockefeller a "monster of capitalism." She stated, "He gives charity and in the same breath he permits the helpless workmen, their wives and children to be shot" (Chernow, 1998: 579). Rockefeller and other industrialists wanted an industrial peace that would not admit unions, not strictly because they disapproved of unions per se but because debates about legalizing unions heightened attention to, and thus jeopardized, CEO control in firms, which some—notably John Dewey—considered incompatible with democracy (O'Connor, 1999a: 119).

Inspired by the work of Durkheim, Janet, Freud, Malinowski, and others, Mayo developed a political-psychological theory according to which workers "agitated" because of anomie in industrialization. Their neurosis took form in grievances and strikes. His solution restored the workers' dignity through the therapeutic interview. The cathartic process calmed workers down (O'Connor, 1999b).

In the 1930s, Donham and his colleagues reframed their mission as nothing less than saving Western civilization. In the aftermath of the Great Depression, Donham wrote two books on national recovery. Remarking favorably on the Soviet Union's use of central planning, he wrote to Selfridge in 1931 about his concern that the United States, too, needed a comprehensive plan to ensure "stability":

It is my belief that the only hope for Western civilization centers in the ability and the leadership of American business, and on their recognition of the fields in which government action is necessary to secure sound results, in their capacity to make and carry out a major plan conceived in the largest terms by men of the highest ability and social objectives. (O'Connor, 1999a: 124, citing Donham)

This mission to build HBS into an elite academy for solving society's greatest problems was not only a legitimacy campaign for business and for Harvard specifically, but also an attempt to resolve grave problems through science and formal education (Donham, 1936). Mayo concurred: "We do not lack an able administrative elite, but the elite of the several civilized powers is at present insufficiently posed in the biological and social facts involved in social organization and control" (Mayo, 1933: 177).

The elite, scientifically informed response, led by Harvard, had to scale up: "The situation would be hopeless if it involved the decisions of millions of business men." Society needed "critically the leadership of a few hundred men in a few hundred corporations" (Donham, 1932: 11–12). This leadership, in turn, needed an elite education "which thinks in terms of broad social problems" rather than in terms of "particular companies" (Donham, 1932: 207). Above all, it needed an "effective understanding of the emotional nature of men" as the strategic factor in social action (Donham, 1936: 270).

Donham also based his legitimacy campaign on the successful example of HLS. As an HLS alumnus, Donham was educated in Dean Christopher Langdell's approach, whereby the law professoriate, a professional research faculty, established the scientific foundation from which the applied science and thus the profession of law derived. As noted earlier, by the end of the nineteenth century, HLS led the nation in training the law professoriate, an entirely new professional category. Thus HLS celebrated the hiring of James Barr Ames in 1873, not because he was a proven attorney but precisely because he was *not* a proven attorney.

Donham had initially intended to use HLS's proven method of establishing foundational principles from which the applied science of management, or applied art of decision, would derive. However, unlike the law school and legal tradition, HBS did not have an existing corpus of cases. In establishing the legal professoriate, then, HLS engaged the legal tradition's very existence *as a tradition*—of historical documents, but more important, of decision based on precedent. Business had neither this tradition nor its artifacts.

HBS's faculty and students thus undertook an extensive case-writing effort institutionalized as the Business Research Bureau (BRB). But contrary to Donham's goal of building a corpus from which researcher-professors would discern general principles, the BRB and the case-writing process followed the VSB's specialist logic. Each subfield wrote its own cases and built its professional community from the academic-practitioner collaborations afforded by case-writing. The individual contributions of each specialty generated sufficiently large revenue to enable the business school to grow autonomously as an administrative entity despite its substantively unrelated parts.

Business schools nationwide adopted the BRB model. The BRB lent new impetus to the business school's growth through specialization, particularly in synergies with the institutionalizing consulting industry (Aaronson, 1992: 181). HBS faculty were expected to earn about a third of their income from consulting (Marshall to Judson, 1-3-23, SCRC-UCL, HPJP, B29: F9). Ironically for Donham, HBS's case method actually furthered specialization by standardizing the genre, giving it the Harvard name, and marketing it to business schools nationwide.

The PSB model implied that students had perfected a skill. For Donham, the case addressed key elements of business education: practice and experience. HBS admitted "specials," students enrolled in single courses rather than degree programs; but it also admitted full-time students continuing straight from college and working toward a degree (Gleeson et al., 1993: 5). The case method satisfied both groups. It "generated interest" among immature and inattentive students (Donham, 1926: 114–16) by bringing "reality" into the classroom. Instructors encouraged lively discussion and debate. Cases enabled students to "practice" "diagnosis," decision-making, and taking responsibility. Finally, the combination of case analysis and class discussion "developed individual personality" (Donham, 1926: 207) and displayed it before professors and peers.

In his retirement years, Donham focused not on the business school but on undergraduate education. He regarded the case method and human relations content as "education for life" (Donham, 1947). Donham experimented extensively with undergraduate education. In particular, he used cases to address topics in human relations (Donham, 1954). In the business school, however, the case and the human relations content took separate paths. Human relations became a new discipline: organizational behavior (O'Connor, 1999a: 129). It supplemented economics' previous monopoly of the foundation for business. The case became the leading pedagogical method in the VSB and put HBS in the publishing business.

HBS's PSB model established leadership for HBS in business education, but it did not establish a foundation of administration. However, it did make business into an applied science in two unrelated ways: human relations was the science of psychology applied to industry, which gave the field a "behavioral" branch distinct from economics; and the case study was a method for integrating state-of-the-art knowledge and for practicing decision-making in specialist fields.

Aaronson (1992) describes a similar process at Columbia University's business school. In the mid-1950s, despite efforts to integrate the curriculum, specialization remained the norm and the faculty was declared "an aggregation of specialists" (Aaronson, 1992: 177).

HBS also succeeded in attracting students: It dominated the field. In 1949, almost half of all MBAs were HBS graduates. HBS's faculty consisted mostly of its own graduates. The majority had either a Doctorate of Commercial Science or Master's in Business Administration (MBA) from HBS. In the late 1970s, over 20 percent of the top three officers of each of the Fortune 500 manufacturing companies had graduated from HBS (Aaronson, 1992: 168, 169, 180, 174).

This very success also drew attention to HBS's academic weaknesses. For example, in 1946, the University of Chicago's business school dean, Garfield Cox, stressed the BRB's overwhelmingly "opportunist" logic:

> The Business Problems Bureau [Chicago's version of the BRB] has brought us financial support for various projects. Although often contributing something of use in teaching, these undertakings have typically been quite limited in scope and objective, and pressure has usually been strong to produce immediately usable results. The more significant research problems are basic ones requiring sustained efforts, and long-time financial support on terms that contribute to confidence in the independence and integrity of the investigation and of the publication that results from it. ("Plans for the School of Business," 1948, SCRC-UCL, GSBA, B2: F2)

The next reform would concentrate on the need for basic science in the business school.

THE CARNEGIE GSIA

Scholars have extensively documented the Carnegie Graduate School of Industrial Administration (GSIA) and its dissemination as the "business school revolution" and "the New Look" (Gleeson, 1997; Gleeson et al., 1993; Gleeson & Schlossman, 1995, 1992; Schlossman & Sedlak, 1988, 1985; Schlossman et al., 1989a, 1989b; 1998, 1998; Sedlak & Schlossman, 1991). The following exposition draws from this research. It also builds on it by tracing this reform to the University of Chicago's Economics Department as well as to the GSIA.

The New Look matched HBS's assembly of researchers, educators, and executives in the BRB. But instead of adopting a human relations orientation and psychotherapeutic techniques, it grounded itself in engineering and tools for "decision science." Far beyond HBS's clannish ties to individual CEOs, it won large, ongoing contracts from the federal government, the military, and policymakers. Socially, technically, and ideologically, the New Look came out of World War II and postwar initiatives (Moore, 2008). It also aligned higher business education with national strategic interests. In the Cold War era, New Look champions hailed business schools as the means to cultivate managers who would make the solid economic, and thus the political and social, cases for democracy over communism (Gleeson & Schlossman, 1995; Schlossman et al., 1998). New Look reformers themselves had extensive wartime experience in macro-scale planning. They rebuilt, reformed, and administered the economies of entire countries, exercising "dizzying levels of control" (Gleeson & Schlossman, 1995: 10).

W. Allen Wallis and George Leland Bach

In early 1975, a group of academics organized to honor George Leland Bach for his contributions to management education by nominating him for the Dow Jones Award, bestowed by the American Assembly of Collegiate Schools of Business (AACSB). Each professor wrote a letter providing evidence as to Bach's exceptional merit. But one noted that W. Allen Wallis also merited at least a passing mention. Its author, Arnold Weber, provost of Carnegie Mellon at the time, disclosed that he had "grown up at Wallis' [sic] feet in Chicago" and merely "inherited" his respect for Professor Bach's "patrimony" at GSIA (Weber to Dow Jones Award, 1-29-75, SC-SUL, GLBP, B8: F14). Wallis served as dean of the Graduate School of Business at the University of Chicago from 1956 to 1962. New Look historians stated that Wallis may have figured more pivotally in the historical record had he stayed longer at Chicago (Schlossman et al., 1998). However, this argument underestimates the ties between Wallis and Bach.

Both Wallis and Bach did graduate work at the University of Chicago's Economics Department in the 1930s. The "Chicago School" developed a strong sense of mission to advance economic science. The school is well known for its commitment to neoclassical and neoliberal economic theory and doctrines. However, it also advanced a rigorous method integrating the ideal of scientific discovery with its execution (Emmett & Kovacek, 2008; Emmett, 2011). In particular, the Chicago School linked research and training to enable "a seamless movement from the entrance into training to advancing the boundaries of the science" (Emmett & Kovacek, 2008: 6). This method also strictly distinguished between undergraduate and graduate education and between pedagogy for social initiation and pedagogy for the cultivation of the scientific mind. Like the Lazzaroni, who elevated the status of science (see Chapter 2), the Chicago School established a separate and elite preserve dedicated to the high ideals and rigorous practice of science. Furthermore, within itself, it recognized a faculty hierarchy based on seniority, and more important, on intellect, regardless of age (Emmett & Kovacek, 2008: 7).

Before the Chicago School, U.S. economics departments had followed or adapted foreign thought schools such as the Verein für Sozialpolitik. As noted in Chapter 3, Wharton organized its School of Finance and

Economy (WSFE) around an intellectual circle devoted to protectionism. The so-called Philadelphia School achieved distinction, but the Chicago School became an intellectual powerhouse: it provides the textbook study on how to develop a thought school. Emmett & Kovacek (2008) note that Chicago may be understood as having one or two thought schools. However, whether one finds one or two, one cannot deny a phenomenon that has lasted three-quarters of a century. Endurance defines the strength of a thought community (Farrell, 2001). Bach and Wallis were inculcated in a scientific ideal and method upheld by an elite community in an elite research university. In social science, this ideal reached fruition in economics and at Chicago. Although some make the case for Chicago's strong sociology tradition (e.g., Abbott, 1999), the Sociology Department was more eclectic and diverse than Economics.

The GSB organized under the scientific ethos epitomized by the Chicago School and the applied-scientific ethos epitomized by the Carnegie Institute of Technology (CIT). Together, these made the research professoriate that produced the professional manager—that is, the decision scientist, skilled in using the new tools from the new discipline of computer science.

Initially, HBS and Carnegie/Chicago seemed to strike a perfect balance: HBS contributed narrative realism through the case study genre and the human relational skill of Donham's psychologically informed executive statesman; and Carnegie/Chicago contributed sophisticated quantitative methods. But in fact, the GSB established a new bipolarity in the business school because it held that engineers made the best managers and that the proper management curriculum began with engineering. However, HBS, the established leader, was a far cry from an engineering school. Because of HBS's standing (Khurana, 2007: 256–58), the human relations–quantitative bipolarity was resolved through the Graduate Management Admissions Test (administered for the first time in 1954): the higher the math GMAT score, the more desirable the applicant.

Bach actually shared Donham's integrative vision for business education in many respects (Gleeson & Schlossman, 1995). Noel Capon noted the irony of GSIA's being exemplary for other schools, although within a decade it "had become dominated by neoclassical economists and operations research specialists"; and "the research that had led to the path-breaking behavioral theory of the firm 'was one of the first victims of the new bias'" (Capon, 1996, citing Simon, 1991: 249). In a personal interview in 1992, Bach acknowledged that his project to achieve a "grand synthesis" of the "various components" of the GSIA into a "unified science of administration" had failed (Gleeson & Schlossman, 1995). Donham thought case work would provide "empirical building blocks for theoretically oriented research," but it succumbed to a "drift to specialization" nonetheless. "Neither the thousands of case studies nor the small human relations group Donham cultivated provided the alternatives to specialized instruction that the dean needed in order to realize his broad educational goals. Generalizable business theories did not spring forth from the case studies (much to the delight of several of Donham's own faculty)" (Gleeson et al., 1993: 17). Similarly, Bach tried to "kee[p] the various strands of GSIA intact as a single organization without trying to solder them together." More specifically, "the more Bach was willing to tolerate the growing chasms between groups, the more he insisted on keeping their work quantitative in order to encourage intellectual exchange at whatever level remained achievable" (Gleeson & Schlossman, 1995: 19). Bach's emphasis on mathematics as a tool to integrate faculties, and his basing of business education in engineering, coincided with the academy's dropping of the foreign language requirement for the Ph.D. Henceforth mathematics would be the lingua franca for the social sciences because it resolved scientific differences (O'Connor, 2008: 417).

With expert organization, generous funding, and status appeal, the New Look achieved considerable homogeneity (Khurana, 2007:263, 276–77). The GSB became institutionalized as a professional school in the research university with faculty from various academic disciplines. The GSB made the business school not only academically legitimate but also academically elite. It also attracted, and in fact created, a new candidate—the executive-scholar.

NEW HEIGHTS IN THE SCHOOL OF OPPORTUNITY: THE EXECUTIVE MBA

Leon Carroll Marshall, dean of the University of Chicago's business school from 1909 to 1924, spoke at the school's fiftieth anniversary in 1948 ("Collegiate Education for Business Faces Challenges," SCRC-UCL, RMHP, B43: F9). Pointing to the strong adult-education programs in business, Marshall asserted, "business education may well be the area of greatest importance in adult education both in terms of the numbers of adults interested and in terms of the pressing needs" for education in a world of rapid social and technological change. In fact, as Marshall spoke, adult business education was only just beginning.

As noted in Chapter 2, the University of Chicago was a pioneer in adult education. Although its president, William Rainey Harper, originally focused on general studies, popular demand leaned toward business. Harper regarded "seriousness"—that is, advancement to a degree—as the biggest challenge of adult education. The institution of the executive-scholar, the development of which was led by the University of Chicago, would go furthest in this respect.

The University of Chicago offered night school for working people at its downtown location known as University College. In 1952, 250 students enrolled on the South Side campus; but 450 attended evening business courses downtown, of whom 226 were formal degree candidates, and more intended to apply for this status. Thus the University College's administration confidently asserted that "the larger volume of the [business] School's work now comes in the area of evening work" (Donohue to Houle, 12-17-52, SCRC-UCL, UEP, B18: F5).

University College began its Executive Program in 1943. Students could opt for a certificate, based on a series of courses, or an MBA. Factoring in age and work experience on a case-by-case basis, the program accommodated students without an undergraduate degree (Graham to Tyler et al., 11-8-46, SCRC-UCL, UEP, B18: F5). The Executive Program fulfilled the mission of University College: "To offer adults an opportunity for improvement of professional competence through advanced training." University College "recognizes that the greater breadth of experience of mature persons opens new areas of knowledge and brings into sharper focus deficiencies in earlier educational experiences. The offerings at the Downtown Center are therefore geared to provide advanced training to the adults who already hold an established place in the political, economic, and social life of the community" (Houle to Cox, 8-29-49, SCRC-UCL, UEP, B18: F5, p. 1). The programs were

designed to reach leaders. The content of any activity should be at a broad and complex level. The activities should be of a pioneering nature. The Downtown Center should cooperate with other professional adult educational agencies and groups which are committed to similar objectives. The Downtown Center should work cooperatively with associations and other groups which are composed of the mature persons it wishes to reach as students (p. 1).

In the late 1890s, University College had offered a few "railroad courses" independent of the on-campus business school. The downtown site served mostly public school teachers, not business people. The business school faculty and administration deliberately restrained its growth owing to competition from Northwestern as well as quality-control considerations. "The School of Business of the University should not enter the field unless it [can] carry to those interested a distinctive program with adequate financing and adequate facilities" ("Adult Education in Business," 1934, SCRC-UCL, RMHP, B385: F10). However, in 1928, the business school, "with considerable hesitation," partnered with University College to offer a "comprehensive program of work" downtown. Within a few years, Chicago's program, despite being "pitched at a high level" and entering a competitive market of evening business programs, attracted "an increasing number of the more competent men in business in the city." Interest grew even more during the Depression. However, reviewing the program in 1933, the business school dean worried about the quality of the program:

Too much emphasis has been placed and is now being placed upon manipulative activities and techniques and too little upon fundamental principles . . . the recommendation is here made that the School of Business, in view of its limited facilities and in view of the genuine uncertainty as to what a sound program of adult education should be, proceed cautiously in the extension of its work in the downtown area of the city. ("Adult Education in Business," 1934, SCRC-UCL, RMHP, B385: F10, p. 11)

After World War II, the business school adopted a policy of helping downtown students earn MBA degrees. "We soon yielded to a demand, coming increasingly from able and mature students with the bachelor's degree, for MBA work at University College that could be pursued at a flexible rate instead of the rigid one provided by the Executive Program" (Cox to Colwell, 8-25-49, SCRC-UCL, RMHP, B43: F8). However, like the Executive Program, the downtown MBA program also accommodated students without a Bachelor's degree (Graham to Tyler et al., 11-8-46, SCRC-UCL, UEP, B18: F5, p. 1). War service gave more license to this accommodation. The business school dean went so far as to recommend that returning veterans not continue with their Bachelor's degrees but advance directly to the MBA program (Cox to Colwell, 12-31-47, SCRC-UCL, RMHP, B43: F8).

University College administrators initially thought this demand for advanced terminal degrees was temporary. They met "the emergency" by "overloading the regular faculty" and by making "the best possible ad hoc appointments." However,

under the exceptionally able leadership of Van den Woestyne the results to date are better than we had reason to expect. The non-faculty instructors are a competent group. The quality of the degree students is high. Ninety per cent of them already hold first degrees. Thus our work in the Downtown Center is assuming a truly graduate character. A plurality of these students are engineers who are now achieving administrative responsibilities and desire a program we are uniquely qualified to offer.

But while student quality rose, the faculty composed of "ad hoc appointments and overworked regulars" did not. The program lacked status and

clout; "Central Administration" assigned a "low priority" to the so-called
"downtown regular program" (Cox to Colwell, 8-25-49, SCRC-UCL,
RMHP, B43: F8, p. 1). In 1949, the School of Business elected to abandon
the downtown MBA program. However, it also admitted an increasing
number of non-degree candidates both on campus and at the downtown
center (Krumbein to Lorie, 3-27-58, SCRC-UCL, UEP, B18: F5).

By 1950, the university had established a new position, director of the
Executive Program at University College. Correspondence between this
individual and the business school dean reveals the degree of thought put
into adult business education at Chicago. University College was deemed
"the University [of Chicago]'s main agency of adult education." In line
with this mission, University College distinguished five "areas of adult
education in business administration": (1) the Executive Program, (2)
"special pioneering programs . . . designed to provide outstanding business men with an increased knowledge and understanding about complex subjects" (e.g., "the new non-credit course in Commercial Financing
and Factoring"); (3) "a program of well-rounded business training provided for those . . . with degrees in such fields as chemistry or the liberal
arts [who] find that the requirements of their career make it imperative
for them to understand business management"; (4) "courses borrowed
from the curriculum of the School of Business and designed to provide
training in a special field for those who need it"; and (5) "a degree program for those who did not have an education while young and are trying now to get it because they need a degree for business advancement"
(Blake to Cox, 11-27-50, SCRC-UCL, UEP, B18: F5).

The head of University College, Cyril Houle, had led wartime training
programs for servicemen at the university. From the mid-1960s through
the 1970s, Houle would receive praise for his contributions to adult
education; he was inducted into the International Adult and Continuing Education Hall of Fame in 1996. Under Lyndon Johnson, he served
two terms on a national advisory body on continuing education. Houle
published extensively. His books include *Continuing Learning in the
Professions (1980)*, *The External Degree (1973)*, *The Inquiring Mind
(1961)*, *The Design of Education (1972)*, and *Patterns of Learning: New
Perspectives on Lifespan Learning* (1984). He co-wrote *The University,
the Citizen, and World Affairs* (with Charles Nelson) in 1956.

Houle led University College from 1944 to 1952. He presided over experiments in adult education and in the Executive Program specifically.
For example, he helped develop an executive seminar including campus,
evening MBA, and local executives to discuss "civic problems of special
concern to business men" (Blake to Houle et al., 2-24-50, SCRC-UCL,
UEP, B18: F5). The seminar experimented with new discussion methods,

including leadership by the students. Another experiment proposed "a new program for supervisors and others not quite eligible for admission to the Executive Program." It established an unprecedented collaboration: its "most distinctive feature" was that Executive Program alumni designed and taught all courses (Graham to alumni, 5-1-46, SCRC-UCL, UEP, B18: F5).

While the business school worried that University College could not deliver distinctive and competitive programs, Houle worried that the business school did not understand the purpose of University College and its contributions to the university and the city. In a memorandum to the business school dean, Houle noted a danger of collapsing groups 3 and 5 (as numbered above), the group supplementing their education and the group playing catch-up. He did not think highly of the latter, whom he viewed as

made up of people who are simply going through the routine of getting an education in business because it is required of them by employers. Usually they have not had very much previous higher education. They are not a stimulating group of students because often they lack basic motivation and ability. I include them as a possible group only because they are usually sincere and because their education will tend generally to improve the business community. Furthermore, the University of Chicago has set a standard for the education of this group which has required the other universities in the city to give serious thought to the improvement of their own programs. (Houle to Cox, 8-29-49, SCRC-UCL, UEP, B 18: F5, p. 2)

He also noted some fluidity among the categories. If the university abandoned the third program, managerial training for specialists, then "this decision would also eliminate the fourth and fifth programs as well." *As a whole*, then, he considered the University College students

of high quality; they and the community will benefit by the kind of instruction we can give them. The program is valid adult education. It provides a standard of complexity and integration which surpasses anything available to adults at other universities in Chicago. It provides an excellent basis of contact between the University and the business community. It serves as a base for the development of other programs and for recruitment for the executive program. I would hope that it might provide the faculty of the School of Business with opportunities for trying out new techniques in teaching and with contacts which would be useful in research. (Houle to Cox, p. 2)

Houle proposed more selective admission to convert group 5 students into group 3 students.

The increasing disparity between the weak academic credentials of the "ad hoc" faculty and the high quality of the students, along with the popular demand for the MBA, dissuaded the business school from continuing the downtown evening MBA program (Van den Woestyne to

Cox, 8-30-49, SCRC-UCL, UEP, B18: F5). The university could not offer a sufficiently "superior" offering:

We are not justified . . . in holding ourselves out as giving professional work at the graduate level with a staff recruited and composed as at present. That is becoming increasingly true with the rising calibre of the downtown students. They deserve a faculty at least the equal of that on campus. Moreover, to execute the present policy is exceedingly difficult, since in considerable measure it involves building a faculty quarter by quarter, or at least year by year. It is impossible to have stability and assure quality on that basis. (Van den Woestyne to Cox, 8-30-49 SCRC-UCL, UEP, B18: F5)

Only closer coordination with the campus-based business school would ensure this outcome.

The many students who began the program as non-degree students and then switched to a degree program held back the level of instruction. Excluding non-degree students altogether would raise faculty, student, and content quality. Whereas the Executive Program enjoyed respect in the Chicago business community—even becoming an exclusive club in which one rising executive referred others (Graham to Fourth Executive Group, 6-23-47, SCRC-UCL, UEP, B18: F5), the "regular [MBA] program" did not enjoy such a reputation (Van den Woestyne to Cox, 8-30-49, SCRC-UCL, UEP, B18: F5). However, success and failure both gave cause for ownership disputes between the business school and University College.

Harlan M. Blake, head of business education at University College, had argued for assigning no priority among the five areas:

[Ranking them] implies that we are willing to pass judgment to the extent of saying that the Executive Program, or an as yet almost undeveloped program of "special courses and conferences," is inherently more appropriate adult education than . . . the MBA program. I can find no reason to think that this is true. A capable junior executive slated for promotion to a position of greater responsibility in his firm is an appropriate candidate for the Executive Program. I do not, however, believe that a program designed to meet his needs is inherently superior to a curriculum (such as the MBA program) which can serve the needs of a person who finds that his job, perhaps as an engineer, chemist or other specialist, requires a broader understanding of business administration, or of a person who discovers, later in life than some, that he is moving into areas of business responsibility that require further professional education. Second, it seems to me that a ranking of this sort *may* result in negative thinking. Rather than stressing the opportunity and obligation of the University to build the best possible programs in all such areas, it may tend to suggest that only one or two (at the top of a list) are worthy of much effort. (Blake to Graham, 12-13-50, SCRC-UCL, UEP, B 18: F5, p. 2)

Suggesting he had "some reason to think that this has happened," Blake criticized "a technique of analysis" that is "open, in my opinion, to misinterpretation." Blake requested more resources so that University College could meet all five objectives.

For approximately five years, the business school's administrators attempted to take control of business education at University College. But this meant removing themselves from it: they constantly expressed reservations about their ability to maintain academic quality, and they in fact voted to discontinue the downtown business programs. Even though they rescinded that decision and took over the downtown programs, University College administrators held that this very act showed that the business school did not understand the purpose of University College and of adult professional education in general. The new head of University College, Maurice Donohue, suggested that the School of Business's vote to abandon the night school—its largest population—showed that the school disregarded its most important constituency. University College, "the official extension division of the university," served the purpose of "strengthen[ing] our University's position in the regional community." The variety of downtown offerings led to "a useful cross-fertilization between business and other disciplines." The "unified mailing list" enabled "simultaneous promotion of many aspects of our program," including liberal education particularly. A formal separation of adult education from University College—"autonomy" for the business school—would sever vital ties connecting the University to the business community and would establish "rivalry from the same institution that is unpleasant and shows a lack of awareness of each other's problems." He observed that "Northwestern has three separate evening programs in business, separately administered, with separate prerequisites, separate requirements, and even separate calendars." Northwestern's system was explained "in a long speech at Atlanta which neither I nor anyone else I talked to understood. How could I as a student choose intelligently?" (Donohue to Houle, 12-17-52, SCRC-UCL, UEP, B18: F5, p. 2). If the business school separated from University College, the latter would still maintain ties to the business and industrial community. University College sustained vital university-city relations:

[N]ot only must University College act as agent for the departments of Economics, Sociology, Psychology, Education, Nursing Education, Union Education Service, Industrial Relations Center and other campus units having something to contribute to business and industry, but contacts with these vital parts of the community are necessary for the major promotional responsibilities of University College. As needs appear, they must be filled or the confidence of the community in University College will be shaken. If we are helping unions organize department stores [the business school offered a program for labor union administrators], we must also be visibly active in teaching department store managers how to deal with unions. (Donohue to Houle, 12-17-52, SCRC-UCL, UEP, B18: F5, p. 2)

Above all, "separation would violate the Chicago concept of what a University ought to be." The argument merits full citation because of its expansive scope:

There is a unity of knowledge, and the organization of the University must exemplify that unity. It must as a single institution of society take all knowledge as its province. It must be able to mobilize all its resources on a single problem. And its ability to do this must be visible to the adult community as part of the justification for the time, money, and energy which society invests in the University.

Therefore, the University must have a unified approach to the general community. Separate departments may make specialized separate approaches to specialized fragments of the community. But the University must show a single face to the adult citizens in its constituency. That face is University College, designed to undertake this responsibility by all ways of communication: face-to-face, mail, radio, television, the lecture hall.

Belief in this concept, which is a noble one, is widely and deeply held. Violation of it by an over-riding loyalty to a small part of the University would align persons who believe in the integrated university as opponents, in campus councils, of the violators: in this case the School of Business.

This would be the result of an unforgivable administrative error in permitting the separation, because the real future of the School of Business lies in summoning to its service the information and insight of the departments of the Division of Social Science in the genuine problems of management. These problems involve interpersonal relations. And business outside the University is discovering the importance to commercial success of a better and deeper humanist culture among its executives. The necessity for constant consultation with the physical and biological sciences as these involve business problems (e.g., relation of food chemistry to refrigeration to retail merchandising) is apparent. So is the necessary link between Business and Law, Business and Industrial Relations, in fact every department of the University that is serving a useful function in the preservation, increase and transmission of knowledge.

The School needs closer alliance with all departments, not a separation from any link it has now won (and earned) with university extension. (Donohue to Houle, 12-17-52, SCRC-UCL, UEP, B18: F5, p. 2)

But in early 1954, the business school dean effectively declared war. He bypassed the chain of command to report on disagreements between himself and the director of the Executive Program. The latter had complained that, under the business school's direction, the executive program had excessive entertainment expenses. The business school dean explained,

It just happens that the men in the Program do not usually drink Coca-Cola . . . a niggardly expense account is not a wise economy measure, especially when the pay-off is substantial. I have no doubt at all that the prime mover in bringing

Carson Pirie Scott & Co. to the University of Chicago for the working out of its Centennial Fellowship program was occasioned by the experience of one of their top management men in the Executive Program. It would be ridiculous to associate that event with the particular issue of the expense account matter, but it is not far fetched to associate his attitude with the way we treat people in the Executive Program—and the discretionary expense account practice is just part of that standard treatment. (Jeuck to Harrison, 2-25-54, SCRC-UCL, UEP, B18: F5, pp. 1–2)

The business school dean also complained that the director of the Executive Program demanded final approval of all printed materials for distribution. "I suspect this may be a censoring operation in response to our failing to have 'University College' imprinted on our latest Executive Program announcements," the dean wrote. He explained that the omission was not "cavalier" but resulted from "the Chancellor's assurance some time ago" that the Executive Program would soon be in the business school's hands (Jeuck to Harrison, 2-25-54, SCRC-UCL, UEP, B18: F5, p. 1).

But the separation did not occur until early 1958. University College's new director committed to the business school's new dean that the college would not offer any instruction "designed primarily to increase professional competence in the discharge of business responsibilities" without the business school's cooperation. Instead, "University College will be primarily concerned with general cultural courses relating to the world of business and to the business society in which we live. These courses will attempt to broaden and 'humanize' the student." University College also pledged to offer no for-credit courses under the title "Commerce." However, it could offer no-credit courses on narrow topics and for specialized audiences. University College also agreed to spin off its certificate programs in accounting to Northwestern (Krumbein to Lorie, 3-27-58, SCRC-UCL, UEP, B18: F5, p. 3).

THE GSB WINS STATUS

The case of University College shows how early business educators pursued an institution that would thrive by linking the university's visionary educators and the city's up-and-coming executives. Over time, as the University of Chicago focused on maintaining the nation's highest research standard, the animating relation was not between the university and the city but between the elite research university and its handful of peers. That is, the meaning of leadership for the university changed, from building the city to building the research reputation of the research university.

The GSB spread throughout the United States and internationally. In the postwar economy, MBA programs could not grow fast enough. The social sciences supplied the demand. In 1949, Harvard awarded almost half of all MBAs (Aaronson, 1992: 168); in the mid-1950s, nine schools did so (Gordon & Howell, 1959: 247). By 1974, 370 schools offered the MBA degree. In 1970, 20,000 MBAs were granted. The figure grew to 50,000 in 1980 and 75,000 in 1990 (Capon, 1996: 20). The rapid growth only reinforced business schools' dependency on the social and quantitative sciences for faculty. Rita McGrath points out that, even today, top-tier business schools prefer to recruit faculty from "disciplinary departments" than from business; furthermore, in hiring, promoting, and tenuring, they assign more prestige to publications in "disciplinary" than in management journals (McGrath, 2007). She concluded, "management seems to suffer from an identity crisis that results in research based on a disciplinary foundation being regarded as superior to work that is integrative and relevant to managerial concerns. Our identity crisis reflects a larger challenge facing the institutions with which we are affiliated" (2007: 1376).

The expression "identity crisis" and the reference to institutional affiliations do not adequately express the business school's bipolar parentage in the academy and industry, its central role in popularizing the professionalization movement, and its post facto remaking into a scientific institution to fit the governing logic of the research university.

Making "the disciplines" the foundation of business provided instant manpower in large numbers to upgrade even the lowliest vocational school of business rapidly. On the opposite end, the elite business school had neither the memory of nor the inclination toward Donham's vision for a discipline of management. The GSB secured "the" scientific foundation—actually, many scientific foundations—for higher education in business. It had also settled the ownership struggles between academic and occupational specialists. Henceforth, management was a hybrid discipline made up of anything in general and nothing in particular.

PART II

Recovering the Lost Foundations
of a Science of Management

By the 1980s, the graduate school of business (GSB) had secured elite status in the university and in industry. The professional manager henceforth received a new kind of liberal education in academic and technical disciplines. This concept abandoned Donham's science of administration, Wharton's principles upon which men would "combine their energies for the accomplishment of any desirable object," and NYUC's administrator who could "handle the reins of a multifarious business on comprehensive principles"—and never looked back.

Working independently but systematically, grounding their research in their experience as executives and institution-builders, Mary Parker Follett and Chester Barnard had already put their life's work into the idea. Follett had integrated the socially divided Boston community into what she called a "functional whole"; and Barnard had formed a statewide utility out of numerous small and local companies in New Jersey. While mainstream professional science increasingly demarcated researchers, subjects/objects, and the nonscientific or lay domain, Follett and Barnard pursued an integrative science that did just the opposite. In particular, it explained their personal experiences in co-creative (Follett) and formally organized (Barnard) action. In this way, they formulated a social science proper, unlike professional science modeled on the natural and physical sciences. Their science did not take subjectivity as a liability; in fact, it exploited the creative possibilities of conscious organization, beginning with organizing oneself. This new science grew not by passive discovery but by a self-directed relation to action that Follett and Barnard called "personal responsibility." For them, it was a scientific, creative, and ethical relation at one and the same time.

CHAPTER 5

Mary Parker Follett's
Science of Reciprocal Relating
and Creative Experience

☽
.

Mary Parker Follett (1868–1933) proposed a new science of relating, which she described as "dynamic," "reciprocal," and "circular" (the terms are used interchangeably). Joan Tonn's definitive biography (2003) and bibliography (2003: 585–90) show the extent to which Follett theorized and tested this science in her executive practice.

Tonn made a seminal contribution precisely by showing the relationship between Follett's science and her life. This chapter draws from Tonn's book as well as other sources to reverse the lens. That is, it explicates Follett's very interweaving of science and practice as, itself, a function of a new relationship to inquiry and action together of which she was the inventor, exemplar, and prototype.

This is an entirely new understanding of Follett because, aside from Tonn, management academicians and historians have focused on a very narrow slice of her work: her business lectures (Metcalf & Urwick, 1941: 315–17; Massie, 1965; Graham, 1995). They have connected this content neither to Follett's seminal theoretical writings (1918; 1924) nor to her institution-building and so-called social work. Some scholars show little or no appreciation of her concrete accomplishments; however, they wrote before Tonn's biography appeared. Nitin Nohria, for example, characterized Follett as a utopian (1995: 162); and Rosabeth Moss Kanter called her a "romantic" who "offered no specific techniques, no step-by-step approach, no strategies for success, no action plan" (1995: xviii). But Tonn demonstrated that Follett worked on challenging problems such as unemployment and social ostracism. More specifically, she built institutions with the capacity to solve these problems. Follett concurred that adjustment was the problem of the day, but she emphasized that in dynamic conditions adjustment was lifelong, and that it worked reciprocally: the individual had to meet industry, but industry also had to meet the individual. Finally, she defined adjustment as a self-reflexive act, not a transitive one: the individual could not be adjusted to industry any more than industry could be adjusted to the individual.

This chapter also corrects the erroneous view that Follett worked with disconnected ideas such as "the law of the situation," "power-with versus power-over," and "constructive conflict" (see, e.g., Feldheim, 2004: 344–47). Kanter described Follett's "diverse writings" on problem-solving, authority, leadership, and the social aspects of business (1995: xiv). Peter Drucker distinguished four postulates in Follett's ideas: constructive conflict, management as a function, management as a discipline, and reinventing the citizen (1995: 4–7). But Follett's close colleague and friend, Richard Cabot, professor of medicine and social ethics at Harvard, stated that Follett "saw one principle running through all [the] social sciences" and lamented that no one connected them. In her theoretical writings, and "throughout all the executive detail" of her professional work, she pursued understanding and mastery of this principle (Cabot, 1934: 81).

OVERVIEW OF RECIPROCAL RELATIONS THEORY

Follett explicated reciprocal relating most extensively in *The New State* (1918) and *Creative Experience* (1924). The first book followed from her leadership of social movements in Boston. Taking her local experience to a national scale, she proposed methods to make democracy more representative. Woodrow Wilson, Theodore Roosevelt, and Herbert Croly, among others, had advocated formal changes. Wilson, for example, had proposed that Cabinet members be made members of Congress. Drawing on her institution-building experience and her research on congressional leadership (see below), Follett instead proposed grass-roots solutions. She believed that neighborhood groups working on pressing local problems led to more representative democracy. As they personally experienced democracy, they made it.

In the second book, Follett went to the heart of this method: What made the process of state-making truly creative? How could one cultivate this process? Follett fastened on a principle or law she found in both philosophy and biology, "the alpha and omega of philosophical teaching: Heraclitus said, 'Nature desires eagerly opposites and out of them it completes its harmony, not out of similars'" (Follett, 1918: 34). "The biological law is growth by the continuous integration of simple, specific responses; in the same way do we build up our characters by uniting diverse tendencies into new action patterns; social progress follows exactly the same law" (Follett, 1924: 174). The theory reconciled unity and heterogeneity without compromising either but only enhancing the parts and whole. Above all, the theory posited a mind perceiving ever-emerging opportunity. Phenomena, coming into being mutually, remain unfinished. They move toward both independence and unity. The tendencies have no logical resolution, but this is not important. What matters is that they establish conditions for creative processes that may be directed. To this end, Follett posited a science of integration that would study relating per se and particularly the creative or destructive tendencies. For example, she observed that favoring independence leads to eccentricity and eventually to separateness, and favoring interdependence leads to the loss of a self with which to relate.

Circular response was not only a science or technique but also a "vital mode of association" for "the quintessential art of living" (Cabot, 1934: 80). For Follett, it entailed obeying a scientific *and* ethical law: "The fundamental law of the universe is the increase of life, the development of human powers, and either you keep yourself in obedience to that law or for you the universe breaks around you and is shattered" (Metcalf & Urwick, 1940: 182).

FOLLETT'S CURSUS

Follett drew from many sources, particularly intellectual and social-reform circles. However, she was equally impatient with professors' talk of "practical ethics" and reformers' complacency that they knew how to help others. She studied pragmatist philosophy as interpreted by William James, John Dewey, Charles Sanders Peirce, Josiah Royce, and others. Community and "social mind" were favorite topics of this school. However, despite the emphasis on cooperation, arguments often remained speculative and even metaphysical. The philosophers led isolated lives (Wilson, 1968: 51, 171–74; Ross, 1991: 136–38, 242–43); and some feared the consequences of immigration (Ross, 1991: 233–35). "Social mind" to them meant minds with which they themselves identified (Wilson, 1968: 172). For example, although James coined the term "compenetration" that inspired Follett (Ramsey, 1993: 109; Follett, 1918: 34), he theorized a self that "floated unfettered by any wider frame of reference or meaning than itself" (Ramsey, 1993: 55). When he did "commune," it was with a "cosmic consciousness" into which "our several minds plunge as into a mother-sea or reservoir." This led to the moral imperative that "we not fence out this surrounding mother-sea consciousness" (Gale, 1999: 5). Follett found this advice impractical. Yet James's method of taking himself as his subject and directing his own mind did interest Follett. James, suffering from mental illness, wrote that he would choose to sustain certain thoughts over others. Inspired by the French philosopher Charles Renouvier, James declared in his diary, "My first act of free will shall be to believe in free will" (James, 1870, cited in Simon, 1998: 127). This focus on individual consciousness and choice is crucial in Follett.

Follett studied at Newnham, the women's college at Cambridge. Oxford and Cambridge followed a moral code conforming to Church tenets, i.e., the Thirty-Nine Articles; but a scientific ethos began to develop. In addition, influenced by Christian Socialism, professors led reforms, such as education for working classes and for women. However, in Follett's terms, these activities did not "react back" on the scholars. For example, the political philosopher Henry Sidgwick argued that British colonialist policy was legitimate, but he could not formulate the principles that made it so (Schultz, 2004: 627).

Different ideas about a science of society emerged from these intellectual and reform circles, but all shared a keen interest in the outcome—a better society. In the United States, the states' incompatible railroad laws forced the issue of a stronger central government and regulatory body such as the Interstate Commerce Commission (Berk, 1994). But the states also protected their individual interests and the general cause of states' rights. Led by farmers, the newly settled Midwestern territories had agrarian economies and populist political orientations in contrast to the mercantile, aristocracy-led East. Debates about "home rule" thus referred both to Ireland and to U.S. localities. New immigrants, particularly the unskilled, worked in the exploitive conditions of unbridled industry. In stark contrast, a new class, "the plutocracy," amassed and controlled unprecedented wealth and drew attention to the social processes entailed in wealth creation and allocation (Bliss, 1898: 1012–16). Public opinion cultivated in newspapers, magazines, pulpits, lectures, and classrooms centered on reconciling adversaries in the union (e.g., capital "versus" labor, class "warfare"). The same public opinion was also losing consensus on the foundation of the social order in the clergy, in Christian ethics, and in the application of Christian ethics by governing bodies (Hofstadter, 1956).

In these circumstances, Follett experimented with processes by which individuals and collectives could govern themselves and more important, *learn to govern themselves,* in the dynamic conditions associated with new state-building and new knowledge discovery, together.

The Thayer Academy

Sylvanus Thayer, founder of the co-educational Thayer Academy, which Follett attended, had also founded an eponymous engineering school at Dartmouth. He had thus proved himself as an academic entrepreneur and reformer. Earlier, Thayer had served as superintendent of West Point and then director of the Army Corps of Engineers. Follett's family moved to Thayer's home town just a few years after Thayer founded his eponymous secondary school there. Although Thayer himself was neutral on the question of co-education, the trustees chose to admit girls, perhaps owing to the influence of civic leaders who had daughters (Tonn, 2003: 21). Thayer Academy offered both a general and a college-preparatory course. At that time, Charles Eliot was campaigning to raise the level of secondary schools in New England in order to upgrade Harvard. Thayer's programs "were expressly designed to be more advanced" than most eastern Massachusetts high schools (Tonn, 2003: 20). Thayer Academy sent its graduates to the finest colleges in New England. Although Harvard did not admit women, Thayer's faculty took pride in the number of its girls who passed Harvard's entrance exam.

The minimum age for admission was 13, and most students entered at 16 or older. Mary Follett was admitted at 11. Thayer had three core faculty—a classics scholar with college teaching experience; a chemistry professor; and Anna Boynton Thompson, who became one of Follett's mentors. Follett's acknowledgement of her in two book prefaces indicates a close and long friendship (Follett, 1896; 1918). Thompson launched Follett academically, training her as a star pupil and introducing her to Albert Bushnell Hart, who taught government at Harvard and mentored her academically and civically.

Thompson counseled selected women students so they would "amount to something" instead of becoming "an ordinary wife and mother" (Tonn, 2003: 42). Writing to one of her thus-favored, Thompson cited Follett as an example of "marked success." She instructed the young woman, "You must [continue your education] that your intelligence may grow and that your wit may make up for your weakness. Otherwise you will not accomplish much in this world . . . I expect a brilliant future for you . . . Look far ahead and make broad plans. Ask yourself now what is the very highest thing you can do for yourself in the next ten years, lay the plan carefully, and then question yourself every day, if you have taken one step towards." Thompson also collaborated with students. When asked to publish articles on her pedagogy, she encouraged her students to do so also or even in her place, inviting them to "become famous, and get a fine position." She encouraged them to make lasting favorable impressions on their professors. "If they recommend you strongly someone will help you." In another letter, she advised, "All you can do to repay [this professor] . . . is to help increase his reputation, by speaking of his generous friendship, when you have the opportunity" (Tonn, 2003: 49).

Thayer reformed secondary education to include science and technology, and Thompson reformed it to include education for democratic citizenship. She thus inculcated this content, method, and ideal in her students, who were "poor, and hard-working, and therefore utilitarian in their views." She worked to convince them that "history is of practical use, something they will need and that will be of service to them in daily life." Thompson also experimented with pedagogy. Conventional secondary-school history emphasized memorizing what Thompson called "a hodgepodge of unassimilated, unrelated facts." "What the pupil of a free republic needs . . . [is] . . . training in the ability to reach his own premises for his own times" (Tonn, 2003: 24). Thompson cultivated students' inductive reasoning. Drawing from multiple and diverse sources, they developed their own premises and conclusions. They defended their arguments, which they outlined on the chalkboard, in front of their teacher and peers. Thompson believed that this public defense forced students to take responsibility for their thinking. "Miss Thompson could not be bluffed, and if anyone did not know the topic, she was extremely quick to find it out" (Tonn, 2003: 25). Then the class as a whole discussed the evidence, reasoning, and conclusions. These processes evidently made a strong impression on Follett. She based her first public talk, "The Schoolmate as Educator," on her classroom experience and especially the student-teacher role reversal.

Thayer also exposed Follett to the emerging field of psychology, which included hypnosis, mesmerism, and "mind cure" (Parker, 1973). William James pioneered in the field, which he demarcated from philosophy. Follett studied pragmatist philosophy/psychology at Thayer and wrote an essay on "mind control" (Tonn, 2003: 26). When ill or in pain, Follett practiced mind control as a cure (Tonn, 2003: 341–42). James's pragmatism emphasized the individual's free choice to adopt beliefs that had positive practical effects. Likewise, Follett chose to believe that "there is a fundamentally blessed relation between self and circumstance." She contrasted this with the "resistance of environment" idea:

It is the philosophy back of [this notion] that I do not agree with. Resistance implies the opposition of nature, suggests, "I am but a pilgrim here, Heaven is my home," gives you a pretty forlorn idea of a self that has strayed out of its orbit. The philosophy involved in "progressive integration" gives us a soul at home and it gives us the crescent self; it shows us that our greatest spiritual nourishment comes . . . in meeting the circumstance. (Follett, 1924: 132)

In this way, her theory is a theory of mind directed to creative processes and outcomes (Follett, 1918: 208).

After graduating from Thayer, Follett began correspondence courses, thereby joining another reform movement—adult and continuing education, the School of Opportunity (SOO) tradition discussed in Chapters 2–4. Anna Ticknor's Society to Encourage Studies at Home served women of all social classes. Accommodating unequal preparation and "difficult personal circumstances," it also took an individual approach to each student (Tonn, 2003: 33). Reviewing the coursework and faculty credentials, Herbert Adams, professor of history at Johns Hopkins University and a pioneer in the adult education movement, called Ticknor's program "an intellectual revolution" (Tonn, 2003: 34). Ticknor's approach resonated with Thompson's. Home study reconciled young women's family life with their personal need for intellectual development, emotional support, and social solidarity. This was particularly true for Follett: only a few months after graduating from Thayer in 1884, she returned home to care for her mother after her father died (Tonn, 2003: 33, 36).

The Annex

In 1888, Follett began studies at the Harvard Annex, later called Radcliffe. Charles Eliot had opposed women's higher education at Harvard; but a civic group, the Society to Encourage Studies at Home, persuaded Eliot to survey faculty on the issue. Forty-one out of fifty-four faculty members approved of women's education. The Annex resulted from a compromise whereby Harvard administered courses through the Society but gave no degree, following the practice of Cambridge. Annex students were mostly "specials" in the SOO tradition, "older and more absorbed in their own responsibilities" (Tonn, 2003: 42). They were employed, or preparing for employment, in secondary-school teaching. As New England schools raised their academic standards, they drew from this growing pool of educated women.

Eliot imposed certain restrictions on Annex students. The women could not walk through Harvard yard. Professors were to give women about half the time they gave to men. When Eliot toured the library with visitors, women students were "hustled out of sight" (Tonn, 2003: 44). Nevertheless, they considered themselves privileged. One of Follett's peers, Esther Pearson, who won an academic competition that was mistakenly opened to Annex students and had to return the prize, wrote:

We acknowledge that we shall never get a degree, that we are wholly dependent on what time and strength the instructors have left from their college courses, and that we run a risk of leading lives isolated from our fellow-students; but to us the spirit of the place outweighs it all. To us the life in Cambridge, with all the advantages which it and Boston offer, the chance to study with men who stand among the ablest in America, the companionship of a picked set of girls representing the best culture of New England, and above all the utter freedom . . . to study what we choose and when, to live with whom we like, in short, to order our lives for ourselves in all those outside matters which are such a help or a hindrance to the inner—all this is what the Annex means to us. (Tonn, 2003: 44–45)

Follett too expressed gratitude for "very unusual privileges" (Follett, 1896: ix).

At the Annex, Follett studied with Albert Bushnell Hart, who became another mentor. Hart taught history and government; like Thompson, he taught them as education for citizenship and life. Hart's method called for students to develop a personal opinion on controversial issues (Hart, 1888: 632–33)—for example, U.S. immigration policy, home rule for Ireland, voting rights for blacks, civil-service reform, and enforcement of federal regulation of interstate commerce. The method was integrative in three respects. Intellectually, students located diverse sources and reasoned inductively from them to develop an argument faithful to the evidence. Subjectively, they cultivated the ability to think sufficiently by and for themselves to experience conviction. Socially, they connected their individual lives to civic life.

Hart's pedagogy was part and parcel of his active public life: he taught by example. He served on numerous municipal and educational policy-making bodies. He gave speeches and wrote magazine articles to cultivate public opinion on contemporary political issues. He regarded the United States as an experiment and a work in progress in which all individuals had the ability and obligation to participate. But first, they had to understand the continuing progress of this experiment. This view defined history as past politics and present politics as future history (Cunningham, 1976). Above all, they had to participate in this experiment themselves. In this regard, scholarship helped them "acquire power as well as information" (Tonn, 2003: 67).

In Hart's seminar, "Topics in American History and Modern Constitutional History," Follett worked on what became her first book. Hart had ambitious plans for his top students. Samuel Eliot Morison, who became a leading U.S. historian, said that Hart encouraged him to work on a topic that "was as astonishing to me, a junior in college, as if he had suggested that I should design a cathedral or run for the presidency" (Tonn, 2003: 69). Hart's Annex seminar consisted of five women. Each worked on an "elaborate thesis" based on original sources. Hart met weekly with each student individually. At the end of the term, he was so impressed with the results that he added a special note to his grade report: "I wish to bear testimony to the extraordinary faithfulness and interest of the class and to their quickness of discernment and ability to use their knowledge wisely" (Tonn, 2003: 51–52). Follett worked on a topic that often appeared on Hart's recommended list—the "chaotic functioning" of the House of Representatives. Hart was not alone in worrying about this problem; in 1889, the Massachusetts statesman Henry Cabot Lodge called the House "a complete travesty upon representative government, upon popular government, and upon government by the majority" (Tonn, 2003: 69–70). Hart focused particularly on the filibuster and on the presidential Cabinet.

In the 1870s, the Congress had considered approximately 37,000 bills. The figure doubled by the mid-1880s. Approval of legislation was already difficult, but interpretation and enforcement were doubly so. Woodrow Wilson proposed structural reforms, such as having Cabinet members vote on legislation. Hart thought that Wilson underestimated the formal and informal power of the Speaker of the House of Representatives. He based this conclusion partly on Thomas B. Reed's handling of the role, which "revolutionized House procedure" and proved the magnitude of the Speaker's power (Tonn, 2003: 75–76). While some saw only personal ambition in the moves, Hart thought they reflected an intelligent evolution of the position. Hart and Wilson squared off in the debate. According to Tonn, Cabinet involvement versus strong Speakership reflected opposing views of the prospects for popular government. Wilson held that the Cabinet brought the healthy influence of an outside body to congressional decision-making. He doubted the idea of "leadership of one man supreme" in the legislature (Tonn, 2003: 77). Follett's research method and findings would draw from and feed into this debate.

Newnham

In 1890, encouraged by Thompson and Hart, Follett continued her studies at Newnham, the women's school at Cambridge. Women enjoyed greater autonomy and status at Newnham than at Harvard. Newnham offered women buildings and dormitories of their own. Newnham women walked freely about the Cambridge campus. Annex professors repeated for the women the courses they taught to men, but Newnham women could also attend lectures at Cambridge. Follett called her experience at Newnham "the great milepost and turning point" in her life (Tonn, 2003: 53).

Henry Sidgwick became another mentor. He was a demanding teacher; in one term, when the only other student in the class withdrew, he taught the class for Follett only (Tonn, 2003: 63). Whereas Hart's influence is evident in Follett's first book, Sidgwick's is less visible but was perhaps more profound. He was intellectually exacting. His writings "set new standards of precision in wording, clarity in exposition, and care in argument" (Schneewind, 1977: 1). Sidgwick belonged to an elite philosophy faculty at a time when the discipline enjoyed considerable prestige. It also held to its grand vision to unify all knowledge. Sidgwick contemplated science's effect on that project. He concurred with John Stuart Mill that it contributed to the breaking up of social consensus. A new consensus could be neither religious nor philosophical. Science could provide the basis for consensus; but it did so through authority, and authority could be misled or manipulated. Therefore, a sound education had to encourage independent thought. Assuming that dissent could be freely expressed, "out of the chaos a new consensus might arise, based on broader experience and clearer insight" (Schneewind, 1977: 21). Sidgwick sought to resolve this social *and* epistemological problem at the individual, subjective level: discerning judgment had to get "as close as it was humanly possible to come to beliefs which one could rightly feel certain were true" (Schneewind, 1977: 62).

Sidgwick worked to reconcile three different ethical systems or "methods"—egoism or the pursuit of one's greatest good, "dogmatic intuitionism" or obedience to virtues such as promise-keeping and truth-telling, and utilitarianism or the pursuit of the greatest good for the greatest number. Sidgwick sought to impartially negotiate among the methods, "all of which he found in himself" (Schultz, 2004: 205). He particularly prized "sympathetic understanding and harmonization" and "the intelligent apprehension of common interests" (Schwartz, 2004: 604).

Sidgwick's admiring students included John Maynard Keynes and Arthur Balfour. Balfour reminisced: "Of all the men I have known he was the readiest to consider every controversy and every controversialist on their merits. He never claimed authority; he never sought to impose his views; he never argued for victory . . . [these qualities gave] Sidgwick the most potent and memorable influence, not so much over the opinions as over the intellectual development of anyone who had the good fortune to be associated with him" (Tonn, 2003: 62). Another colleague characterized Sidgwick as "seeing in a moment the point of an argument, seizing on distinctions which others had failed to perceive, suggesting new aspects from which a question might be regarded, and enlivening every topic by a keen yet sweet and kindly wit" (Tonn, 2003: 60). A Newnham student described her private tutoring from Sidgwick:

[H]e would say something of this sort: "I want you to begin at the beginning, as if you were explaining to somebody who knew nothing about it [the argument]"

... And, in a series of Socratic questionings, he would proceed to clear away the rubbish and open up the line of thought ... he presented me with a very difficult standard of intellectual integrity: to observe, to record, to deduce with no aim but the truth, as nearly as one could hit it. No stress of after years could shake the result of this discipline. No easy path to difficult conclusions could satisfy. Truth is not simple. (Tonn, 2003: 63)

Follett, returning to Boston, wrote to Sidgwick: "Perhaps . . . the best way in which a pupil can thank her teacher is in trying to give others something of what she herself has received. And this I shall try to do" (Tonn, 2003: 64).

Leadership Research:
The Speaker of the House of Representatives

Following Thompson and Hart, Follett taught secondary school in the reform tradition that combined science, history, and citizenship (Cunningham, 1976). She also completed the book she had begun in Hart's course, which was published in 1896 as *The Speaker of the House of Representatives*. Methodologically, Hart encouraged students to consult "diaries, travels, autobiographies, letters, and speeches" because they were "more real and more human." He also had students read about the "social, political, and occasionally economic conditions, to show how ordinary people lived" (Tonn, 2003: 82). Taking this approach, Follett gained intimate knowledge of formal and informal power at the highest level of government. In this way, her academic research was also an initiation into leadership.

Hart publicly praised Follett's research and predicted that she would become the "acknowledged authority" on congressional leadership. He said her work exemplified his ideal of the "impartial and scientific" approach to "solve a knotty problem in history and practical government" by seeking "the truth" (Hart, 1896: xvi). But reviewers, distinguishing between her historical research and her views on policy, took issue with the latter (Tonn, 2003: 86). Nevertheless the book showed the informal dynamics of the speakership. Tonn notes that Follett thus anticipated Barnard's research on informal organization and the subjective aspect of authority (2003: 92; see Chapter 6).

In her preface, Follett stated that because speakers relied so much on "unwritten practice," only a House member of long experience could perform a "proper" study. Yet her capturing of this element is precisely what Theodore Roosevelt praised in reviewing her book. He had such experience; and he commended Follett for getting at the truth of the "practical work" of Congress, about which "theoretical students" were "almost absolutely blind" (Roosevelt, 1896: 176).

The book also anticipated Follett's work on reciprocal relations. In essence, she posited an emerging office. Then, in a series of case studies, she showed the emerging individual relating to emerging circumstances and redefining the office. For example, concerning a young politician of "mediocre talents" elected during a time of "great political excitement," she explained that he enjoyed an advantage from "being free from the weight of a career" (Follett, 1896: 95). "[N]otably ignorant of the practice of the House," he "did not know enough of parliamentary law to manipulate it for his personal or for party advantage. He was not enough of a politician to extract from the Speakership its political power, and he was too honest and upright to become the tool of the corrupt elements" (Follett, 1896: 95–96). Concerning Henry Clay, Follett explained not only his acquisition of power but also his colleagues' deference to his doing so. She argued that Clay was the most powerful man in the United States from 1811 to 1825. He added power to the Speakership, but no one charged him with abuse of office because of his "personal qualifications" and especially his "remarkable tact" in relating to House members as well as in "interpret[ing]" his "own privileges." Clay distinguished himself from others by knowing "how to measure [his] power so as to obtain the utmost possible, and yet not go beyond that unwritten standard of 'fairness' which exists in every House of Representatives: how to observe the subtle yet essential difference between 'political' and 'partisan' action" (Follett, 1896: 80). Follett criticized another officeholder for "separating himself from his constituents" (Follett, 1896: 85). She accused the men who used the position for personal or party ends of abuse of office. Defending an officeholder who exercised individual judgment rather than catering to majorities or minorities, she said he "was only carrying out an honest conception of the Speakership" (Follett, 1896: 116). In this way, Follett was already using reciprocal relations theory by studying the co-emerging individual and institution.

At the Center of Action

Follett wanted to "make some practical significance of what she had learned" (Tonn, 2003: 111). In 1891, she told Sidgwick that she would use her knowledge of political science and political philosophy to "infiltrate much into her pupils and make history much more valuable to them than it could ever be by learning a string of facts" (Tonn, 2003: 66). She taught girls aged 17–20 in Pauline Agassiz Shaw's private secondary school. Shaw became Follett's principal benefactor. An immigrant from Switzerland, Shaw was the daughter of Louis Agassiz, a leader of the Lazzaroni movement (see Chapter 2). Shaw was also the stepdaughter of Elizabeth Cabot Cary Agassiz, who negotiated the formal ties between the Annex and Harvard, ran the Annex as president of the Society for the Collegiate Instruction of Women, and became the first president of Radcliffe (the Annex's new name).

Pauline Agassiz had married Quincy Adams Shaw, a member of Boston high society, the so-called Brahmins. He made his fortune from copper mines in Michigan. In 1880, Pauline Shaw opened a private school serving this society (Tonn, 2003: 64). It offered a traditional curriculum but also innovative subjects and methods, notably "sloyd," a type of manual training that Shaw admired for its "synthesis of physical labor" with values such as "respect for work, self-reliance, and habits of order, accuracy and neatness" (Tonn, 2003: 66). In addition to secondary school political science, Shaw conducted other educational experiments such as the kindergarten and the settlement house (see below).

In 1898, Follett left teaching to become a clerk in a law office. According to Tonn, her search for meaningful work led her to the Settlement House Movement (SHM). Although it is tempting to say that Follett "joined" this movement, it is more accurate to say that she marshaled the necessary resources to solve what she thought were the pressing problems of the day.

Cooperation among financiers, engineers, and politicians had enabled the construction of the transcontinental railroad and helped coordinate a unified domestic economy. The SHM, the Municipal Reform Movement (MRM), the Vocational Education Movement (VEM), and the Women's Club Movement (WCM) pursued the grass-roots analogue of such extensive cooperation. They worked across gender, generational, and class differences. In Boston, the movements were interlinked through a common biological bond, the Brahmin families (Farrell, 1993), and a moral bond, the Massachusetts commonwealth idea. Dating to the Puritan era, the commonwealth posited and pursued a common good. The Brahmins, the longstanding governing class perpetuated through intermarriage, were custodians of this value (Dalzell, 1987; Jaher, 1982).

Massachusetts was among the first states to industrialize as the Brahmins transitioned from whaling to textiles. Industrialization in the United States, and famine and political upheaval outside the country, brought waves of immigrants to U.S. shores, and to Boston particularly. Immigration peaked at the turn of the century (Tager, 1985a, 1985b). The dire working and living conditions of immigrants posed problems for the Brahmins and "their" city and commonwealth (Follett, 1924:

186). Religious and political differences were pronounced and divisive: the Irish were Catholic and Democratic; the Yankees, Protestant and Republican. "Habits of thought" differed with regard to power relations (Handlin, 1973: 181, 327). Immigrants and natives clashed over different moral codes (Hofstadter, 1955: 9). Although immigrants and "their" patronage systems were blamed for corruption, "the bosses and grafting politicians were usually of native stock" (Schlesinger, 1933: 392). Second-generation immigrants expected more than their parents' lot. The Brahmins divided and weakened over these issues (O'Connor, 1984: 138–39; Solomon, 1952).

The MRM formed "municipal leagues" advocating "municipal home rule" over state or federal government rule (Patton, 1940). The Boston MRM sought to integrate the city's native and new populations. Hart was one of its leaders (Stewart, 1950: 206–08), serving as an officer from 1910 to 1911. The MRM instructed the "ignorant classes" as to the abuses of boss and patronage systems (Bliss & Binder, 1908: 795–800). It rallied the "educated classes" from apathy to civic action (Hart, 1918 [1903]: 213–14; Bliss & Binder, 1908: 325–26). Follett saw that self-governance crossed class, gender, and cultural differences. However, she found that paternalism, values inculcation, and similar methods were doomed because they reinforced dependency. Thus, when asked to prepare a "civic primer" or a textbook on how to be a good citizen, Follett instead formed junior city councils that engaged students in the civic process (Tonn, 2003: 168–69).

In this respect, Follett drew from the women's club, an institution dating to the early seventeenth century, when Anne Hutchinson offered Bible studies for women in her home (Martin, 1987: 5). The club ran on the SOO's do-it-yourself logic. In a gender-segregated society, the club enabled women to pursue active lives (Blair, 1980; Breckinridge, 1933). According to Jane Croly, mother of Herbert and founder of Sorosis, a New York club for professional women, the purpose was to overcome isolation (Stettner, 1993: 12). In the nineteenth century, women's clubs transitioned from religious and recreational to political purposes, particularly abolitionism (Martin, 1987; Scott, 1991). The U.S. Sanitary Commission (USSC) took previously uncoordinated local clubs to a national scale. Organizing women's voluntary services for the Union army in the Civil War, the USSC gave its members a new and high level of leadership experience. Boston had a particularly strong USSC chapter (Sklar, 1995: 73) that included the social reformer Caroline Severance, social activist and abolitionist Julia Ward Howe, and journalist and women's rights advocate Mary Livermore. After the war, the USSC started clubs organized around suffragism and other political causes. Undertaking a new political or civic initiative, club women began with an investigation, or a "survey," which they called "social science" (Carson, 1990: 24; Muncy, 1991: 31). This genre flourished in the early twentieth century. Surveys appeared in magazines, reformers' journals, and newspapers. The classic exemplar is Florence Kelley's study of the Hull House neighborhood and sweat shops (Oberschall, 1972: 197).

Clubs thus developed women's research, writing, and speaking skills. Club women also practiced debate and consensus-building (Evans, 1993: 130). Politically oriented clubs organized themselves by congressional district. They taught parliamentary procedure, legislative processes, advocacy, and public relations (Sharer, 2004: 22–25). Boston clubs had a particularly successful track record. They helped Massachusetts become the first state to win compulsory education (1852); regulate interstate commerce (1869, predating the federal body by eighteen years); limit women's work hours (1874), and elect women to public school boards (1873—although women could not vote for themselves until 1889).

In Boston, clubs were segregated by gender. The MRM leagues were for men only (Stewart, 1950: 14); women formed the Women's Municipal League (WML). Boston had a particularly strong chapter, the Women's Municipal League of Boston (WMLB). This club, with Shaw's help, funded Follett's work in Boston. Nationally, the MRM's central challenge was inconstant public opinion and support due to skepticism (Patton, 1940: 33) and inertia (Bliss & Binder, 1908: 325). The voluntaristic WCM had strong leadership and member participation. In Boston, shared Brahmin ties gave the women access to political decision-making and the men greater public consensus on their decisions. This tie also voluntarily redistributed wealth and wealth-creating mechanisms, Follett's Placement Bureau being a textbook example (see below).

Katherine Lowell Bowlker, the WMLB's founder, came from the bluest of Brahmin blood—Lawrence on her mother's side and Lowell on her father's. They were the largest textile manufacturers in New England (Worrell, 1943: xiii). Her brother, a former president of Harvard, had been active in the MRM (Stewart, 1950: 208). Bowlker attracted Boston's wealthiest women to the WMLB. She earned a national reputation as a leader of a WCM splinter movement known as domestic feminism or municipal housekeeping (Skocpol, 1992: 332; Bowlker, 1909, 1912). Women were divided over which cause, suffragism or municipal reform, should take priority. Bowlker appealed to both interests:

If the suffrage shall eventually come, we believe that the League will have proved its usefulness in serving as the best possible means of educating women to vote intelligently. If the suffrage should never come, we believe that the League will equally have proved its value in showing how great is the work that women can do, without the vote. (Bowlker, 1909: 7)

Bowlker was a consummate organizer, with a vision and a method. At the WMLB's first "public meeting," she stated that although women had always "had a keen sense of their individual duties and responsibilities to their homes, their charities, their hospitals, their various organizations," they were now "awaking more and more to a sense of communal consciousness." The "time seems ripe now when all women can unite together to form an intelligent, concerted body of public opinion, which shall be so representative, and so influential, that no public official can disregard its desires" (Bowlker, 1909: 2–3). Bowlker cited the "tremendous power" of public opinion:

[T]here is no limit to what it can accomplish if it be only strong enough, if it be only reasonably and wisely guided. In a representative government such as ours, the people eventually obtain what the people really demand, be it good government or mis-government. If the public opinion of women is to gain the convincing power, and authority, that it can have, if the justice of its demands is to be recognized and obeyed, it must first become an educated opinion. (Bowlker, 1909: 3)

Bowlker's method had three steps. First, the women had to learn "the relation of the City government to its citizens," for example, the "statutes and regulations of the city, all the laws, in accordance with which the public officials perform their duties" as well as the "hindrances and handicaps, which often make it difficult for such officials to act as they desire." They also had to learn "the relation of the citizens to the government"; that is:

they must realize their duty in helping the government to carry out the laws, they must understand that unless they themselves cooperate with it, no government can ever make the city clean, or healthy, or happy. When they have learned exactly what the citizen has a right to expect from the government, by law; when they have learned exactly what the government has a right to demand from its citizens in return; when they are fulfilling their share of this bargain, then the opinion of women will have gained a weight and a prestige which are beyond the power of words to measure. (Bowlker, 1909: 4)

Second, the women had to study public service organizations in the city, learn what they had done, join them, and avoid duplicate effort. "[T]he sympathy, the intimate touch, the mutual confidence of membership, will put the League in a position where it can give the help." Third, the women had to conduct "object lessons." "[E]xperiments must be tried if the world is to advance, and there are some experiments which seem so sure of success, that it becomes almost imperative to try them. This can only be done by private initiative." The League would select the experiments deemed to be most sound and "prove themselves to be of such enduring benefit to the community" that the city would incorporate the experiments (Bowlker, 1909: 5). The League did so successfully (Worrell, 1943).

Bowlker emphasized that although the WMLB had aroused interest, it had to prove itself—"it must do good work" and "actually accomplis[h] some definite, concrete pieces of work, which shall be so useful and so important, so prominent in the city, that they cannot be overlooked." She reported on the first two methods, which she called "investigation" and "cooperation." Her report on the third, "initiatory experiments of civic interest," was the most extensive. It described Follett's work in detail (Cabot, 1909: 12–13). Thus Follett had already contributed substantively to the WMLB's most pressing goal to accomplish concrete work and "justify itself before the people of the city" (Bowlker, 1909: 8).

Through Shaw and other Brahmins, the WLMB had interlocking relationships with the SHM. Jane Addams is credited with leading the national SHM at Hull House in Chicago, modeled after Samuel Augustus Barnett's British institution, Toynbee Hall.

Settlement "methods" called for "settlement workers" to live (settle) in local communities. The idea was that one best helped the poor by living among them. The haves were not superior to the have-nots because in settlements, all parties both gained and gave. The U.S. SHM collaborated with other movements such as the MRM. For example, Addams led campaigns to replace a ward boss. Robert Woods, a leader of the Boston SHM, collaborated with local MRM leaders (Curley, 1957). Shaw and Follett were recognized leaders of all the social movements described in this chapter.

In particular, the U.S. SHM joined forces with the new and rising population of women college graduates seeking an active life outside of secondary school teaching. A contemporary resource for reformers listed settlement houses as "women's college settlements" (Bliss, 1898: 307). One historian compared the SHM to a post-doc for women (Sklar, 1995: 187;1993: 67). Ninety percent of settlement workers had attended college, and 80 percent held the Bachelor's degree (Davis, 1984: 33). An 1896 survey of settlements showed that a majority of head residents were women, two-thirds of all residents were women, and three-fourths of the clientele were women (Sklar, 1995: 202). Thus, in the U.S. context, a more accurate term for the Settlement House Movement is the Women's College Settlement House Movement.

Follett said her work was "conducted on Settlement principles and in the Settlement spirit" (Tonn, 2003: 140). She spent time in the neighborhood. She spoke with employers, teachers, headmasters, and residents (Tonn, 2003: 137). A high school principal introduced Follett to a group of boys who had played baseball together. "[T]o stimulate an intelligent

interest in local economic questions," she formed a "debate club," Highland Union, with them (Tonn, 2003: 125–26; 138–39). The club integrated what Follett had learned in her formal and informal education:
content such as parliamentary procedure but also initiation into governing one's individual and collective, and personal and civic, life. Follett
"had a knack for stirring one's ambitions. More than a few Roxbury
young men got their first stimulus to 'amount to something,' as she used
to say, from Miss Follett," stated James Mulroy, who became her star
protégé. He started with her debate club in 1902; in 1917, he replaced her
as head of the Boston Placement Bureau (Tonn, 2003: 141, 255). Of the
seventy-five original members of Highland Union, many others also went
on to careers in municipal and state politics (Tonn, 2003: 127, 141, 145).

The School Center Movement and Self-Governance

Follett recombined ideas and momentum from various social movements:
vocational education and guidance, adult education, and the extended-
use public school. In 1902, she received funding and political support
from James Storrow, head of the Boston School Committee, a local-
citizens' body that oversaw primary and secondary public education.
Storrow proposed using public schools after hours to educate adolescents
who had quit school. Led by Edward J. Ward and Gustav Strauben-
muller, in Rochester and New York, respectively (Tonn, 2003: 185), the
School Center Movement (SCM) had tested this policy.

In Massachusetts, students could leave school at 14. In Irish neighborhoods, almost all did so (Tonn, 2003: 159). Unemployment was high, so
many did not work. A Vocational Education Movement (VEM) argued
that students would stay in schools that offered industrial or "manual"
education (Bennett, 1937: 507–52; Brewer, 1942). Advocates also viewed
this as citizenship training: "Young people drifting into various kinds of
work on the basis of ignorance both of their own abilities and of the characteristics of occupational life present a condition menacing to free government" (Brewer, 1942: 8). The VEM also inculcated ambition (Brewer,
1942: 1–52). It captured the Massachusetts governor's attention. In 1905
he set up a commission on industrial education led by a former U.S. labor
commissioner. The commission's final report found that 25,000 children
ages 14 to 16 were either working or not attending school. The commission identified a gap between students' interests and the high school curriculum. It recommended adding "elements of productive industry," including
"agriculture and the mechanic and domestic arts," to the offerings. It also
recommended that the mathematics and science curricula "show the application and use of these subjects in industrial life" (Bennett, 1937: 514–15).

A Vocational Guidance Movement (VGM) took the VEM a step further. It fit students to jobs while they were still in school; that is, students selected courses based on their occupational interests. "The necessity for choosing, in turn, brought forward the idea of assistance in making such important choices" (Bennett, 1937: 537). This echoes Charles Eliot's argument that the elective system cultivated students' decision-making skills and responsibility (see Chapter 2). Bennett credits Frank Parsons with initiating the VEM in Boston as a cooperative venture among the Women's Club Movement, the Municipal Reform Movement, and the Settlement House Movement (Bennett, 1937: 538).

The Boston VEM organized the Boston Vocation Bureau. "The Bureau did not attempt to decide for any boy what occupation he should choose, but aimed to help him investigate and then come to his own conclusion" (Bennett, 1937: 538). The decision process entailed self-understanding, knowledge of different lines of work, and "true reasoning on the relations of these two groups of facts" (Bennett, 1937: 538). Psychological tests and profiles helped operationalize this idea (Brewer, 1918: 266–70).

Follett addressed this issue more holistically, as education for life. She launched her WMLB work by distinguishing it from the SHM. Adolescents disliked the settlements' condescending attitude. Unemployed and out of school, they took to the streets and saloons. Likewise, settlement workers were uncomfortable with adolescents, especially unruly young men. Follett cited her success with the Highland Union debate club, which she had made into a social club by adding classes and recreational activities (Tonn, 2003: 166). The SCM used public schools after hours for adult and industrial education. This idea appealed to adolescents because its base in a school, not a house, took away the maternalistic associations and replaced them with civic ones: meeting in a public building encouraged "dignity, responsibility, and loyalty to the city." Also, public schools had the large spaces conducive to adolescents' favorite activities, athletics and dancing. Follett explained, "If we did not have a place large enough to play basketball, we could not belong to the Athletic League, and the success of our whole organization would be doubtful" (Follett, 1909: 15).

But Follett also took the reformers' standard line: "We use our social and recreative features as a bait for more serious work." From the initial attraction, the adolescents "may then be influenced to join classes" in vocational training and in citizenship. Follett also appealed to standards of decency and common sense:

There are thousands of young men who have no place to go to nights. There are thousands of girls who used to stay at home in the country, but who have been brought by our changed industrial conditions to the cities to work in shops and factories. Many of these will be in the streets nights unless we provide some decent recreation for them. Thus on the one hand there is this urgent need, on the other there are all these empty buildings upon which we have spent literally millions and millions of our money. Such a waste of capital seems bad business management on our part. (Follett, 1909: 16)

Above all, Follett emphasized self-capacity. As early as 1902 she had organized her centers into "self-governed and self-officered groups" (Tonn, 2003: 166). Setting up industrial education for working girls, she spoke of clubs taking their "first steps toward self-government" (Follett, 1911: 18). Describing her work to members of the Playground and Recreation Association of America, Follett articulated the "most important principle" of "our particular form of organization": "we have only *clubs*, no classes." Groups met for "a definite purpose, and this seems to me very important (that they *should* meet for a definite purpose and for some form of self-development)" (emphasis in original). Groups organized into "clubs with their own officers and con-stitution and rules." They worked on deliverables such as musical performances and sports tournaments. They kept and managed the revenues they earned. They held weekly "business meetings," where they learned "parliamentary law and self-government. And we feel not only that this form of organization is more educational, but that we shall thereby hold our young people, give them an esprit de corps, a greater interest, and a greater individual responsibility" (Follett, 1913b: 387). A delegate from each club served on a central committee oversee-ing the whole center. "The plan is that the delegates shall report back to their clubs and get instructions, and thus all our four hundred and fifty members can take part by a representative system in the manage-ment of the social center." In this way, members might feel that they belonged to "something larger than a glee club or a gymnastic or dra-matic club." It might

make them feel that they are part of a living and radiating center of municipal activity, and that *they* are responsible for its success and for its accomplishment of the aims it has set before itself, aims which they *approve* merely at pres-ent, but which in the future we expect they will help to initiate, formulate and execute. They will incidentally learn self-government, how to work for larger things than their own self-development, and eventually be helped to any social or civic work for their community for which they show willingness and aptitude. (Follett, 1913b: 387)

Speaking to SCM advocates, Follett criticized the tendency to focus on form and forget purpose. The very phrase "extended use of public schools" directed attention to the secondary rather than the primary purpose:

I am speaking to you today as chairman of a committee on the extended use of school buildings. The name is misleading because I have no interest in the extended use of school buildings in itself. I stand for a great unmet need in our community, and I believe that we can meet that need with our schoolhouses. The title of my committee might rather be The Educational Recreation of Young Workers from fourteen to twenty-one. I am pleading for an extension of our educational system, rather than for the extended use of school buildings. (Follett, 1913b: 390)

Follett also criticized reformers' regulatory tendencies. "You can force a moral code on people from above yet this will change them very little, but by a system of self-governing clubs with leaders who know how to lead, we can make real progress in educating people to higher standards" (Follett, 1913d: 266). Writing up her experiences in Boston, she stated, "I am constantly being acted upon, no one is encouraging me to act . . . Thus am I robbed of my most precious possession—my responsibilities—for only the active process of participation can shape me for the social purpose" (Follett, 1918: 235). Reform movements had to start by *reforming themselves* into a "wise and trained leadership" that could realize its greatest possibilities:

You study by yourself, many forms of work you perform by yourself, you can take exercise by yourself. Now the most striking characteristic of the present time is that people are doing more things together. They are coming together more than ever before in municipal movements, for national purposes, in labor unions, in associations of employers and employees. The key-note of the twentieth century is the passion for solidarity. That this is so is the great hope of our future democracy. To train people for that larger degree of democracy which we see coming, to help them learn how to work and play together, how to live together harmoniously and effectively, is the great mission of adult recreation and what makes it loom up so large at the present moment. (Follett, 1913d: 267–68)

Follett pursued "an atmosphere of high if unformulated ideals, and real, if intangible influence" (Follett, 1913b: 392). This atmosphere was physical, based on the public nature of the buildings and the large spaces that accommodated dances and competitions. It was also a professional atmosphere: unlike the settlements, the centers paid their leaders and managers. They were also formally trained in leadership and in management—by Follett. Although she won recognition for her leadership, she discouraged others from believing "that we as leaders emanat[e] something regenerating from our mere presence . . . We know now that we must get people to do their own regenerating" (Follett, 1913d: 267). Although admitting that this technique had "to be worked out," she in fact operationalized it in her training program, quoted extensively here (Follett, 1913a) because it is unpublished.

Follett's Training Program: "Aims and Duties of Managers and Leaders"   Addressing her staff of approximately one hundred center leaders and managers, Follett demonstrated as well as described her idea of good management and leadership. She divided her remarks into two parts, the first addressed to the leaders (all of the following quotations are from Follett, 1913a: 3–20). She began by stating the opportunity before them. "You are the first leaders of the Boston evening centers—it is for you to blaze the way and show all the possibilities of these centers, and to solve some of the many problems connected with the working out of the evening center idea." But they had to remember that the centers ran according to definite principles. Boston centers held that "community obligation to the child should not end at fourteen because of the accident of the child's being obliged to go to work at fourteen." They focused on the many thousands of young people aged 14 to 21 who attended neither high school nor night school. To this group, the centers offered "a lighter form of education." Follett left further interpretation to her audience. "What this shall mean in the life of the child depends on the leaders of the centers." Follett urged a focus not on the "negative value" of the social center—keeping adolescents out of trouble—but on the "positive gain of building up character and developing the social sense of our young people." She defined this broadly as "the sense which makes us useful members of society." She underscored the leaders' singular importance: Because at this age adolescents separated from family, the leaders' influence "may perhaps be almost the only direct and positive influence for good in many of these children's lives."

The centers' purposes, then, were "to make the young people have a good time in a wholesome way; to stimulate individual growth of character; to develop the true social spirit,—how to work and play harmoniously together, and to encourage responsibility." Subjects had to be taught as a means, not an end. "[The leader's] usefulness to the center ceases when he looks upon it as an end." Leaders must ask themselves, "How can I accomplish the aims of the center through my subject?" Further, they should ask: Did they hold the boys' and girls' interest? Did they lead them to "pull together"? Did they attract "large enough numbers to make [their] center valuable to the neighborhood"? The true test was to reach as many as possible, as deeply as possible. "An athletic leader who picks fourteen of the young men of the neighborhood for two basket ball teams . . . and does not devise some way of interesting larger numbers . . . has failed from the evening center point of view." Leaders had to "see how the things which we want to teach"—"self-control, fair play, patience, steadiness, generosity of feeling toward the efforts of others, perseverance, courageous facing of difficulties"—are taught through the activity. "That athletic club is successful, from the evening center point of view, not which wins the game, but which shows clean play, pluck and perseverance . . . In a minstrel show . . . that show is successful, from the evening center point of view, not which gives the most finished performance, but which has produced the best spirit in the preparation for that performance." Teachers taught their subjects primarily and other things secondarily. "Their incidental aims are your chief aims . . . the leaders of the evening centers are engaged primarily to provide a guiding influence in the life of young people at a time when many other influences are withdrawn, and to stimulate the social life of the center."

The club spirit was inculcated through "business meetings," which trained members "how to bear each his proper part and yet to subordinate himself sufficiently to the whole so that there shall be concerted action." These meetings could, improperly managed, "become a farce." They degenerated into "a lot of classes with a school atmosphere—just what we are trying to avoid." She admitted that the process began with artificiality. But human nature would kick in: "As each naturally wishes his club to be the best in the center, every member can be asked to bring into the next meeting some suggestion for the improvement of the club. This will make discussion."

Follett concluded by reinforcing the centers' priorities. They were not founded to make actors, musicians, or athletes:

These centers have been established to provide for the leisure hours of working boys and girls wholesome recreation, and activities which will raise the tone and level of their lives and tend to make them better citizens, better workmen, better members of their families and of society generally. Every leader must ask himself constantly what *he* is doing to accomplish these ends, how far he is being successful, and what more he can do.

She insisted, she *personalized*:

Please don't haze over this matter to yourselves. Do not think vaguely, "Yes, I know the evening centers exist for these ends, but that is not my part; *I* must teach this boy to be . . . a good cornetist, or a good basket ball player; some one else will teach him these other things." Don't make this mistake. There *is* no one else. There are only the leaders and the manager, and the manager has other duties. What the thousands of young people will get out of the evening centers will depend largely on the leaders.

She warned of the trap of "helping":

We must be careful . . . that the attitude of manager and leaders is that all are there to help the young people get what they want . . . At the same time, indirect as your influence may be, your very name emphasizes the idea of a real influence . . . You are called leaders—you must show the power of leadership, your power of leading that part of your community which you have before you.

Turning to the managers, Follett enumerated their formal tasks: "custodianship of a public school building," "keep[ing] order, to see that the leaders come on time and that the records are kept." But she underscored their "organic and vital" relation to the center:

I think the manager is above everything else the link which connects the community with the center, the center with the community. If the center becomes an integral part of the life of the community, and that is the final test of the success of the center, this end will be accomplished by the manager.

She encouraged the managers to ask themselves, "What is the relation of the center to the neighborhood? What is it to mean in the life of the neighborhood?" Therefore, managers had to know their neighborhoods, the residents' wishes, and how to reach them. Many of the answers to these questions

indicate only surface characteristics. After all these things have been discovered the neighborhood must be studied to find out its underlying forces. In every community there are certain underlying forces which make for righteousness; these differ in different places; they must be got hold of and fostered and nurtured until they come to their full fruition.

Understanding the neighborhood was the first step. Then the manager must "secur[e] the cooperation of the neighborhood with the center." The manager had to

secur[e] the embodiment of the needs and aspirations of the people in the activities of the center through their own initiative and effort. It is not enough for the manager to know what the people of his district need and want, he must know how to help them to develop the machinery by which they themselves can furnish the satisfaction of their desires.

The Boston SCM was a means and an end.

The evening center movement gives the greatest possibility we have ever had in city life for a full expression of the people by themselves, for all to get together to express the best in themselves, not the best in yourself or the best in myself, but the best in themselves. He is not the best manager who imposes the most progressive ideas on his district—he is the best manager who guides the people of his district to express and develop the best in themselves.

Managers had to understand leaders' duties and help train them "in the aims of a center and their own relation to it." Managers had to ensure that activities met the centers' primary aims. They had to impress on leaders "the objects of the evening center and the methods by which it has been decided those objects can best be obtained." Managers had to know if leaders were teaching "in the way best calculated to get the results aimed at by the evening center movement." Managers also needed to take part in center activities. "You have to have points of contact with people . . . It is an additional advantage if he [the manager] happens to do some of [the activities] well enough to win the admiration of the people."

Follett told managers that they held matters of life and death in their hands: "The whole success of the centers" depended on the growth of self-government. "If I cannot impress this upon you I see no hope for the evening center movement in Boston." Only children, not adolescents, could be forced to frequent the centers. Adolescents would come only "if they feel that they have a place and a part there, that the centers are theirs . . . give [them] the power and the responsibility, and . . . it is *their* affair and they work for its success." Managers chaired central councils that "decide[d] on all matters relating to the center as a whole." Behind self-government was a process of posing questions "in such a way that their consideration of them should be a real training in self-government." This process entailed far more than a simple vote. Members had to be genuinely interested. If they were, and if they took decision-making responsibility, and if managers gave them final decision authority, then heated debate would ensue and the group would prepare itself "for a future of real self-government."

Finally, she asked managers to relate more broadly, to "understand the social center movement throughout the United States" and "study the different ways proposed of approaching the problem." They should also "try to understand what it might mean in Boston, how rapidly it can be developed, and its relation to the whole educational and recreational problem of the city." Members "will come to the evening center unformed children." The center would prepare them for "their home, their industrial, their social, their civic life." By training the child in his social and civic duties, the center would "react on the whole life of the community." As she had burdened the leaders with their definite responsibility, she likewise informed the managers: "Whether this aim shall be accomplished rests upon the manager more than upon anyone else."

What this recitation fails to show is that Follett came to her audience with experience and accomplishments to command their respect (Cabot,

1909: 12). They attended not only to her instructions but also to her example. She had succeeded in doing, herself, what she asked of them. She grew the centers not by building an institution but by relating to the needs and desires of the residents and circumstances (Tonn, 2003: 136–37).

Once the city had integrated the centers into the public budget, Follett had to convince the city *as a whole* of the value of the local entities. Because she had grown the centers organically, they had to be justified at the city level post facto. Follett successfully intervened twice when the mayor's office threatened to cut the centers' budgets. In 1914, she wrote a persuasive account of the centers' activities in a Boston newspaper (Follett, 1914b). In 1916, she convened a special public hearing of the Boston School Committee to fight proposed budget cuts to the salaries of center directors and managers and assembled more than a hundred citizens to speak out (Tonn, 2003: 229–32). In formal speeches, each speaker emphasized a different benefit of the centers. At the end, one of the committee members spoke of "the strong hold the evening school centre plan had on the people of Boston." He also said that "it was farthest from his mind to vote in favor of stopping the work" (Tonn, 2003: 232). Later, a review by outside consultants found that "no city has yet devised a better solution of [sic] the problem presented by its adult foreigners . . . In Boston this work is being carried on effectively at a small cost entirely out of proportion to the value of the service rendered" (Tonn, 2003: 232).

The Centers and the Placement Bureau:
"A Giant Combination for the Good of the Whole City"

As the city added centers, Follett added a new piece to them: vocational guidance. She called it the Placement Bureau, but it was really a means to integrate the adolescents' recreational, economic, and civic lives and to convert work experience into continuing education for life. Even successful businessmen had difficulty fitting themselves into professional and industrial life (Rogers, 1912: 32).

Her first priority was getting the children back in school, and approximately one-fourth returned (Follett, 1914a: 24). Her second priority was long-term follow-up for those in the workforce. She described this as creating a future for the child through his vital connection to the community:

The aim is to find for each that work . . . which will give him the largest amount of development and training of which he is capable, and which will at the same time enable him to give to society what *he* is particularly fitted to give. To "get on" in life, in the best sense of the word, and to fit one's self into the social scheme of things, to find one's social value, is surely what each individual most needs. (Follett, 1914a: 22)

One's first job is "the most important decision in the life of the adolescent," too important to leave to commercial agencies or to chance. Conventional job bureaus served neither the child nor the employer, "having neither intimate knowledge of one nor personal interest in the other." Follett distinguished placement, with a long-term and developmental focus, from "employment" and "blind-alley jobs . . . into which we would not conscientiously direct any child" (Follett, 1912b: 25).

The bureau provided "minute, careful and conscious correlating" of the knowledge of the child and of the job. Follow-up, via synergistic relations with the centers, was its crucial role. Solidarity among center participants established bonds between the individual and the community:

By this close and constant touch, the [Bureau counselors] will get to know those [youth] they are fitting into the life of the community in a way impossible in isolated interviews, and guidance can be given at all times as far as tact and good sense dictate, and the young people will allow.

Citywide, social centers and placement bureaus were "acting and reacting on each other, playing directly and indirectly into each other's hands, and the two together forming a giant combination for the good of the city" (Follett, 1912b: 15–17).

As we are finding out by our own experience, very effective follow-up work can be done merely by meeting a girl in the corridor of the Centre on her way to a sewing or a folk-dancing club. A girl thus met . . . was asked how she was getting on. It was discovered that she had been dismissed although in such a way that it was possible for her to go back . . . The girl, however, was much too frightened to go back without encouragement. This encouragement she received at the Centre, but if she had not been seen by the placement secretary at the Centre, the placement secretary would not have known she had been dismissed in time to take any steps in the matter. (Follett, 1912b: 15)

Likewise Follett described

a young man who had fallen in with rough companions, and whom we told we would find a place if he would stop drinking and change his companions. We got him a place four months ago, he has been doing very well in it . . . But please notice, this happy result could not have been obtained through the placement secretary's necessarily meager knowledge of that young man. In this case the result was due entirely to the head of that Centre having intimate knowledge of that young man and his immediate temptations and needs . . . I do want you to see just how these two pieces of work—the Evening Centres and the Placement Bureau—dovetail together. (Follett, 1914a: 28)

The bureau raised standards for employers and adolescents alike. The qualifying process served as much to shape behavior as to screen it. Each youth interviewed with his school headmaster, a placement counselor, a teacher, and a nurse. Data taken included "physical characteristics," academic record, "general mental and moral characteristics" (virtues, vices, moods, attention, memory, special talents, suggestions for future occupation) and "social interests" (church, club, recreation, reason for leaving school, wages expected, preferred work and why). Counselors met the youths' parents and visited their homes to learn "at first hand the parents' preference for the child's future career, the reasons for sending him to work, the hereditary tendencies of the family—physical and occupational—and the general conditions and incentives in the family life." Parents and children attended lectures where employers discussed subjects such as "How to apply for a position—with practical demonstrations" and "What the employer expects of the employee." Nurses discussed occupational health. The youths visited companies and factories. The orientation gave them "an enlarged vision of the industrial possibilities and a clearer notion of what was expected of them." To employers, the bureau increased the chances of getting employees "of greater seriousness and in directness of approach." Adolescents showed "greater self-confidence and definiteness as to the type of work desired or disliked." Counselors did not attend job interviews because the boys and girls were instructed to prove themselves, by themselves, for the job: "Finding work for the child weakens the child's character and stifles his power of initiative" (Rogers, 1912: 30).

Employers also had to meet standards. Initially, 1,600 companies employing minors were identified and researched. Bureau researchers, many of whom were college students earning academic credit, investigated each opening—required tasks, working conditions (hours, lighting, ventilation, cleanliness, "class of fellow employees," sexes, race, wage scale, advancement opportunities). By 1915, they had completed over 5,200 profiles. Follett viewed the investigations as occasions "to describe and interpret the Bureau to employers" (Follett, 1915: 28). Fewer than half of the firms met Follett's qualifications. To be rejected from the bureau was perhaps an embarrassment for employers in reputation-conscious Boston. But the companies that were accepted enjoyed tangible benefits. The bureau helped them meet legal requirements. It facilitated communication between youths and employers and reduced turnover. Such advantages led employers to improve their working conditions and raise wages to access the bureau's desirable job candidates (Rogers, 1912: 31).

In 1913, a Boston Chamber of Commerce report stated that the bureau's placements were up despite high unemployment (Tonn, 2003:

538). The bureau achieved a national reputation (Rogers, 1912: 29). By 1913, it served all public schools in a central office. In 1915, Follett declared her mission accomplished. So many employers offered positions that it was no longer necessary to search for openings. Follett applauded the "closer connection" and "more sympathetic relation" between teachers and employers. She described individual children whose experiences demonstrated "a change in the whole direction and value of their life" (Follett, 1915). She cited one boy as an example of "the difference between a man giving his full value to the community and one plodding along using only half of what is in him" (Follett, 1915: 26). The bureau met the interests of the employer and the child. "While the child himself stands as the centre of all our work and must be the primary consideration of our Bureau, yet we have always felt that we must hold before us both points of view, the employer's and the child's." Follett cited the bureau, coordinating with the social center, as the WMLB's contribution to the Vocational Guidance Movement (Follett, 1915: 14–15). The mainstream VGM had focused on immediate needs—placement and job-finding (Brewer, 1942: 78–79). In Follett's view, it abandoned the central task, continued "relating" between the individual and coworkers.

The VGM split between those who thought they were helping adolescents by getting them jobs quickly and those who used the dropout rate to lobby for vocational training in high school and night school. The missing element was the child: Could young people be "induce[d] . . . to look in upon themselves that they will come to a satisfactory gauge of their own talents and limitations"? (Lane, 1912: 228). Lane noted the advances of professional psychologists and their new statistical tests for better fit in hiring, but he did not mention Follett's contribution. Yet this was precisely the problem she had solved.

FORMALIZING EXPERIENCE: *THE NEW STATE* (1918) AND *CREATIVE EXPERIENCE* (1924)

Follett wrote about her experiences in *The New State* (1918). She initially intended to produce "simply a chronicle" of her work for the School Center Movement (Cabot, 1934). Probably because of the heated and high-profile debates about democratic reform, she attached this account as an appendix (Follett, 1918: 363–73) and instead devoted the book to proposing "group organization" as "the solution to popular government."

In *The New State*, Follett argued that democracy was not a quantitative exercise of adding votes and majority rule. It was a personally and socially creative process "bringing forth . . . genuine collective will" and unforeseeable outcomes. The new "political science" would discover this method of self-government and self-making. "Vital group process," she argued, was "the key to democracy" and the "secret of collective life." The group is a technology for satisfying individual desires, *and* it alters those desires at the same time. The very condition of "united states" disproved the old idea of "the isolated individual as the unit" and a government that saw its chief function as protecting individual and individual states' rights. Such a logic "was hardly adequate to unite our colonies with all their separate instincts" (Follett, 1918: 165).

In *Creative Experience*, Follett went further to examine the methods underlying the vital group process. The group technology had to be cultivated. In 1918, she had already stated the necessity for "an attitude of learning" (Follett, 1918: 370). But *Creative Experience* investigated the creative process associated with this "creative attitude" (Follett, 1924: 217). Follett emphasized "relating," the present participle, over "relation," the "static" noun. Relating had to be "freeing" (130) and "developing" (82). This creative attitude called for "a qualitative change in our thinking" (163). It relaxed distinctions between cause and effect. It viewed conflict as an opportunity rather than a threat (301). It gave "legitimate play" to difference (6). The creative attitude dissolved the apparent concreteness of value-laden labels (10) and symbols (222). Static expressions are "stopping places to thought, and when man cannot think any further it is dangerous" (58). "[W]ould it be possible for the executive policy to be presented in such a way that we do not have to take a for or against attitude?" How can the executive office, "which is at first a functional agency of the whole body," be prevented from "acquiring a solidarity of its own and drifting apart from the rank and file which created it?" (217).

She dismantled commonly held beliefs: that one can do things for other people (Follett, 1924: 204, 237), that power-seeking should be "the predominant feature of our life" (180). In particular, she attacked the idea that cooperation requires shared concepts. "All the different nations are presenting their pictures of the world . . . they think that if they can only paint their pictures with sufficient skill and in vivid enough colors, the other nations will see them with their minds. They never will. Because we do not see with our minds" (148); nor do we think with our minds (198). "The creating is always done through concrete activity, never, except very partially, through intellectual activity . . . Many Christians pray to God to change their characters; yet most of us learn gradually and painfully that the only way to change our characters is by *doing* things" (143).

Dynamic relating undid common sense about seemingly self-evident matters:

There is no use chasing through the universe for a "real" you or a "real" me; it is more useful to study our interactions, these are certainly real. What happens when I meet another person for the first time? He comes to me always pushing in front of him his picture of himself; as I get to know him, do I see that picture gradually disappear, leaving his real self? Not at all, I put my own interpretative picture in its place. Where, then, is the real person—for me? It is in his behaving (and his account of his behaving is part of his behavior) plus my interpretation of his behavior *as shown by my behaving*. (Follett, 1924: 177)

When I realize fully that there are no things-in-themselves, struggle simply fades away; then I know that Mr. X and I are two flowing streams of activity which must meet for larger ends than either could pursue alone. (97) . . . As we no longer think of personality as a static entity, but as "so far integrated behavior," so the collective will is also "so far" integrated behavior. (Follett, 1924: 207)

Follett lamented the term "integrated organism" in a psychology text, which she called an "unfortunate" use and reification because in fact "the organism is the continuing activity of self-organizing" (Follett, 1924: 58).

This is the real challenge of Follett. One knows only the so-far-known (Follett, 1918: 38). Language, a door to understanding, also interferes with understanding. For example, the description "extended school use" rallied people to keep public schools open after hours—to do what? The label drew attention to form at the expense of content. The "Placement Bureau" connected employers and adolescents, but the term did not do justice to a relating and adjusting period of lifelong duration. Relating to meet ever-emerging desires was Follett's deepest wish, to "live in such a manner that the fulness of life may come to all" (Follett, 1918: 353).

Words do not adequately capture dynamic processes. They also add the weight of received ideas and habits. In sentences that literally fight with themselves, Follett struggled to define reciprocal relating:

In human relations . . . this is obvious: I never react to you but to you-plus-me; or to be more accurate, it is I-plus-you reacting to you-plus-me. "I" can never influence "you" because you have already influenced me; that is, in the very process of meeting, by the very process of meeting, we both become something different. It begins even before we meet, in the anticipation of meeting. We see this clearly in conferences. Does anyone wish to find the point where the change begins? He never will. Every movement we make is made up of a thousand reflex arcs and the organization of those arcs began before our birth . . . Accurately speaking the matter cannot be expressed even by the phrase used above, I-plus-you meeting you-plus-me. It is I plus the-interweaving-between-you-and-me meeting you plus the-interweaving-between-you-and-me, etc., etc. (Follett, 1924: 62–63)

She codified "the basic truth for all the social sciences."

First, my changing activity is a response to an activity which is also changing; and the changes in my activity are in part caused by the changes in the activity of that to which I am in relation and vice versa. My response is not to a crystallized product of the past, static for the moment of meeting; *while* I am behaving, the environment is changing because of my behaving, and my behavior is a response to the new situation which I, in part, have created. Thus we see involved the third point, namely, that the responding is not merely to another activity but to the relating between the self-activity and the other activity.

Follett called this a "differential calculus" of human relating (Follett, 1924: 63–64).

The Pivot of Business Success

After World War I, Follett found that business organizations provided the most fertile conditions for experimenting with reciprocal relating. In 1918, she had already observed "growing recognition of the group principle in the business world" (Follett, 1918: 112). Follett gave several reasons for this interest. She found "the greatest vitality of thinking to-day" among businessmen, "and I like to do my thinking where it is most alive." Furthermore,

I find the thinking of business men to-day in line with the deepest and best thinking we have ever had. The last word in science—in biology—is the principle of unifying. The most profound philosophers have always given us unifying as the fundamental principle of life. And now business men are finding it is the way to run a successful business. Here the ideal and the practical have joined hands. That is why I am working at business management, because, while I care for the ideal, it is only because I want to help bring it into our everyday affairs. (Metcalf & Urwick, 1940: 17–18)

Also,

[I]ndustry is the most important field of human activity, and management is the fundamental element in industry . . . management is the pivot of business success. It is good management that draws credit, that draws workers, that draws customers. Moreover, whatever changes should come, whether industry is owned by individual capitalists, or by the State, or by the workers, it will always have to be managed. Management is a permanent function of business. (Metcalf & Urwick, 1940: 18)

Her belief in control, shared with "our most progressive business men," led her to management.

I believe in the individual not trusting to fate or chance or inheritance or environment, but learning how to control his own life. And nowhere do I see such a complete acceptance of this as in business thinking, the thinking of more progressive business men. They are taking the mysticism out of business. They do not believe that there is anything fatalistic about the business cycle that is wholly beyond the comprehension of men; they believe that it can be studied and to some extent controlled. (Metcalf & Urwick, 1940: 18)

Finally, she appreciated that "so many business men . . . are willing to try experiments." She cited discussions on centralization versus decentralization in which "men were not theorizing or dogmatizing; they were thinking of what they had actually done and they were willing to try new ways the next morning . . . Business . . . is pioneer work . . . in the organized relations of human beings." Thus it "offer[s] as thrilling an experience as going into a new country and building railroads over new mountains." Problems solved in business management

may help towards the solution of world problems, since the principles of organization and administration which are discovered as best for business can be applied to government or international relations. Indeed, the solution of world problems must eventually be built up from all the little bits of experience wherever people are consciously trying to solve problems of relation. And this attempt is being made more consciously and deliberately in industry than anywhere else. (Metcalf & Urwick, 1940: 18–19)

Follett took up the same work and used the same principles as before, with slight modifications. Instead of speaking of local groups that scaled to state and federal levels, she spoke of coordinated parts that scaled to productive wholes: "The first test of business administration . . . should be whether you have a business with all its parts so co-ordinated, so moving together in their closely knit and adjusting activities, so linking, interlocking, interrelating, that they make a working unit" (Metcalf & Urwick, 1940: 71). The leader relates "all the complex outer forces and all the complex inner forces." Yet "[o]ne man seldom knows enough about the matter in hand to impose his will on others." Integrating, then, requires "the reciprocally modified judgment" of all concerned (Metcalf & Urwick, 1940: 284)—the same group process of *The New State* and the dynamic relating of *Creative Experience.* Follett saw that the formal complexity of organization led it to fracture into smaller, unrelated parts—executives, departments, functions. Thus she observed the correcting need for group technique and creative experience. "It isn't enough to do my part well and leave the matter there. I must study how my part fits into every other part and change my work if necessary so that all parts can work harmoniously and effectively together" (Urwick, 1987 [1949]: 76). Decision-makers must consider what is good for their department but above all "the good of the business as viewed from their department." This differs from "what is good for the whole business" (Metcalf & Urwick, 1940: 73–74). This discussion anticipated what Barnard later called "moral complexity" (see Chapter 6).

Follett worried about how local loyalties affected one's relating to the whole, an expansive view that she associated with management. Citing a salaried manager who thought about how to improve the business during off-hours, she wondered if those paid by hourly wage thought likewise. "Can business reach its maximum of efficiency and service unless it is so organized" that wage earners would have such a relation to the business? (Metcalf & Urwick, 1940: 71). Likewise, she considered how to "foster local initiative and at the same time get the advantages of centralization." As with her 1918 theory of scaled relating, linking the individual and the state, Follett argued that individuals related to the whole by relating to local functions and groups (81–82). She thus collapsed the distinction between managers and others (88): "Workers are sometimes managing" (85). The worker who decides how to execute an assigned task is managing (85). Most people have managing ability, "and opportunity should be given each man to exercise what he has on his actual job . . . We want to make use of what they have" (86). However, as in the case of governance, this relation was grounded in personal experience: "[W]hen men are allowed to use their own judgment in regard to the manner of executing orders, *and accept the responsibility involved in that*, they are managing" (88; emphasis in original). This derived from her deeply held view that responsibility cannot be transferred.

Follett approached business as a promising field for continuing to build the basic science and applied art of dynamic relating that she began at the turn of the century. In fact, complex formal organization made integrative practices more explicit and analyzable than the social center. It also raised the stakes for the individual who could master these practices and move from creative vision to execution—the project taken up by Barnard.

Follett richly documented principles and processes of conscious coordination to build value. Her example demonstrates the power of a free play of difference toward individual and societal becoming: "The more power I have over myself the more capable I am of joining fruitfully with you and with you developing power in the new unit thus formed—our two selves" (Follett, 1924: 189–90). This called for "intellectual team-work" (Follett, 1924: 97), a qualitative change of mental and practical habits.

At the end of her life, Follett focused on organization as a means in this process (Metcalf & Urwick, 1940: 164). That is, organization "gives scope for the development of individuality." However, hierarchical relations could also obscure responsibility: "[W]hen you are constantly in contact with those above you, there is a tendency to think that the man over you will bear the brunt of the responsibility. To be sure, you bear it for those under you, but it is all too easy to pass it on up the line." If businesspersons interacted with "equals," they could overcome this tendency to shirk responsibility. They could also overcome it through "independence of thinking." Theorizing formal organization as an experimental condition and method, Chester Barnard took up these ideas.

CHAPTER 6

Chester Barnard's
Science of Responsible Experience

☽

This chapter interprets Chester Barnard as a co-founder, along with Follett, of
management science. Barnard cited Follett only once (1968 [1938]: 122), and
no scholars have systematically pursued the connections between the two. Yet
their theory and methods were remarkably similar.

Barnard began more narrowly than Follett, with a structure that he called
"formal organization," which he believed entailed an entirely new condi-
tion for the individual and for society. He theorized formal organization as
a method that developed the individual and society mutually. He also pur-
sued a science that created knowledge about these processes. Initially, Barnard
understood the "executive-leader" in the formal organization as the alpha and
omega of value(s) creation. But after his World War II experience with volun-
tary organizations, Barnard's thinking grew closer to Follett's more expan-
sive concept of personal responsibility. Whereas he had previously theorized a
leader as taking on responsibilities shunned by an organization's members and
delegated upward, he now theorized one whose key function was to cultivate
responsibility in others.

Barnard was convinced of the explanatory power of "things unseen"
(Barnard, 1968 [1938: 284), particularly the "moral judgments" that give
meaning to human striving (Wolf & Iino, 1986: 137). In his last publication, he recognized the "general failure" to accept such reasoning (1958).
This failure continues today, and it remains an obstacle to understanding
Barnard. A prevailing moral code is to ignore the importance of moral
codes. Also, the scientific community's empirical ethos disregards the unseen; and as Barnard pointed out to his 1958 audience, most people are
not inclined to engage in self-analysis and self-expression. In addition,

"morals are in many respects felt to be private, not appropriate or seemly for public expression" (1958: 5). Barnard had long thought that moral codes explain individual and collective action; but he did not publicly address the looming gap between himself and others on this matter until the last years of his life.

Barnard did not simply discuss moral codes and point out their importance. He used them to form himself and the organizations of which he was a part. Specifically, he governed himself throughout his life according to a moral code of self-development attached to increasing personal responsibility in the formal organization. Beginning in 1909, he was promoted from statistician to commercial engineer (1915), to assistant vice president (1922), to general manager (1926) to president of New Jersey Bell Telephone (1927), where he remained until his retirement in 1948. In the mid-1930s he accepted the further responsibility of directing the emergency relief administration of the state of New Jersey during the Depression. In the mid-1940s he accepted the additional position of president of the United Service Organizations (USO), the morale-building agency of the U.S. armed forces in World War II. In 1948, Barnard served on President Herbert Hoover's committee to study the reorganization of the executive branch of the federal government. From 1948 to 1952, he presided over the Rockefeller Foundation. From 1950 to 1956, he served on the board of the National Science Foundation. Shortly thereafter, he published his views on science policy, particularly the organization of knowledge (Barnard, 1957). As a consultant to the federal Office of Scientific Research and Development, Barnard co-authored a report on atomic energy that became the basis for national policy. (For a more complete description of Barnard's public and private service, see Wolf, 1973: 56–58.)

Barnard's moral code emphasized education. In his view, all education was fundamentally self-education (CIBP, Book 2: 1-798), that is, learning by oneself from one's personal experience. For Barnard, "experience" has two meanings. It has the ordinary sense, as in "work experience" on a résumé. But it also has a subjective sense, as in the "felt experience" of a particular individual in concrete circumstances. This interpretation thus includes unconscious experience and knowledge (see below). Furthermore, in relating his formal responsibility, the first meaning, and his subjectively felt responsibility, the second meaning, Barnard interpreted himself as participating in an experimental condition. Barnard described this condition as an "interested, intimate, habitual" relation to experience, with the latter term incorporating unconscious experience. For Barnard, it was also a scientific condition, as he tested hypotheses and documented findings throughout his lifetime. Specifically, he encountered situations that he called "dilemmas." He reflected on these again and again and wrote on them, sometimes years apart, but always showing a trajectory of thought. Barnard prized knowledge derived from experience because it gives insight into "the vital aspect of all social practice": its "assimilation and acceptance in fact below the level of consciousness by those affected by it" (Wolf & Iino, 1986: 85). He used writing as a tool to explain his "mental processes" and findings to himself. After discovering that he was not alone in his experience of organization and that others found his experience interesting, he offered it for scrutiny and to build the field of management. Barnard particularly objected when he heard statements from people in positions of responsibility that contradicted his experience. He also criticized those whose moral codes devalued experience and knowledge obtained from experience, particularly academics and intellectuals (1968 [1938]: 301–22). He especially objected to this attitude in light of the increasing status afforded to, and exploited by, professional scientists, believing that it led to separation and arrogance. The first was fatal to cooperation, the second to a science of cooperation.

Barnard also distinguished between "book learning" and what he called "local and personal knowledge of the everyday and commonplace matters," which "many people are unwilling to grant . . . is knowledge at all." This included "knowledge of the particular individuals with whom we come in contact in all our various situations, knowledge of the specific materials with which we work, familiarity with the specific times and places with which we are concerned . . . [including] what one learns in Al Smith's famous College of Hard Knocks." This "personal, on-the-spot knowledge . . . is absolutely indispensable for the acceptance and the discharge of responsibility for all and any action, and the capacity for responsibility is a vital component in the execution of useful work" (Wolf & Iino, 1986: 135).

Barnard deliberately used formal responsibility as a means to develop the ability to govern himself and others. "Nothing so much develops individuals within the limits of their capacity as responsibility" (Wolf & Iino, 1986: 22). This followed naturally from "adapting one's self to the varieties of conditions and by acquiring the sense of the appropriate in variations of action" (Barnard, 1948 [1940]: 105). When a colleague asked him about his extensive professional obligations ("Why do you waste your time with these people?"), Barnard replied, 'Look, every one of these things that I get connected with has two things: one is the immediate, practical, pragmatic question of what you can do to help out, but the second is it's always a laboratory for me.' This is where I found out how people really work . . . You have to be on the inside to do that" (Wolf, 1973: 13). After giving a lecture, Barnard answered a thank-you letter: "As so often happens in connection with these little services, in the end I get more out of them than any one else." He explained that had he not given the lecture, "I never should have made the analysis of my experience . . . and should not have gotten out of it as much of interest and value as I think I now have" (CIBP, Book 5: 1-1975).

Barnard went further: he organized his experience. Although he did not keep a diary, he developed the habit of using professional commitments, such as speaking engagements, to analyze and probe his experience. He also reformulated his experience repeatedly in order to capture it more fully. Barnard stated that he rewrote *The Functions of the Executive* entirely sixteen times, "and there is scarcely a word in it that has not been thoroughly weighed" (Wolf, 1974: 19). Furthermore, as described below, Barnard reworked *The Functions* throughout his life.

He also analyzed his experience informally, in his conversation and correspondence. Perhaps Barnard best explained the usefulness of this practice in a write-up of his impressions from a 1939 trip to Russia:

[T]he stream not only flows very rapidly in Russia, but the speed with which we acquire experience in these days leads to radical changes in our individual appraisals of conditions and sometimes alters the opinions we hold. So it seemed to me that in this case I might find it of interest to recall later not only the principal observations I made, but also what I thought of them, and what ideas they stimulated. (CIBP, looseleaf document, 5780)

Correspondence was a particularly productive outlet. In prefacing *The Functions*, Barnard acknowledged the help of Major Edward S. Johnston, who had suggested that Barnard develop his ideas on comradeship, a topic on which Barnard then wrote three pages. He explained to Johnston, "Your letter stimulated the above, which may be nothing more than a rather boring preliminary work-out of what I might find pertinent to include in the book" (CIBP, Book 5: 1-2006–08). In fact, Barnard put several of these paragraphs verbatim in the book, which suggests that he took pains with the letter. Barnard also corresponded extensively with Lawrence Henderson, a chemistry professor at Harvard (see Chapter 4). The two had planned to collaborate on a book about Vilfredo Pareto's sociological theory, but Barnard found the intellectual quality of their early drafts lacking. However, he used the correspondence to test Pareto's concepts and Henderson's interpretations of them against his experience. He also developed his own ideas relative to those of Pareto and Henderson, and he wrestled with the general problem of defining a science of organization (see Chapter 7).

Thus for Barnard, writing structured experience and enabled learning. But experience came from assuming responsibility—not just a demand-

ing position but also a personal relation to the position with burdensome physiological effects. In this way, Barnard focused on the knower's
relation to knowing, the actor's relation to acting, and the interaction
between the two. Barnard hypothesized that this personal relation and
experience of physical burden heightened the powers of observation, en-
abling one to take in more, unconsciously, than one could otherwise.
Afterward, in a Proustian way, one accessed the unconscious by verbal-
izing and writing. As he wrote in 1938:

What I mean by responsibility is the willingness deliberately to make choices
of courses of action where there is adequate recognition of the risks of error involved. That willingness and recognition create a state of tension, I should guess,
which greatly expands the scope and increases the sensitivity of the perceptual
processes so that partly consciously and much more unconsciously a much larger
proportion of the concrete is absorbed. Of course, this is a mere guess on my part,
but it seems to me to be as good as other assumptions which are well decorated
with words. (CIBP, Book 6: 1-2016)

What is singular in Barnard's case was the degree to which he felt this
burden. That is, he experienced organization, and the leadership position
specifically, as entailing a quantity and quality of responsibility that few
understood and fewer could articulate. Then he felt the further burden
of codifying and disseminating this experience to build a science of management. For this reason, he declined Harvard's offer of a permanent
professorship in the business school: he recognized that his productivity
depended on "conditions of considerable administrative stress and activity" (Walter-Busch, 1985: 142).

Yet Barnard collaborated extensively with Harvard Business School
dean Wallace Donham and with Lawrence Henderson while continuing
his independent work. As noted in Chapter 4, HBS had rejected economics as an academic foundation for business. It found the contemporary
psychology insufficiently social and U.S. sociology uncomfortably close
to the Social Gospel and to theology. With encouragement from his colleagues at Harvard, Barnard offered his documentation of his "mental
processes" to "inspection"—first in a lecture series at Harvard, then in
his classic book. "If [the book] has any further value it will lie in the
suggestion it may give to more competent inquiry . . . The test of it will
come from its application to social phenomena as a whole, as they present themselves to others—many others" (Barnard, 1968 [1938]: 262).
Although the field did not test Barnard with seriousness matching his
own, he himself did so; and he reported the results to a field that had
narrower concerns (Barnard, 1948, 1958).

As Barnard achieved distinction for his leadership in business, government, and civic life, others asked him for personal advice and to take

on more responsibility. In what appears to be a draft of the preface to *The Functions*, initially entitled "One Way to Look at the World" and retitled "Background for Advice," Barnard observed that often a person "really wants to know about the world he has to live in and how to meet [it]." But this advice required contextualization, "for which there is no time," so he always feared either misunderstanding or ineffective application of the advice. "Even if there were time, the difficulties of expressing much that should be said, and the need for time to absorb gradually what should be said preclude satisfactory discourse on these occasions." Barnard's book came "[o]ut of this dilemma." He wrote it

chiefly for pleasure and to clarify my own understanding of the world in which I have lived . . . What I have written however is neither a story of my experience or a treatise on any of their subjects. It is rather a description of the world about me as I understand it through this process of experience and study. Least of all is it a book of advice. It is what I think ought to be known of my mind in order to understand or to appraise advice that I might give. (CIBP, looseleaf document, 5458–59)

INTELLECTUAL BIOGRAPHY

Apart from Wolf's summary (1974: 5–45), the field lacks a biography of Barnard. Yet because Barnard made science a personal practice, and responsibility-taking a practical experiment, all of his writings shed light on his life. This section draws from Barnard's published and unpublished writings, in chronological order. It also incorporates Barnard's retrospective reflections. For example, although Barnard apparently did not document his experience with increased responsibility from 1909 to 1927 as he did later, Barnard did reflect in 1934 that this period presented him with what he called the "dilemma of individualism versus collectivism." In Follett's terms, he had difficulty integrating his youth with his corporate life. Drafting and finalizing *The Functions*, Barnard analyzed how he eventually did so. In fact, Barnard's highest "executive function" involved precisely this integrative capacity (Barnard, 1958). That is, whereas this particular dilemma consumed him in the prime of his life, in his later life he took it as one example of a larger and more pressing problem of reconciling different moral codes.

For Follett and Barnard, management was only just becoming a profession and a science; and it held promise for individuals and society. In 1959, Barnard called "the art of formal organization" the single most important development "in determining the character of our society" in the past 150 years (CIBP, Book 11: 1-4104). To understand this view requires understanding Barnard himself.

The Individual in the Organization: Barnard at New Jersey Bell

In 1934, Barnard addressed engineers at the Stevens Institute of Technology's engineering camp (Wolf & Iino, 1986: 9–27). They had assembled to appraise the economic aspects of the New Deal. Barnard argued that any program "concerned with the management of human affairs and the improvement of the conditions of society" had to consider industry as a particular case of the more fundamental problem of human relations governing society. Thus he proposed "a somewhat philosophical discussion of collectivism and individualism in general and their significance in human affairs," for which he used the concrete example of his experience.

In his youth, he had considered the individual as "almost the sole factor in human progress" and "systematized group activities" as "of incidental importance." He attributed this attitude to his education but also to his observations of economic and political life. "I had been taught by the reiteration of precept that individual initiative, individual effort, individual thrift, individual ambition, individual character, were the main elements in civilized life and progress . . . to the neglect of the facts and the problems of cooperation, organization and collective effort." Barnard mentioned but did not elaborate upon "having been thrown on my own resources at an early date." In fact, owing to his father's financial ruin, Barnard not only paid his way through secondary school and college but also selected and gained admittance to these institutions, the finest in New England (Wolf, 1974: 5). He also kept his own double-entry accounting books and carefully managed his finances. Evidently Barnard left Harvard with more money that he had upon entering it (Biles & Bolton, 1994: 1109).

Barnard told his audience that in his youth he had compared himself to the farmer who gives credit for the harvest to his own efforts, which are in fact "quite superficial and incidental," instead of to "the energy of the sun, the chemistry of the soil, the vital but undefinable processes of life" that are the true sources.

Somewhat similarly I looked upon the family, the social groups of which I was a part, the schools and universities, the railroads, the organizations of industry, the government, as things made available to me by nature rather than by the deliberate and largely conscious effort of men acting in cooperation. (Wolf & Iino, 1986: 10)

"In this state of mind," Barnard joined the telephone organization, "one of the greatest and most complex collective enterprises ever organized on a commercial basis." Hundreds of thousands of investors supplied its capital; hundreds of thousands of employees operated it. Thousands, "carefully arranged in a hierarchy of positions and authorities," managed it. The "collectivity called the State" legally authorized it. Its "conduct, rights, its privileges were governed not only by an immense body of general law and custom, derived from collective action through many generations by also by specific statutes and regulatory authorities similarly evolved and created by society for the regulation of the business. Even the service itself depended upon a collective social condition so that it was not possible in general to sell to any individual . . . unless many other individuals also were subscribers." Barnard "quickly learned that all of this collective operation . . . possessed tremendous power which transcended the sum of the efforts of the individuals directly concerned in it, and that it also accomplished many things impossible except by cooperation on a grand scale" (Wolf & Iino, 1986: 10–11).

Looking to the "things unseen," Barnard evoked the "constantly expressed phrases" of the organization, such as "the service as a whole" and "the good of the organization." He also alluded to the organization's longstanding code of uninterrupted service, even in emergencies. He initially experienced this code as "repression of the individual who was becoming less and less significant." He felt this repression particularly in the "intangible barriers of departments, grades and ranks, policies, appropriations, laws, prejudices and economic limitations of consumers." He "experienced a reaction away from the rugged individualism with which I entered the service, toward the conception that facts and principles and organizations and collective action were everything, and the individual was and could be nothing." But this idea was "as destructive as that of extreme individualism." The supervisors "continued to regard me as an individual" and "society continued to treat me . . . as an individual . . . I could not eliminate myself from myself." He risked "falling into a complete lethargy" due to an "inability to reconcile two apparently contradictory states of affairs" (Wolf & Iino, 1986: 11): "attempting to treat myself either as a slightly conscious and unimportant cog in a gigantic machine" or "as an anarchist determined to assert my individuality in destructive action." Society is full of people "whose escape from the dilemma due to the existence of individual life and the university of collective society has been through one of the[se] three doors." Social workers call these individuals "maladjusted." Barnard credited his supervisors for his escape through "the fourth door," that of "directing my individual efforts not only in conformance with, but in furtherance of the objectives of the organization." He "gradually learned that properly understood and with intelligent adjustment the individual can secure from collective organization great expansion of individual opportunity for accomplishment and for self-expression." Yet he still noticed ongoing tensions "between one's duty to one's self and one's duty to the ever present collectivities of which one is inescapably a part" (Wolf & Iino, 1986: 11–12).

Barnard eventually considered this dilemma universal as well as personal. Accepting "minor" managerial responsibilities, he studied it "philosophically." He hoped to solve the problem for himself, for others, and for the organization. World War I, "with its tremendous cooperation and regimentation of people," led him to understand that "one and perhaps the most vital of all problems of human life is how effectively to develop and how practically to harmonize two principles of life which in isolation seem to be utterly opposed—the one, systematic arrangements of human affairs, cooperation, organization, regimentation, collectivity; and the other the dynamic individual" Wolf & Iino, 1986: 12). The individual, the "dynamic element in all systems of collectivity," makes an "independent and voluntary" decision to "either promote the collective interest" or "oppose it" or "become a dead weight against collective progress" through inaction. Russian Communism and Italian Fascism answered this dilemma. That is, societies had four ways to win individual support—coercion, emulation, personal loyalty, and "a cultivation of automatic incentives and inducements not only in material rewards but in grades and ranks" that bestowed status and prestige (Wolf & Iino, 1986: 13–14). Anticipating his extensive discussion of individual incentives in *The Functions*, Barnard described how collective effort had to recognize individual differences because the individual is the "source of energy by which collective action is operated or is resisted." Satisfaction or lack of satisfaction of individual motives explains individual contributions of energy. "The essential problem is then one of developing both plans of cooperative action and the individual in such ways that they reinforce each other and operate harmoniously in conjunction" (Wolf & Iino, 1986: 17). As individuals develop, cooperation advances. Highly developed collectivism and highly developed individualism were "mutually dependent conditions" and "equally indispensable to any high degree of civilization." However, "the emphasis requires to be put on the development of the individual rather than upon the development of organization" (Wolf & Iino, 1986: 18). The individual's "initiative, enthusiasm, cooperative spirit and training and competence" lend necessary "vitality" to organization. Barnard based this assertion on his experience in the telephone organization and on "the standard of education and the vigor of the individual which is available in the American people" (Wolf & Iino, 1986: 23).

Barnard then isolated management as the pivotal but elusive factor in reconciling individualism and collectivism. The guiding principle was

that men shall be able to design groupings of human beings for joint or cooperative action in adjustment to the material and other conditions of operation and in adjustment to the individualism of those who compose the group, capable of leading and inspiring that individualism into effective cooperation without destroying—and indeed while increasing—the individual energy necessary. (Wolf & Iino, 1986: 23)

This required "a considerable amount of knowledge, frequently highly technical, analytical ability and a substantial degree of imagination." It required "personal traits such as stability in character, acceptable personality, force and persuasiveness." It called for "a dynamic individualism which will express itself in initiative and resourcefulness together with control evidenced in patience and restraint." Finally, "all of the conflict of forces which underlie the ebbs and flows of collective operations and individualism must not only be understood or felt but are experienced within the individual manager himself."

These qualities had to be possessed to a degree above the average in the general population. In the individual, they had to be "possessed in proper balance," changing according to the circumstances. Training required "persistent and long effort" as well as "intensive experience so that there is necessary not merely more than average intellectual capacity and more than average character and personal qualifications but a high degree of vitality to withstand the severe work, high pressures, and moral strains which are the lot of most managers for long periods in their careers" (Wolf & Iino, 1986: 24).

Alluding to the Depression, Barnard explained a "major cause of difficulty in our present affairs": the lack of adequate "management material." Collective organization had advanced, but the development of the individual for the conditions of management had not kept pace. This "poverty of material" crucially obstructed progress. Barnard focused, then, on incentives that would "induce the effort for self-development, without which there can be no great degree of managerial ability." These included "highly developed individualism" less subject than the general population to fear, discouragement, and "lack of appreciation." For such individuals, "such motives as self-esteem, individual recognition and prestige are more potent than with the average person." No amount of money would suffice to motivate such persons given the "larger responsibility and the greater restriction of freedom" entailed by the managerial condition. "Hence . . . the real incentive to the development and application of the world's limited supply of managerial talent is the culture of the individual so that great desires make great effort worthwhile" (Wolf & Iino, 1986: 27). Barnard also feared the consequences of lack of leadership on "stable cooperation" in societies (1948 [1940]: 83).

At or around this occasion, Barnard deliberately took responsibility for cultivating these desires in himself and in others. As he said to military men and businessmen in 1940:

> [T]hough we can as yet apparently do little in a formal way to develop leaders, we can encourage potential leaders to develop themselves, to seek for themselves the occasions and opportunities when leadership is needed, to learn the ways of making themselves sought as leaders, to acquire experience in leading by doing it. I have myself been so encouraged and inspired in my youth . . . so that to give such encouragement seems to me an important private and social duty; but I believe whatever we do in this respect will be harmful if not done in full realization that there is no substitute for the experience of recognizing and seizing opportunities, or for making one's own place unaided and against interference and obstacles; for these kinds of ability are precisely those that followers expect in leaders. (1948 [1940]: 105–6)

As Barnard made these observations, he was building the Bell system and his reputation in and around it. In 1909, immediately after leaving Harvard, Barnard began working as a statistician. Using his knowledge of German, French, and Italian, he reviewed international practices in the industry. According to Iino's bibliography, Barnard published his first article in 1914, while serving in the statistical department: "An Analysis of a Speech of the Hon. D. J. Lewis Comparing Governmental and Private Telegraph and Telephone Utilities" (Wolf, 1974: 125). In 1915 he was promoted to commercial engineer.

In World War I, Barnard was appointed as a technical adviser on rates to the New Jersey State commission and to the U.S. Telephone Administration. In 1922 he was promoted to assistant vice president and general manager of the Bell Telephone Company of Pennsylvania. Also that year, Barnard published his first article on executive development (Wolf, 1974: 11). He followed this up with another article on the same topic in 1925, which anticipates many ideas in *The Functions* (Wolf, 1974: 11). In 1926, Barnard was promoted to vice president of Pennsylvania Bell. He oversaw the consolidation of "duplicate" phone systems in "little independent companies" and set up a monopolistic service, "very much to the public's relief." He explained, "It's just a false idea to have competition in a thing like telephone." Barnard "was very much engaged . . . in building and rearranging and readapting the organization, which is an endless job . . . Conditions change and they change rapidly; if you are properly alert you begin to mold the organization to fit the conditions" (Wolf, 1974: 13). In particular, he integrated "two entirely different organizations" in the North and the South.

> [It was a] very fascinating kind of thing to do because you're dealing not only with differences in tradition, you're dealing with differences of personality and differences in training and outlook. The New York Telephone Company was

dominated by the ideas that are essential to the operation of a complete big city. The other company was operating in a number of small places . . . That's the kind of problem that you have with amalgamation. (Wolf, 1974: 13)

Asked to explain his method, Barnard spoke of transfers and new hires. He also mentioned "constantly preaching" to the organization.

An executive is a teacher; most people don't think of him that way, but that's what he is. He can't do very much unless he can teach people. He does not do it by any formally organized classes or seminars . . . He has conferences that are seminars in which either he or other people who are involved do the instruction and teach themselves. That's absolutely essential. You can't just pick out people and stick them in a job and say go ahead and do it. You've got to give them a philosophy to work against, you've got to state the goals, you've got to indicate the limitations and the methods. (Wolf, 1974: 13–14)

In 1927, Barnard was promoted to president of New Jersey Bell Telephone. According to a 1936 biographical sketch, his interest in creating an amalgamated phone system for a larger and more diverse geographic area also directed his attention to "the orderly development of [the] area." Barnard participated in a variety of activities formally outside but still related to the telephone business statewide (Wolf, 1974:14).

In 1928 he gave an address, "Some Problems in the Future Development of New Jersey," to the state's Chamber of Commerce (CIBP, Book 6: 1-2572–84). Barnard stated that although he took a "great personal interest" in the subject, he was not an expert on it, nor did such interest qualify him to speak. Instead, he cited his official position: New Jersey Bell was the only corporation in New Jersey that did business throughout the state, so it had a responsibility to consider the state's future (CIBP, Book 6, 1-2572). He based his authority, then, on "attention which we have given to the trend and character of the growth and development" of New Jersey, leading him to form "an opinion as to the nature of the growth . . . and of the problems which arise from that growth." Barnard discussed population and expansion. He noted the "unique condition which vitalizes every other"—the state's "position . . . between two very large centers of growing population," New York City and Philadelphia. Quality of life, not just growth, was of concern—would New Jersey become a better place to live; would "the wealth and well-being" of its residents improve? Only "conscious constructive effort" would tell. "In any large business . . . only intelligent advance planning and construction effort could be . . . a promising basis for future prosperity."

Barnard favorably reviewed the work of public agencies in transportation, commerce, and power but found them "not sufficiently integrated, or co-ordinated." He noted difficulties with "the popular attitude and

understanding"; "deficiencies in the business community for developing, focusing, and presenting its knowledge and opinion on local and
statewide questions constructively and effectively"; problems in zoning,
planning, taxation, regulation, and education. Barnard asserted that the
public did not think of itself as one community:

[T]hey take little part even in local community affairs, do not read New Jersey
newspapers . . . , frequently bank in institutions outside the State; take little
interest or part in political problems of the State beyond reading of them . . .
and patronize, even at great inconvenience, mercantile establishments outside the
State . . . thereby limiting the development of even better markets for their needs.
(CIPB, Book 6: 1-2576)

Barnard called on "political leaders, merchants, banks, newspapers and
employers" to exert "persistent efforts" to change those attitudes and practices. Fundamentally, New Jersey had two different "dispositions," one
favoring New York, the other, Philadelphia. "Our conceptions of policies
and practice are based subconsciously upon solutions developed east and
west of us, rather than upon an independent approach to the New Jersey
problems," which bore no resemblance to those of Philadelphia and New
York. This attitude prevented "the development of an adequate conception
of the State as a whole." Improvements depended on "a popular realization
that New Jersey is fundamentally one entity": "I am convinced from my
constant traveling and contact throughout the State that not merely as a
political fact but as an industrial and social condition the entire State now
should be recognized as a single commonwealth" (CIBP, Book 6, 1-2577).

Barnard expressed concern about disputes among localities, which
he attributed to "local pride." This characteristic had virtues, but "only
when in proper coordination and in proper subordination to larger and
more fundamental interests, just as individualism is to be cultivated provided it is subject to general social cooperation." The policy of "local
independence and isolation" posed problems in the new condition of
rapidly increasing population. This problem found its analogue in the
question of centralization and decentralization in a business. With "thor-
ough understanding throughout an organization," it could be resolved.
Thus Barnard called upon leaders to abandon their own "excessive local
pride" and to use their "own temperate examples . . . to induce a fair and
intelligent attitude" in local matters.

He emphasized that the Chamber was a statewide organization.
It constituted a body of "representative men in close daily contact on
concrete matters with the people and affairs of the community." It adequately represented business men and institutions, "by far the most
important group for ascertaining the facts and for formulating public re-

quirement" on a wide range of collective interests. The individuals making up the Chamber "know by daily experience not only what people say but what they actually do." The Chamber had a unique opportunity to develop a "State System of Chambers of Commerce" in "vigor, size, financial resources and federation." After the state legislature and political parties, "a stronger State Chamber comes next . . . in importance in promoting the best solution of the numerous vital problems confronting the State as a whole" (CIBP, Book 6, 1-2580). Barnard did not cite Follett, but he clearly subscribed to her belief in group organization as the basis of large-scale representation.

From 1931 to 1933, during the Depression, Barnard became the first state director of emergency relief for New Jersey. "Relief" meant food and jobs for the many hungry and unemployed. In 1934, Barnard gave an address, titled "Education and Social Welfare," to the New Jersey State Teachers' Association in this capacity and as CEO of New Jersey Bell (CIBP, Book 6: 1-2301–25). As he had done with his Chamber audience, he encouraged the statewide point of view. He also demonstrated what he meant later in *The Functions* when he spoke of the executive's task to create moral codes that give meaning to material effort. The speech concerned the long-term moral implications of the Depression. Thus Barnard introduced himself not as an educator but as one concerned with the "social results" of education.

In this speech, Barnard urged his audience to abandon "the dominant view" of the purpose of education, which he found excessively individualistic, sentimental, and utilitarian. This view, reinforced by the Depression, regarded education as a "method of preparing the individual to earn a livelihood, a means to the attainment individually of a higher social status, a process of culture permitting greater individual enjoyment of the benefits of civilization." He called these "secondary or intermediate results." Instead, Barnard distinguished three aspects of education: "the foundation for the productive capacity of society"; the "vital element in purchasing power"; and a cost limited by other social initiatives (CIBP, Book 6, 1-2303).

On the first point, he argued that productive capacity had been "won through centuries of slow progress," but society took it for granted. Moreover, the Depression might lead people to believe that progress was "imaginary" or "nullified." The advance of civilization showed a trade-off between serving the basic needs of greater numbers and raising the standard of living for fewer. Both conditions demanded increased productivity; otherwise, mankind would face lower living standards, higher poverty, or reduced population from war or starvation. Education was "the basic process" of productive capacity—not, as commonly believed, by increasing individual capacity to produce but by increasing "the *effectiveness* of individual capacity to produce" through "social cooperation," which "depends primarily upon education." He explained, "My convictions . . . are induced by considering the helplessness of the most able individuals in the absence of social support, and by reviewing the requirements for maintaining any large society in a stable and cohesive state" (CIBP, Book 6, 1-2306–07).

He cited his readings about the African exploits of Stanley and Livingstone, the lives of the explorer-scouts of the far western U.S. territories, and "the incredible privation of small and remote pioneer communities." This knowledge "will convince anyone, I believe, that the ablest and most educated person, having lost all contact with and all products of industrial civilization, say, by accident, is powerless to do more than barely keep alive, and would fail in that in all probability in a short time, even though possessed of an intimate and expert knowledge of raw nature." Civilization required more cooperation, and "increased individual ability is chiefly also a result of this enlarged cooperation." Education fostered a "civilized society of high productive capacity," not just leaders but also "recruits": "Captains are limited by the character, spirit, and ability of the men they command." Large organizations showed the diversity of ability and education among personnel as well as the problem of "the ineducable and the unemployable." "The mere transmission of facts, of orders, and the recording of data . . . in a highly effective society, call obviously for a wide diffusion of ability to read, write, enumerate and compute." Finally, education developed "final legislative authority" in a democracy. "[M]any defects of democratic government are due in large part to lack of a sufficiently developed intelligence in the people as a whole" (CIBP, Book 6, 1-2307–08).

Barnard then reminded his audience that he spoke of practical matters. The major justification for education was that "this is, has been, and will continue to be a bread and butter world for most of its inhabitants." The differentiating factor in wealth creation was the inculcation of desire. Barnard cited Franklin Roosevelt, who spoke a "great truth" by saying that "true wealth is not a static thing. It is a living thing made out of the *disposition* [Barnard's emphasis] of men to create and to distribute the good things of life with a rising standard of living." If undesired, products were useless. Thus desire, a powerful phenomenon, was entirely taken for granted. Yet "per capita wants and desires" in fact differentiated individuals, nations, and societies (CIBP, Book 6, 1-2309).

Furthermore, he said, few people understand that

wants and desires have to be inculcated in people, taught to them, and that logically the stimulation of a want precedes production to satisfy it, whether reference is made to the services of a particular man, the product of a specific business, or the material achievements of a civilization. Every civilization that has retrograded must have first lost its desire to have things.

Education develops "those wants and desires which are the real basis of all production. This it is which creates values, and energizes the capacity to produce things." Barnard asked his audience to observe ordinary human behavior. Managers, teachers, and social workers repeatedly lamented "'lack of ambition' of those under their supervision as workers, pupils, or 'cases' as a most serious problem in industrial production, in educational progress, or in social and economic rehabilitation." The term "lack of ambition" really meant the lack of incentives to exert personal effort. But these incentives—recognition, influence, money—"are largely but expression of desires created by social influence and education." Even money, except when seen as an end in itself, "is normally desired only as a means of satisfying wants and gratifying tastes which are cultivated." Also, desires, once cultivated, are easily destroyed. "A sense of injustice, repeated frustration of effort, hopelessness of achievement, accomplish the deadening effect" (CIBP, Book 6, 1-2311).

Even higher incentives may be required to restore lost desire:

The inner standard of life which must precede any realized standard of living, has been largely destroyed. In a large proportion of the people, habitual adjustment to poverty kills an effective desire for better things. In our midst we can see the destruction of culture in individuals, and with it the destruction of the power for sustained effort. (CIBP, Book 6, 1-2311)

Barnard referred to the Depression as well as to impoverished populations. "The starvation . . . is not primarily due to lack of knowledge, but to lack of effective belief that continuity of the means of bare subsistence is worth a new type of effort to make advance provision for it." Only "daily contact with a higher civilization" enabled such "readjustment" of attitude. Barnard summarized: production depended upon production technique, which depended upon education. The will to acquire this technique, "which calls for both individual exertion and substantial social sacrifice, and the determination to apply it," depended on a "cultural attitude, a standard of life, an acceptance of values," which in turn depended upon education. "To inculcate and develop this culture is the primary educational necessity, because it is the basis of the social will to live" (CIBP, Book 6, 1-2313).

Barnard then criticized educators for emphasizing utilitarian over cultural values. This was a matter of balance, for both were necessary. Acquisition of production technique "must develop in step with the cultural status" at the individual and societal levels. The balance could also tip toward excess cultural bias, thus the "personal traged[y]" shown in the saying, "champagne taste and beer pocketbook." Barnard found this "a source of waste" in higher education particularly. Nor could society afford to inculcate living standards beyond its productive state, which risked productivity decreases and social disintegration. Education, "the foundation of social welfare in a dense population," had to balance cultural and technological-productive emphases (CIBP, Book 6, 1-2313).

Barnard concluded with remarks on competing priorities. In essence, he urged the educators to consider that whereas taxation supported education, it also could reduce society's desire to produce. He thus put them in what he called the state of "moral complexity" in *The Functions*: as educators, they might favor greater disbursements for education; as citizens, they had to weigh education alongside other social programs.

That same year, Barnard gave the speech on individualism and collectivism discussed earlier. The next year, 1935, he spoke at an industrial conference at Princeton on "Some Principles and Basic Considerations in Personnel Relations" (Barnard, 1948: 3–23). In this speech, Barnard developed his ideas about the importance of the individual. He argued that the formal personnel administration, organized to advance the individual, actually undermined the individual. He cautioned his audience that although the topic of the individual might appear philosophical, it was in fact "intensely practical." Industrial conferences usually focused on specific programs. But the "danger is that we shall lose sight of the general problem and forget to formulate the major and ultimate objectives by which all else must finally be tested."

Barnard described the "state of mind" and "conditions of modern life" that obscure the individual economically and socially. The "whole complex of thought, except when our immediate personal concerns are involved, relates to the cooperative and social aspects of life. We are so engrossed constantly with the problems of organization that we neglect the unit of organization and are quite unaware of our neglect." The "progress of civilization" had "minimiz[ed] the individual, barring exceptional men, as a factor in progress." This showed in the feudal system, the guild, the monarchy, and the nation-state. The American and French Revolutions worked against this tendency, as did the settlement of western territories and the universal education movement. The theory of evolution and the emergence of social science began to change "habits of thought" on this matter. The modern corporation and organized labor movements emphasized "interdependence, cooperation, regimentation" as "the essential aspects of life, as the constructive forces of civilization, until the subservience of individual to state, society, economic machinery is the habitual attitude."

Of all occupations, he said, only the psychologist, psychiatrist, physician, clergyman, and teacher recognized the individual rather than the "statistical unit." Although the interdependence of humankind precluded overemphasizing the individual, "[i]t is individuals who are being organized, and the effectiveness of the group depends not only upon the scheme of grouping and function, but upon the quality of the elementary units" (Barnard, 1948: 5).

In his industrial relations experience, Barnard wrote that he had "seen again and again . . . that either the wrong thing is done or the right thing is done very badly, because of the attempt to find a short cut which fails to take into account the individual as the key to the effective operation of all these plans and schemes of coordination." Citing Elton Mayo's research (see Chapter 4), Barnard explained, "My own belief is strong that the capacity, development, and state of mind of employees as individuals must be the focal point of all policy and practice relating to personnel." Mayo's key finding concerned "the mental reaction of the employee to the individualized atmosphere." With this sensibility, the employer can "adjust his treatment of the individual employee to the state of mind and the condition of the man as he is" (Barnard, 1948: 7).

The "key to dynamic effort in all industry is the individual and his willingness to develop in it": When he had first heard this idea in conferences and trainings, he rejected it as too idealistic. "Since then continual observation and the analysis of my own experience in public and private organizations has convinced me that this idealization . . . of personnel objectives is highly practical in the long view." The problem was in the execution:

If this development of the individual is to be a central consideration in all personnel work, it should be so genuinely, not merely as a matter of tactics, nor merely or chiefly a matter of industrial efficiency. It will ultimately fail if it is merely a high sounding fiction for stimulating production and good morale. Hypocrisy is fatal in the management of personnel. (Barnard, 1948: 9)

Personnel policies had to facilitate collaboration towards concrete goals. Barnard found this secondary but "equally important" to developing the individual. "[T]he two together constitute the entire legitimate purpose of management so far as the personnel is concerned." Personnel policies focused on "technics [sic], practices, schemes, plans, organizations, schedules, devices." But these, in turn, involve "one major problem to which I have seldom seen conscious attention given—the willingness, desire, and interest of the individual in cooperative effort." This required "the ability to function in conjunction with others in specific ways, a technic of operation or production, a management or control or directing agency, and the will to collaborate," the latter encompassing "loyalty, esprit de corps, desire for team play, etc." The will to collaborate was "the weakest link in the chain of cooperative effort." "[T]hough we are loath to admit it . . . our hands are held back again and again in doing things known to be technically or commercially feasible, because of the fear that the human beings with whom we work will not sufficiently collaborate with us or with each other." We fail to see the possibilities of accomplishment "if we knew how to get people better to work together wholeheartedly for common purposes only remotely related to individual purposes." The critical factor was "a lack of confidence in the sincerity and integrity of management." This "discourages the most promising developments . . . so the advancement of the interests of all is retarded" (Barnard, 1948: 11).

Barnard went further, to find the heart of this lack of confidence: Management's insincerity derived from "a strange trait of human nature—the love of smart tricks."

[A] gamble on "getting away with" unsound or dishonest tactics seems to entice men of honest and sound purpose, just as the desire to take chances induces men to occasional gambles in financial matters, contrary to their judgment and principles. I know of nothing more difficult to check in a management organization of tried, experienced men of integrity and of fine purpose in personnel relations than this sporadic propensity to be smart, to avoid an issue, to withhold an unpleasant truth, to decline to admit an error, when honesty, sincerity, and even good sense clearly condemn such lapses. (Barnard, 1948: 12)

This "fair and honest" ethic showed in small enterprises particularly. But Barnard observed it in his own very large organization and especially in times of adversity:

I have myself seen large groups of employees voluntarily and wholeheartedly cooperate to increase individual and collective efficiency and production in order to reduce expenses when it was recognized that the immediate effect was to the pecuniary disadvantage of the employees themselves. The importance of such collaboration to all involved is incalculable. It is neither justified, nor can it be obtained, except on the basis of confidence inspired by experience. The respect of an organization or of a management can be acquired only as is that of the individual—not by what he says today or said yesterday but by both word and deed through a succession of many days. (Barnard, 1948: 12)

Formal personnel programs thus substituted for "a positive management of personnel." They developed neither the individual nor the will to collaborate—"the two essential aims . . . of sound personnel policy." They enabled management to rationalize that it had organized constructive relations with employees when in fact the attitude was paternalistic or philanthropic, "an attempt to 'buy off' hostile states of mind" or avoid paying proper wages. Thus management was "blind" to the essential problems (Barnard, 1948: 13).

Barnard probed this blindness. "[F]alse ideas regarding business and its conduct" obscured proper attention to personnel matters. Businessmen too often used, and the public too often accepted, economic criteria. But his "observation in several different well-managed businesses" persuaded him that other criteria prevailed:

> Prestige, competitive reputation, social philosophy, social standing, philanthropic interests, combativeness, love of intrigue, dislike of friction, technical interest, Napoleonic dreams, love of accomplishing useful things, desire for regard of employees, love of publicity, fear of publicity, a long catalogue of non-economic motives actually condition the management of business, and nothing but the balance sheet keeps these non-economic motives from running wild. Yet without all these incentives I think most business would be a lifeless failure. There is not enough vitality in dollars to keep business running on any such scale as we experience it, nor are the things which can be directly purchased with money an adequate incentive. (Barnard, 1948: 15)

The underlying problem was that "the business man can't admit this:"

> [He] feels it necessary to take a "hard-boiled" attitude . . . But if you will stop taking the business man at his word and quietly watch him when he is off guard, you will find he is taking care of poor old John who couldn't be placed anywhere else, that he is risking both profit and failure rather than cut wages, that he continues an unprofitable venture on nothing but hope rather than throw his men out of work. (Barnard, 1948: 15)

The same logic applied to employee motives: "[T]here can be no understanding of the personnel problem if it is assumed that wages can buy peace or satisfaction." Likewise, although payrolls had to be met, it was not profit that explained business, but rather fear of loss (Barnard, 1948: 16).

Barnard asserted that most of those who "talk about 'labor,' and ostensibly on its behalf," knew very little about "the actual problems" of daily personnel work. Thus their proposals to improve industrial relations through, for example, "collective bargaining," rang false. The legalization of collective bargaining per se did not endanger industrial progress, but "the philosophy, habit of thought, the moral attitude that is inherent in it" did. It impeded a cooperative state of mind; it "assumed that 'cooperation' is merely a cover for a completely one-sided state of affairs." Collective bargaining posited employees versus employers. It hypothesized a "marginal fund" from which "either higher wages and improved working conditions or profits can be taken" and its distribution based on power struggles. Collective bargaining ignored cooperation to focus on these struggles specifically and on maintaining them through "expensive professionalism, emphasis upon artificialities, exaggeration of details, promotion of lack of confidence and distrust, and polemic attitudes." It also withheld any cooperation beyond the strict limits of formal agreement. It reinforced the idea that "labor is only a commodity to be bought in the market or by contract as cheaply as possible" and a "cold-blooded attitude toward employment, lay-offs, and the merits of individuals." It encouraged "secrecy, distrust, and unwillingness to recognize that employees have any stake or interest in the business" (Barnard, 1948: 19).

In contrast to collective bargaining, Barnard posited "collective cooperation" oriented around "the real and basic interest of employees and the maintenance of a close and free working relationship . . . opportunity for attention to the real conditions of business and mutual adjustments to serve the interests of all; enhanced interest in work, confidence, and stability." Collective bargaining hardened differences between workers and managers, employees and employers. It was "fundamentally opposed to cooperative attitudes and the development of sound personnel objectives." Barnard did not envision a perfect world under collective cooperation, but he argued that it encouraged "first principles," a foundation or habit of thought that accorded with the proper aims of personnel relations: developing the individual and promoting the will to collaborate. Reviewing the speech fourteen years later, Barnard stated that the Wagner Act, which institutionalized collective bargaining, "really was the instrument for destroying what had been accomplished. It promoted industrial warfare, not industrial peace" (Barnard, 1948: 23).

In 1936, Barnard gave a commencement address entitled "Persistent Dilemmas of Social Progress" (Wolf & Iino, 1986: 28–45). Colleagues encouraged him to publish the speech, so he reworked it.

It then seemed to me that the word "organization" which recurred throughout might mean less or something different to those who had little experience in the management and development of organization than to me. Upon further reflection I was not sure I knew what I meant myself, and I was certain that the reduction of my conception to intelligible language was a matter of no small difficulty. I thereupon abandoned the revision pending an effort, which has proved a long one, to describe what I mean by "organization." (Wolf, 1974: 21)

The Functions of the Executive was the result.

In the address, Barnard identified three dilemmas associated with obtaining social progress through cooperation, beginning with choosing between individualism and collectivism, which he reframed as the "effect of regimentation upon the supply of men of initiative, ambition, and sense of responsibility to lead and manage cooperation." Organization "becomes an end in itself instead of a means to an end." Delegation helps resolve this dilemma. Although the state and the church had taken control of different aspects of life in the United States, national and state sovereignties ran in parallel. This situation exposed the superstructural idea that "man has certain fundamental inherent rights coming not from States, but from God and Nature, which no government or State, in fact no human organization, can override on the plea of its own necessities." This idea enabled "the greatest aggregate real cooperation with the greatest individual freedom and development" (Wolf & Iino, 1986: 38).

The second dilemma was "how to allocate Authority and responsibility" to increase social cooperation "without destroying the initiative and ability of the individual" and preventing "domination of any one of the great social forces over any one of the others." All solutions call, above all, for tolerance. "The elaboration of cooperation and the multiplied allocations of Authority of modern western civilization would have been impossible except for the development socially of the faculty of toleration." Thus the third dilemma, finding a way "to secure toleration." Toleration involves "emotional control and the accommodation of opposing aims . . . How to attain it, it is evident, is a matter of state of mind and of methods and practices discovered and evolved through long periods of time." Barnard called intolerance "the dangerous and disruptive element threatening world and domestic peace." "Machine utilization of power" was a newly destabilizing force. Until recently, "economic activities . . . were almost entirely personal and local" and "governed by local custom." Power machinery and cheap transportation and communication "both permitted and required" the "widespread organization of economic cooperation." Social experiments in Russia, Germany, and Italy solved this problem by organizing their societies "on the purely materialistic and economic base"—either "complete economic subordination to political form" or a partnership with religious authority (Wolf & Iino, 1986: 42).

As noted, Barnard presented these ideas in a commencement address, an enduring form of the classical college's initiation function (see Chapter 2). He concluded by personalizing his remarks:

I have been stating to you the conditions and essential problems of your personal life. Emerson said that in History every man found the record of his own life. Is the question of individualism and social cooperation a personal problem? Most assuredly, one of the most acute. For you must often be torn between conflicting loyalties—to yourself and your family, your business associations and obligations, your State, to your nation, your Church. Sacrifice, accommodation, toleration are the constant necessities of personal life; and the greater your place and responsibilities the more complex and acute they become. Do the great social forces interact within your being? In a physical world in which friction and resistence [sic] are attributes, you must expend energy to do work; as an animal you wring food from your environment; as a social being you must at least both govern yourself and be governed; though mortal, you press toward immortality. In the manifold nature of your being lies the perpetual struggle of which you have already often been aware, that is repeated in the social world of which all are a part. It is this conflict of the moral being that gives your great duty and opportunity. (Wolf & Iino, 1986: 44–45)

Also in 1936, Barnard spoke on "Mind and Everyday Affairs," which he attached as an appendix to *The Functions* (1968 [1938]: 301–22). In this speech at Princeton, he spoke of the moral codes of intellectuals and academics, which he found dangerous and irresponsible because of their overvaluation of formal knowledge and devaluation of personal knowledge.

Barnard acknowledged advances in natural and social science, but he found them hard to apply "in everyday affairs." He based his talk on his experience with many different individuals, positions, and occupations. He singled out two difficulties. One stemmed from his experiences of adjusting to new positions in organizations. "A different point of view seemed to call for a rather complete mental readjustment." The other had to do with "attaining a mutual understanding between persons or groups." This did not concern differences in factual knowledge but "a difference in mental processes quite independent of knowledge or experience." Mental processes were either logical or nonlogical. The former category lent itself to words and reasoning; the latter did not and often had to be inferred (Barnard, 1968 [1938]: 302).

Different occupations cultivated and reinforced particular mental processes. Barnard's intellectual and academic audience was biased toward logical processes. Yet whereas most people insist on the importance of logic, they do not display it and do not accept others' use of it. "The validity of much reasoning is not accepted in practice, though not formally denied." Much reasoning is of course erroneous, which explains the insistence on experimentation in science. We accept reasoning "because it confirms what we already understand or believe, or because it is the expression of an authority which we would accept without such reasoning." In fact, "reasoning is a social rather than an individual function." Thus Barnard observed an overemphasis on reasoning and an underemphasis on "intuitions, habits, sense ('common sense')" and "the quick mental processes" (Barnard, 1968 [1938]: 303).

He analyzed different occupations according to their mental processes. He found usefulness in the *variety*: "the improvement of personal development and conduct, especially as respects the promotion of mutual understanding, and . . . a better appreciation of some of the problems of our social world." Recognition of both processes' importance would eradicate the "false sense of intellectual superiority which closes the mind of many to the powers and the merits of others, either of inferior formal education or of education in other fields" as well as the "serious misjudgment of the importance of personal experience and of deliberately acquiring it." Also, nonlogical processes could be developed by "'conditioning' the mind." It "will be stocked by experience and by study. Experience means doing things, action, the taking of responsibility . . . There seems to be no substitute for using the mind, applying it, working it, to develop its power" (Barnard, 1968 [1938]: 321).

Barnard then developed the moral code justifying both logical and nonlogical faculties: "intellectual honesty." The overarching task was "how socially to make mind more effective." Increased specialization generated "inconsistencies of method and purpose" and misunderstandings. The remedy was "the feeling mind that senses the end result, the net balance, the interest of the all and of the spirit that perceiving the concrete parts encompasses also the intangibles of the whole" (Barnard, 1968 [1938]: 322). Barnard would find and articulate this mind in what he called "the functions of the executive" and his personal experience at New Jersey Bell.

In Barnard's 1937 lecture series and 1938 book, he synthesized the ideas he had been developing since the mid-1920s, particularly his definition of organization and his resolution of the individualism-collectivism dilemma. These activities also began Barnard's extensive collaboration with the emerging leader in higher business education, the Harvard Business School.

Barnard wrote *The Functions* midway through his tenure as chief executive of New Jersey Bell. It was a theoretical treatise on "the" organization, but it was also a deep reflection on his personal experience of organization. As noted above, he had already isolated management as a key element in social progress through its ability to encourage the desire to cooperate, which led to productivity, which developed the individual, society, and civilization. Barnard had further isolated a key element of management's ability to encourage this desire—its relations with and among individuals. *The Functions* thus focused on the leader's relation with himself and with his experience.

Although he retrospectively analyzed his book as having two parts— the "skeleton" and the "physiology" of organization, associated with Parts I/II and III/IV, respectively (Barnard, 1948 [1940]: 133), it actually had three parts. The third part deals with the leader, specifically the leader that is Barnard himself, who provides the vital element or the heart of the physiology. Consistent with his typical process, Barnard's structure shows a continuous unpeeling of layers down to the core element. In *The Functions*, this element is the personally created moral code to which the leader, the particular leader who is Barnard, subordinates himself.

Barnard initially set forth "executive functions" not associated with one person but rather distributed—for example, informal executive organization (Barnard, 1968 [1938]: 223–27). However, in Part IV, he focused on the senior-most executive and in particular, this person's "concrete expression" of the "moral factor" of personal responsibility. Here, the discussion became intimate. Barnard had already stated that at the core of responsibility lies a personal decision to subordinate oneself to the organization's moral codes; thus "the moral imperative of uninterrupted service" illustrated by the incident of the switchboard operator remaining at her station while she saw her house burning down with her mother inside (1968 [1938]: 269). The executive, however, not only subordinated himself but also created and lived the codes. This occurred through the "sincerity and honesty" in leaders' convictions that "what they do for the good of organization they *personally* believe to be right" (281, emphasis in original).

Barnard shifted smoothly from discussing the executive to discussing the leader, but the distinction is crucial. It follows from differences in the authority imputed by others. Organizational members impute authority based on the executive's position and/or his "knowledge and understanding." When they impute authority based on both, "compliance [becomes] an inducement in itself" (Barnard, 1968 [1938]: 174). Yet this state is highly tenuous:

Let these "positions" . . . in fact show ineptness, ignorance of conditions, failure to communicate what ought to be said, or let leadership fail (chiefly by its concrete action) to recognize implicitly *its dependence upon the essential character of the relationship of the individual to the organization*, and the authority if tested disappears. (174, emphasis added)

Thus the test of executive responsibility consists in the vital relation or "coalescence" that

carries "conviction" to . . . that informal organization underlying all formal organization that senses nothing more quickly than insincerity. Without it, all organization is dying, because it is the indispensable element in creating that desire for adherence—for which no incentive is a substitute—on the part of those whose efforts willingly contributed constitute organization . . . Leadership . . . inspires the personal conviction that produces the vital cohesiveness without which cooperation is impossible. (281–283)

The vital relation gives life from the organization to the executive and from the executive to the organization. Furthermore, "the people cannot be fooled." Thus Barnard's epigraph to the book, a citation from Aristotle, stated that whereas "slaves and animals have little common responsibility and act for the most part at random," most of the leader's actions are "preordained" (2).

Barnard then drilled down to the vital element of the vital relation— "the" leader's self-governing moral code, but in fact Barnard's personal credo:

I believe in the power of the cooperation of men of free will to make men free to cooperate; that only as they choose to work together can they achieve the fullness of personal development; that only as each accepts a responsibility for choice can they enter into that communion of men from which arise the higher purposes of individual and of cooperative behavior alike. I believe that the expansion of cooperation and the development of the individual are mutually dependent realities, and that a due proportion or balance between them is a necessary condition of human welfare. Because it is subjective with respect both to a society as a whole and to the individual, what this proportion is I believe science cannot say. It is a question for philosophy and religion. (296)

The Functions is not only a theoretical treatise on organization. It derives from and demonstrates the personal basis of organizational knowledge and the organizational basis of personal knowledge for Barnard personally.

Moral Codes in Action: Executive Correspondence

As head of New Jersey Bell, Barnard interpreted the telephone organization to the public and vice versa. In particular, he corrected attitudes that harmed the organization's morale, the public's interest in the organization, and the public interest per se.

In 1934 he answered a complaint from a customer who was also a stockholder. The customer complained that the phone representative had tried to persuade him to continue his service. Barnard acknowledged the customer's annoyance but said that the policy of double-checking cancellations with customers did retain service.

[T]his we believe is of real advantage to our customers as well as to ourselves. I am somewhat surprised that as a Stockholder you do not realize that this effort is one of the many which, among other things, protects your investment, and that as a customer you do not appreciate that keeping telephones in service and selling additional telephone service is not merely a matter of dollars and cents but is a very vital factor in the service itself, for . . . a reduction in the number of telephones distinctly lessens in the long run the value of telephone service, just as the addition of telephones increases its value, because the usefulness and availability of service is thereby increased to all who are connected with the system . . . [Furthermore, the efforts] increase the public respect for this organization which, although it is necessarily monopolistic in character, is as energetically after business as any other concern. The public likes this attitude, and it certainly has the effect of keeping everyone within the organization alive and alert to give good service and to take properly into account the customers' points of view and desires. I have no doubt that in their zeal employees occasionally over-step the limits of good sense in sales work and cause irritation . . . We, of course, regret such conditions and do as much as we can to avoid them without killing that interest and zeal which we believe is important alike to the public and to our stockholders. (CIBP, Book 1: 1-73)

To a customer who complained about bill collectors, Barnard replied, "From the standpoint of relations with our customers as a whole, it is unquestionably true that we will create more disfavor by laxity in our collection methods than we will by reasonably systematic and prompt collection treatment." He admitted greater laxity during the Depression,

[but] with 500,000 customers, many of whom are distinctly unreliable or irresponsible, it is not possible for us to assume that credit should be extended beyond normal periods . . . [considering that] . . . most of our accounts are small and the cost of special treatment for small accounts easily becomes a great financial burden and would substantially increase the cost of telephone service. (CIBP, Book 1: 1-78)

Then Barnard expressed frustration:

It is always interesting to me to observe that a customer who has been irritated . . . should at once jump to the conclusion that the difficulty is due to the fact that we are a monopoly. For years I have been critically observing the practice of all sorts of people in competitive business and, excepting the cases of bad management, it has at least been my experience that the usual run of competitive business men are really less liberal than are we, and are less disposed to make adjustments, excepting where they expect to recoup in some other way. (CIBP, Book 1: 1-79)

The only discernible difference was the phone company's inability to choose customers, many of which "are so difficult and unreliable that only constant caution and effort is sufficient to relieve us of serious losses." Thus the "systematic collection methods" benefited "our customers as a whole" (CIBP, Book 1: 1-79).

A letter from a man proposing that women married to employed husbands be dismissed indicates that Barnard wielded influence on personnel policy generally. Barnard rejected the proposal because he could not assume that the wife's income was unnecessary, and this would mean prying into private family matters. Also, the policy would discourage marriage and encourage "secret marriage and other forms of deceit." Change in conditions "would require continuous reversals of decisions." Together, "these things would undoubtedly react adversely on the spirit and efficiency of the organization and would cause criticism by our employees and by the general public." Above all, an employer, "to keep within his prerogatives and for the best interest of the general welfare as well as his business," had to hire based solely on fitness for the job (CIBP, Book 1: 1-81).

In 1940, Barnard sent a four-page reply to a customer who had criticized the company's advertising. Expounding on institutional theory, he distinguished sales from institutional advertising. He proposed three purposes of advertising: educating the consumer, increasing the overall value of the service as new subscribers joined, and using the sales occasion to evaluate the service. He suggested that those monopolies that did not have professional sales initiatives "may be guilty of serious failure to discharge their service obligations." Institutional advertising "secure[d] an attitude and practice of cooperation on the part of customers and of the general public." In a monopoly, the need for "a cooperative attitude and practice" on the public's part was even greater:

I . . . refer to the fact of very common personal experience, that when our own attitude as individuals toward others doing something for us is hostile and non-cooperative it is difficult for the other persons to do anything well either from their point of view or our own, even though the performance is practically perfect. (CIBP, Book 1: 100-101)

The telephone system's complex physical operations required "great delicacy of the coordination of efforts of large numbers of people including the public." Smooth operations "are easily disturbed by public abuses, by non-cooperation, and by hostile attitudes." Institutional advertising clarified the company's "intentions, policies, and effort." Specifically, it affected "the morale and interest of employees": "There is no greater incentive to good work than a public profession to it." He elaborated,

If we back up what we profess by active measures within the organization to make good, then the mere profession stimulates the interest, enthusiasm and effort of all who are connected with the institution. By our institutional advertising we say to ourselves that we are engaged in an undertaking of public importance, that it is worth while to do it well, and that we are trying to insure that the public not only appreciates what we are doing but endeavors to cooperate with us in our efforts.

To prove his position, Barnard cited an industrial explosion that had occurred only days earlier:

Within ten minutes of that explosion every single off-duty operator of our [local] exchange had called the Chief Operator to see if she was needed to help out in the inevitable overload on our service. Operators are not trained or instructed to do this and are under no obligations to the Company to do so. They evidently regard themselves under obligations to the service and to the public.

Institutional advertising, he said, "back[ed] up" this spirit (CIBP, Book 1: 100-101).

Barnard's correspondence shows how he used himself to relate to the public and the organization. His USO experience developed his thinking and experience much further in this regard.

Barnard's Leadership of the United Service Organizations

The USO was the morale organization of the U.S. military during World War II; and Barnard, its leader, was the moral center of the organization's morale. At its height in 1944, the USO consisted of 3,000 clubs domestically and overseas. Barnard oversaw the USO's expansion from serving 50,000 to over 12 million people. With a skeletal staff of fewer than 2,000, the USO was a superstructure—thus the plural form, "Organizations," in its name—connecting six organizations with longstanding ties to local communities: the Young Men's Christian Association, the Young Women's Christian Association, National Catholic Community Service, the Jewish Welfare Board, the Salvation Army, and the National Travelers Aid Association.

The USO was Barnard's most complete expression of his ideas about organization as an instrumentality to serve the individual and the whole. He built the USO in the prime of his life and at the height of his powers.

Barnard interpreted the USO, a new institution, as "the most constructive attempt yet made on a large scale to find the way in which social welfare and individual welfare, cooperation and independence, coordination and individuality, may simultaneously be achieved." Structurally and morally, he defined the USO as "the cooperation and coordination of the activities of six agencies, of three faiths and of several races, without discrimination between those served, yet with emphasis upon the maintenance of the particular and peculiar services of each agency" (CIBP, Book 8: 1-3026).

Taking charge of the USO, Barnard confronted his ideal experimental condition of "administrative stress" at a new level of intensity. At New Jersey Bell, although he developed moral codes to integrate the organization, he also worked with the long-established and widely inculcated moral code of uninterrupted service. Barnard's speeches to telephone workers consistently recount the year's disasters and how workers mobilized voluntarily, after hours and in dire conditions, to restore service. Walter Gifford, CEO of AT&T, had told Barnard that, according to "his people all over the country," the USO's reputation "was very low." Nevertheless, at the urging of John D. Rockefeller Jr., Barnard accepted the post. After a few weeks on the job, he felt "almost certain that the organization would fail and the effort would collapse," but "I made up my mind to stay with the sinking ship" (CIBP, Book 11: 1-4160). In the interview with Wolf, just three months before his death, Barnard stated that presiding over the USO "was one of the toughest jobs I have had," perhaps because of these negative attitudes. However, the voluntaristic nature of the work also presented challenges, and more important, gave insights that forced Barnard to issue a correction to *The Functions* (see below).

Barnard structured the USO such that each member agency had a senior officer who was both an agency officer and a USO officer. His administrative method called for "cooperative planning" among the agencies, their officers, and the USO (CIBP, Book 8: 1-3133). In this way, Barnard made the USO into a superstructure. He articulated the overarching moral code: to foster "self-respect and personal integrity in men and women . . . when the necessities of war try to tear those persons apart, and to detach them from the societies of which they are a part and which are a part of them" (CIBP, Book 10: 1-3669). This code shows the scope and depth of his vision. It substantiates that Barnard saw what he said others "could never see"—not the USO's military role but how it "maintained cohesion" (Wolf, 1973: 37). The USO,

being in the nature of an experiment, had to improvize [sic] from the start, as it discovered the needs and interests of men in uniform. The program was not set rigidly in advance. The chief discovery was this: What the men crave most is to resume contact in some form with civilian life . . . to re-establish associations as near as possible like the ones they left at home.

Volunteers offered companionship and provided

the assurance that the "home folks," as they say, are with them. This assurance is extremely important, for "morale"—I use the word for want of a better one—is nourished by three things—opportunities for diversion, faith in the cause for which one is fighting, and the knowledge of a loyal home front. (CIBP, Book 15: 1-5698)

The cooperation achieved at the top of the USO worked down to the grass roots. Barnard stressed "the democratic manner in which programs are arranged and conducted . . . the result of a democratic give and take on the part of servicemen and USO. Many activities are proposed or organized by the men themselves." Military men "are interested in cultural matters—good books, study classes in languages, history, mathematics, classical music and kindred art forms." For example, the USO exhibited works by fifty leading American artists. Barnard pointed out the local character of USO activities, with snow- and ice-based activities in northern clubs and boating and fishing expeditions at clubs near water. Programs appealed to "men drawn from all walks of life—sports and games of all kinds, debates, current event nights, quiz programs, music appreciation hours, stunt nights, handicrafts, hobby groups, club radio broadcasts" (CIBP, Book 15, 1-5701).

Barnard also had to change the military's bias that the USO was "mollycoddling" men "who are supposed to develop the vigors of cruelty in organized form." Barnard noted that the USO gradually won the respect of previously skeptical high-ranking officers. "They tell us that the soldier's self-respect is the foundation of his capacity to be a good soldier; that foundation is to be accomplished not alone by *what* we do, but by *how* we do it and the *intention* with which we do it" (CIBP, Book 10: 1-3669, emphasis in original).

Barnard developed a moral code for the USO that not only integrated it with the war effort but also made it a reason for fighting and winning. In 1942, Barnard interpreted the USO to the National Council of Young Men's Christian Associations (CIBP, Book 10: 1-3667-72): The USO exemplified "the new meaning of democracy." Almost apologizing for the subjective nature of moral-code creation, he confessed "a perhaps too personal view of the basic philosophy of the USO." He then distinguished true morale from recreation, education, entertainment, and hospitality. Morale had to do with self-respect and personal integrity in wartime conditions that undermined both. It also involved "the ultimate and deeper objective" to "maintain, in both directions, the communication of the civilization of peace in the organization for war." He cited celebrities' performances at overseas bases:

I was amazed to find that the thing which [entertainers] emphasized most was the opportunity to talk personally with the men, to make the men feel that they were in touch with the civilization back home. If they could go again, these actresses and actors said, they would like more time in which to maintain that personal touch with men who are located in the midst of a high though somewhat different civilization." (CIBP, Book 10, 1-3669)

Critics asked why government did not pay for the USO and why it undertook "campaigns and solicitations and quotas and collections and arguments with community and war fund organizations." Barnard replied:

We go to all this trouble because it is desirable for us, as a people, so far as we can, to conduct our society on a basis of voluntary cooperation . . . Why? Because in so many aspects of our lives we must now be regimented. These are times when governments tell people what to do . . . These are times when governments tell people what they may not eat and may not wear . . . These are times when governments tell people they shall not travel, except when the government says so; that a man shall not be with his family if his country's interests require that he be elsewhere; that he shall not write to his family, except as the government passes on what he writes; that his loved ones shall not even know where he is until the government is ready to have them know. (CIBP, Book 10, 1-3669–70)

Patriotism or fear might dictate these conditions.

But they are exceedingly destructive, not only of our normal and habitual behavior and relationships but they are destructive in considerable measure to our normal outlook on life and our philosophy of how we as Americans, as individuals in groups and families ought to behave. Under such conditions, the ability to say, without compulsion, "I do this of my own free will, because I want to do it, because I believe it is the thing I ought to do," is enormously important in maintaining the spirit of American civilization. (CIBP, Book 10, 1-3670)

Barnard described the six agencies' differences "of program, of philosophy, of personal attitudes." The alternative to cooperation was "an inescapable standardization of operations and the creation of a bureaucracy . . . which focuses its mind on the details of doughnuts and coffee, of pennies saved, and volume of service rendered." This organization would lose sight of "the spirit of essential service of the USO—its emphasis upon self-respect, personal integrity, and maintenance of communication with our civilization." The "glory of publicity about what great things are done with efficiency or economy" would replace this essence or vitality. "We cannot publicize the really great things we do for they are too deep and too sacred to be publicized by direct effort. Without the six agencies I would give two years only before the USO would degenerate into a merely secular operation." The agencies' independence enabled the USO to "adapt its program and its leadership to the specific situations in which the men find themselves and to the individual who easily gets lost from the publicly organized consciousness in times such as we are in" (CIBP, Book 10, 1-3671).

The "utmost in democracy" enabled cooperation among the agencies, "representing three great faiths and many races." "It is not merely the democracy of votes, but the higher and deeper democracy of consonance of opinion and judgment, of judgment and decision, reached after each has yielded something it thinks important . . . Every agency that is involved in these operations has made them work by a democracy based on the final harmony of true agreement." Moreover, "mere deciding is not enough. There must be full acceptance of the decision if it is to be the kind of democracy that goes forward." Thus Barnard interpreted the USO as a "noble experiment" in "techniques of democracy." The agencies and the whole functioned operationally because they adhered to the unifying moral code. In other words, the value-added of the USO was precisely its integrative moral code (CIBP, Book 10, 1-3671).

It is something new in the world. The agencies that came together and founded the USO and persuaded the Government to make it a partner in its interest and responsibility said more than the Constitution of the United States said when it established religious freedom. Each agency said, "We insist on our right not only to practice *our* faith but on the right and obligation of you to see that those of *your* faith are also served: that you of a different race are adequately cared for; and that you of no faith shall be respected in your independence. (CIBP, Book 10: 1-3671)

He elaborated, "I just cannot accept your creed but I will fight for the right of the people of your faith to be served by you who believe that creed." This idea

goes much further than we have ever gone, at least on a large scale, in this country. But we can go even farther than that . . . this means that every USO club is to be conducted so that any man in uniform may feel completely welcome: that there can be no discrimination by reason of creed, race, or color. That is fundamental in the philosophy of this organization. (CIBP, Book 10: 1-3672)

Barnard added that, in general, the USO operations had conformed to this philosophy. He had of course observed "irreconcilable differences" but found them fewer than he expected to find in any "reasonably well-run corporation" and among "any six government departments—state or national." He concluded:

[W]hat we are developing in USO is the very antithesis of Hitlerism. Can you conceive of such a thing being accomplished in a totalitarian state or atmosphere? I cannot. And when I say that USO is the antithesis of Hitlerism, I wonder if I am not saying that it is one stage higher in Americanism. I think it is. (CIBP, Book 10: 1-3672)

In 1945, Barnard spoke at Bloomfield College and Seminary on "Ethics and the Modern Organization" (CIBP, Book 13: 1-5330–37). He argued that social organization could meet the material and cultural needs of men without destroying their personal morals and religions. But in the long run, this would happen "only if there is universally accepted an ethics as yet undeveloped which governs the impersonal behavior of organized effort in a manner which will be inevitably different from that which ought to govern the conduct of individuals and which yet can be consistent with the latter" (CIBP, Book 13: 1-5337).

Barnard cited the example of decision-makers whose religious tenets prohibit them from eating pork but who would make decisions in a world government concerned with population sustenance. This created a dilemma:

So long as they are not officially related to the raising and distribution of pork products, their personal morals are involved only in the tolerance of customs offensive to themselves personally, but as soon as they become officials of a government which is not itself under the restraint of moral scruples against the use of pork, they obviously become seriously involved, yet it is apparent that it would be difficult on many practical grounds to have it generally accepted as either morally acceptable or inacceptable that the government should or should not act in this field. (CIBP, Book 13: 1-5336)

Nazism, Fascism, and communism were "ethical systems" (setting moral codes) to resolve conflicts among individual codes by establishing "the good of the state and the good of the party dominating, the state supreme as against all other moral direction, and subordinat[ing] the individual drastically to the good of organization." But a new science of organization might develop the "ethics as yet undeveloped" that reconciled different moral codes without compromising individual choice and freedom. This view conformed to his ideas from the early 1930s and even his reflections on his first organizational experience in the early 1900s. However, his USO experience led him to develop these ideas on a new scale and with new urgency. As he wrote to a colleague in 1946:

My experience in the management of the USO where there occasionally developed conflicts of a moral character between Protestants, Catholics and Jews indicates that by inventiveness and also by the development of new ethical approaches it is practically possible to reconcile behavior which has diverse meanings in the different moral codes. (CIBP, Book 13: 1-5169)

The USO case sheds important light on Barnard's personal inventiveness in this regard.

In his USO experience, he was struck by the power of individual choice. In his interview with Wolf, he said that this experience forced him to change his thinking about organization in general, particularly on the matter of responsibility without authority. He thus found that his book's "greatest weakness" was an overemphasis on authority. Barnard reflected to Wolf,

The USO was feasible only on the moral basis of acceptance in order to make it work. I can say, "I now hold you responsible for this," but if you don't accept that then there's nothing I can do about it . . . Now if you stop to think of it, almost everything that's done does not depend so much on the formal requirements . . . nearly everything depends on the moral commitment. I'm perfectly confident that, with occasional lapses, if I make a date with you, whom I have never met, you'll keep it and you'll feel confident that I'll keep it; and there's absolutely nothing binding that makes us do it. And yet the world runs on that . . . You can't operate a large organization unless you can delegate responsibility, not authority but responsibility. (Wolf, 1973: 35)

In this way, formal authority serves those who accept personal responsibility. For example, "by authoritative creation of the position," territorial sales positions keep others out.

Barnard clarified this view in a 1950 book review (Wolf & Iino, 1986: 152). Delegation does not relieve the delegator of responsibility; instead it increases responsibility because it involves even more judgment as to how to execute the delegation. "[T]he administrator may formally make the same delegation to subordinate A as to subordinate B, but he is free to supervise, coach, or interfere with A, and to pay little attention to B. This kind of discrimination is required . . . his responsibility involves this kind of judgment." Delegation may require the delegator to change or reverse a subordinate's decision. The "burden of disposing of appeals and complaints," the level of technical knowledge involved, considerations of "enhancing the prestige of the subordinate and of maintaining the morale of subordinate groups," deference to the "moral attitude of the community" or the "rule of fair-play" enter into that decision. The delegator must also decide what level of responsibility to impose upon the subordinate. In this way, he intermingles and trades off the responsibility for the decision and the responsibility for the method of the decision. He may see the inadvisability of the subordinate's decision but decide not to intervene based on the higher purpose of raising the level of responsibility imposed on the subordinate. This point illuminates the claim that "under the appearance of fixing responsibility," the delegation of authority actually limits responsibility. It also explains why Barnard cautioned that formal organization encourages people to "beat the game" by "overemphasiz[ing] the importance of mere machinery, one important effect of which is to tie the hands of the higher officials" (CIBP, Book 13: 1-5283).

The most serious difficulties . . . come from supposing that specification of formal authorities by law secures responsibility, whereas it does the reverse except in the most restricted technical sense . . . The centralization of responsibility, which Americans seem to fear, permits and requires the delegation of responsibility and the magnifying of the moral forces by which primarily, I think, bureaucracy can be controlled. (Wolf & Iino, 1986: 154)

Barnard held fast to this view even several years later. In 1959, he wrote to a colleague, "In two sentences the art of management focuses on the ability to delegate responsibility. Responsibility in formal organizations has to exceed any delegation of formal authority, and in many cases responsibility has to be discharged without authority. In other words, I think the old bromide that authority and responsibility are commensurate and even correlative, is contrary to experience" (CIBP, Book 11, 1-4104).

Furthermore, Barnard applied this view wholeheartedly in his management practice. In his 1959 annual report to the Rockefeller Foundation trustees, he wrote, "My view is that the President of a corporation or an organization is responsible for everything that goes on in it, unless he is specifically relieved of certain duties" (CIBP, Book 11: 1-4153).

Barnard's Final Publication

Barnard's last article, "Elementary Conditions of Business Morals" (1958: 1–13), addressed the larger barrier to understanding responsibility—that is, "the general failure to recognize how much of business behavior is motivated by moral considerations." In this speech and essay, Barnard recognized the great gap between his own and the prevailing attitudes about moral codes per se. He reflected that in writing *The Functions* he had surprised himself by realizing that formal organizations are social systems with "implicit assumptions as to the world . . . that make them largely autonomous moral institutions" and that "to a large extent management decisions are concerned with moral issues." The further idea "that cooperation among men [in formal organization] creates moralities" was "to me, in 1938, a startling conception." Barnard collapsed his writing of *The Functions* with his USO experience in articulating a new dilemma, the reconciliation of personal, organizational, and societal codes. In this reformulation, Barnard's integration of individualism and collectivism was not as important as his ability to integrate different moral codes per se.

Barnard noted the dominant moral codes of "Judeo-Christian ethics, the Ten Commandments, the Sermon on the Mount, the Golden Rule." They had "little application or relevance to the moral problems of the world of affairs" in modern, morally complex Western civilization. He cited the Chicago School economist Frank Knight: A "pure personal-relations ethic . . . can hardly furnish rules for such activities as international trade, or any dealings with people too numerous and remote to have reality for us as individuals" (Barnard, 1958: 2).

Barnard referenced a 1944 conference, led by clergymen and theologians, on world peace. John Foster Dulles had invited him to attend with the request that he "help keep their feet on the ground." Barnard found their attitudes unrealistic, and he told them so. "They didn't know what they were talking about when they were talking about the economic system or the business system or the social system." He recalled, "I said to an Episcopalian Bishop, 'I listened to this discussion, and you're talking about a world I don't know anything about. I live in this world that you are talking about, but it isn't at all like what you say it is'" (Wolf, 1973: 40). Theologians talked in terms of an ethic of nomadic agricultural life, and economists spoke of "highly abstract aggregates of behavior" and "highly artificial assumptions of the maximizations of profits as the principle of economic behavior," which he found "not merely misleading but abortive." (In 1947, Barnard wrote, "Nothing has done so much harm in the field of social science as the emphasis on maximization of profits as the dominant concept in the description of the behavior of either individuals or business organizations"; CIBP, Book 9: 1-3537.)

Moreover, Barnard found businessmen "singularly inarticulate except in the technical language of their heterogeneous shops." Thus he called for "empirical studies of behavior in business . . . and the moralities they create" stated "in language facilitating communication with those whose concern is with general problems of ethics." As president of the Rockefeller Foundation from 1948 to 1952, Barnard supported a book series along these lines. Although the series did not have the desired empirical thrust, it illuminated "approaches and considerations" in understanding business morality (Barnard, 1958: 4).

Barnard acknowledged the difficulties of this subject. Most people do not recognize the extent to which behavior is determined by moral attitudes. Also, the term is associated with "perfectionist standards." Apparent failure depends on circumstances; "the degree of 'temptation' to deviance must be taken into account." Economic or legal justifications hide deeper motivations that one is too inarticulate, unaware, or private to discuss. Finally, most moral systems are not explicitly formulated but they manifest unconsciously and play out habitually. Recognizing these burdensome associations with the word "moral," Barnard used "responsibility" and "loyalty" instead, which he defined as "behavior . . . which is governed by beliefs or feelings of what is right or wrong regardless of self-interest or immediate consequences of a decision to do or not to do specific things under particular conditions." He presented a taxonomy of responsibilities—personal, official, corporate, organizational, economic, technical, and legal. He discussed conflict, "the most crucial testing of behavior from the standpoint of morals in business." The "main burden" of administration consists in "the thousands of moral dilemmas hidden from public view or discussion" (Barnard, 1958: 10).

He outlined three methods of resolution. The judicial method involves narrowing and delimiting the areas of responsibilities. The reconciliation method shows that conflicts are pseudo-conflicts based on false assumptions or ignorance of the facts. The third method is "the invention of concrete solutions": to "construct another proposal which will effectively accomplish the ends initially desired without involving the deleterious effects to be avoided." This "need for invention of alternative means" required "imagination, fine discrimination, and persistence." It also explained the frequent "moral collapses" of individuals in responsible positions (Barnard, 1958: 11–12).

Barnard thus reformulated the problem he faced as a young man but at a level of consummate complexity and scale—world cooperation: "How to secure the essential degree of coordination of a vast system of activities while securing the degree of decentralization and autonomy essential to initiative and, indeed, to responsible behavior." Local decision-making required such initiative and responsibility. Otherwise, "the burden placed upon centralized authority for securing appropriate behavior over vast areas is in fact an impossible one." Despite training and inculcation, "authority could not sufficiently operate if it were not for the development, whether inculcated or spontaneous, of the moral sense to which we broadly give the name 'sense of responsibility.'" Responsibility cannot be delegated and, "therefore, a high degree of effective autonomous behavior cannot be secured except as responsibility is freely accepted. When so accepted the possibility of effective autonomous behavior is realized" (Barnard, 1958: 13).

Barnard had experienced the power of organization as a new instrumentality for setting new moral codes, particularly those that could reconcile contradictions among a variety of other codes. But he met with what he found a most elementary obstacle: the failure to see that business involved any morality at all. While he called upon the academy to investigate (1958), he also showed how its own moral codes kept it from doing so: It held itself apart from organization. "[W]ithout ever having been a scientist myself, I am most cordially and seriously interested, more from a humanistic than from a practical standpoint, in science and scientists, but I think they are very much injuring their own cause by false emphasis and exaggeration. It just simply is not true that technology on the whole rests on purely scientific discoveries" (CIBP, Book 16, 1-5479–80).

Scientists, he believed, did not appreciate "the immense amount of inventive genius necessary to apply pure scientific knowledge to practical purposes, and this inventive genius does not stop at the level of gadgetry, it includes organization for practical purposes and it also includes salesmanship." Barnard cited a former supervisor, H. E. Thayer, who was president of Western Electric. Thayer told Barnard that "probably five times as much money was required to make a discovery useful than was required to make the discovery . . . my guess would be that on the whole the ratio is very much larger than Mr. Thayer at that time recognized." Barnard criticized scientists' "excessive claims for the necessity of freedom for everyone to do as he darn pleases." Scientists compared themselves to artists in their individualism and their disassociation from "practical considerations," which Barnard contradicted by citing relations of contract and patronage in the fine arts. "I think scientists also hurt their cause by an emphasis on 'pure' motivation as against the quality and significance of the results of their investigations" (CIBP, Book 16: 1-5479–80). In other words, scientists had to consider the fundamental aspects of organization that Barnard had studied all his life.

INTEGRATING BARNARD

Barnard recognized a new empirical condition in the combination of the formal organization, executive, and leader: processes whereby followers imputed power based on the leader's continuing subordination to self-created codes and conscious appropriation of that power to create value and values for the organization, the members, and the whole. This, in turn, required dynamic relating between the leader's conscious and unconscious processes so that he "sensed the whole" of the organization including his relating. The leader systematically codified knowledge by writing and rewriting. He fed the fruits back into the subjective processes and started the cycle again.

Chapter 5 discussed how Follett struggled to verbalize her ideas about circular response. Similarly, Barnard looked back on the sixteenth and final version of his book. He found faults due to the new nature of his subject. He apologized for the inadequate treatment of technical material. But "[s]till more do I regret the failure to convey the sense of organization, the dramatic and aesthetic feeling that surpasses the possibilities of exposition, which derives chiefly from the intimate habitual interested experience." Those who lack an interest in the science of organization "are oblivious to the arts of organizing, not perceiving the significant elements. They miss the structure of the symphony, the art of its composition, and the skill of its execution, because they cannot hear the tones" (Barnard, 1968 [1938]: xxxiv).

After he finished *The Functions*, Barnard told Henderson, "What most convinces me that the thing is worthwhile has been its reaction on my capacity to understand and to observe what is going on before my eyes." He wanted to use the book "as a base for the accumulation of evidence; say, through a period of ten years" and then "do the whole job over again." He realized this probably would not happen and that instead, he would "treat [the book] strictly in the nature of a hobby" (Barnard to Henderson, in Walter-Busch, 1985: 140). Yet, as noted above, Barnard did issue major corrections to *The Functions* in his speeches, correspondence, and interview. In particular, his USO experience led him to focus on personal responsibility. Barnard shifted from the specific dilemma of reconciling individualism and collectivism to the idea of creating superstructures that transcended different, even conflicting, codes. However, at the end of his life, speaking to a general audience, he began at the beginning. Observing "the general failure to recognize how much of business behavior is motivated by moral considerations" (Barnard, 1958: 1), he interpreted for businessmen what he had found, lifelong, to be the essence of their practice and foundation of their science.

Barnard admitted his exceptionality in combining scholarship and executive work (Wolf, 1973: 13). In a little-known and difficult text, the focus of Chapter 7, Barnard explained the creative and scientific opportunity he saw before him. He also explained how knowledge institutions could not integrate either his or Follett's science.

The Private Argument between Chester Barnard and Herbert Simon about the Boundaries of Management Science

Building on Chapter 6, this chapter discusses Chester Barnard's epistemology for a management science, which helps explain why the professionalizing management academy did not integrate his work. In particular, the chapter focuses on a turning point in management science, the interaction between Barnard and the more celebrated founder of organization science, Herbert Simon. This exchange set the field's conceptual limits, which remain in place today. In essence, Simon did for the management professoriate what James Barr Ames did for the legal professoriate: he separated research from experience and in doing so established the boundaries between management science and practice. However, instead of drawing from cases to develop the new science's governing principles, he drew extensively from one text and his experience with it: Barnard's The Functions of the Executive. *Barnard's epistemology of applied social science, explicated in this chapter, asserts that each new science demarcates a new field distinct from ordinary action. Simon operated within these parameters, but Barnard formulated a science that explained parameter-setting per se.*

Barnard and Simon corresponded extensively as Simon revised his classic work, Administrative Behavior *(1947), which became a pillar of the Carnegie School (Gavetti et al., 2007). Barnard supported Simon's research because he believed that a science of management required greater formalization than the human relations and case methods used by Wallace Donham at HBS. At the same time, Barnard thought that Simon rationalized away the hard problems at the heart of an applied social science. But Barnard never published his own foundational document, which he began drafting in 1940. This chapter draws from that document and quotes it extensively to revive and expand the Barnard-Simon conversation about the epistemological foundations of management science.*

A defining moment in management scholarship was the rupture of what Wolf (1955b) called "the Barnard-Simon connection." This break was never systematically probed even by the two authors.

In Chapter 4 I discussed how the graduate school of business (GSB), the Carnegie and Chicago Schools, and decision science constituted a sweeping reform package that integrated the practices of the professional school of business (PSB), the Harvard Business School (HBS), and the case method with professional science. The management academy, a fledgling community, needed governing assumptions in order to grow rapidly but coherently. Simon and the Carnegie School provided these. Gaining consensus, they generated a productive and academically respected community (Augier et al., 2005).

Although Barnard found Simon's assumptions institutionally convenient, he also found them intellectually weak and narrow. Yet his own proposal was so demanding that Barnard himself could not sustain it. In essence, Barnard required that organization be explained ex nihilo, whereas Simon took organization as an empirically existing condition. The point merits elaboration: for Barnard, an executive and a leader, organization was an ongoing accomplishment imposing great demands on persons who consciously took not only formal but also informal responsibility—that is, experiencing the condition as a physical and moral burden. Simply put, the challenge was to endure, specifically to keep securing contributions from individuals such that the necessary value and values were created at the total-organizational (objective) and individual (subjective) levels, respectively, over time and in constantly changing conditions. The leader is the quintessential instrument of dynamic relating between the organizational member and the necessary fiction of the whole—necessary because the organization, not existing empirically, must exist imaginatively if it exists at all. The leader, subordinating himself to his vision and experience of the whole and the whole-making process, makes the fiction a condition of his concrete action and thus real; that is, he and others experience it as real. What Barnard knew as the hard work of maintaining tenuous phenomena at best, Simon took as objectively existing.

Simon and Barnard corresponded over this problem but never reached an understanding. They simply talked past each other.

THE BARNARD-SIMON DISCONNECTION

This section draws from Wolf's fragments of the correspondence between Barnard and Simon (1995b) and Wolf's incomplete text of Barnard's epistemology for an organic applied social science (1995a). The correspondence is supplemented by two items: Simon's letter of May 18, 1945, to Barnard, found in Wolf's papers (CIBP, Book 12: 1-4935–37); and Barnard's commentary on the draft of *Administrative Behavior* (Carnegie-Mellon University Archives, "Memorandum of Detailed Observations on 'Administrative Behavior' by Professor Simon," Barnard to Simon, June 24, 1945). The epistemology is supplemented by Note XII, which Wolf (1995b) stated was missing but that I found during the research for this book (CIBP, Book 10: 1-3787–89).

For Simon, management science had to differentiate codified practice (what Simon called "proverbs"; 1946) from economics. Thus Simon articulated the ideas of "bounded rationality" and "satisficing," in contrast to economics' rational actor theory. Simon also explicitly rejected the "classicists," who proposed rules of thumb such as the correct ratio of superiors to subordinates. Simon said his criticisms "derived almost purely from the logical structure and internal consistency of the principles themselves. No experience of organization was required to detect it, just a taste for rigor in reasoning" (Simon, 1991: 87). Simon and his co-author, James March, considered the co-founders of organization science, specified a pressing need to "mak[e] operational the definitions of key variables" and to "provid[e] empirical verification for those propositions that can be made operational" (March & Simon, 1958: 33). The thrust was to reduce the complexity involved, win consensus on basic assumptions, and expedite a coherent research program. Thus Simon broke with the complex reciprocal logic of pragmatism (Cohen, 2007).

Simon breaks with viewing fact and value as entangled, and prefers to treat ends and means as aspects of choice situations that are stably related and largely pre-distinguished . . . With this shift in foundations, the prevailing ideal metaphor for means and ends can be a stable hierarchy rather than a tangled and dynamic web. Rationality can be seen as selecting the most appropriate means for achieving currently preferred ends . . . Organization theories are thus cast as theories of how an approximation of rationality might be collectively achieved. (Cohen, 2007: 504–5)

Simon also limited the scope from action to decision. "Decision making could become the central focus of organizational research whereas action could be treated as less problematic, following more or less automatically from choice" (Cohen, 2007: 505). Simon saw *Administrative Behavior* as the foundation of his life's work:

[T]wo interrelated ideas have been at the core of my whole intellectual activity: (1) human beings are able to achieve only a very bounded rationality, and (2) as one consequence of their cognitive limitations, they are prone to identify with subgoals. I would not object to having my whole scientific output described as largely a gloss—a rather elaborate gloss . . . on the pages of *Administrative Behavior* where these ideas are first set forth. (Simon, 1991: 88)

Simon took subgoals as a given, whereas Barnard saw them as the executive's and leader's responsibility to resolve by establishing an overarching organizational purpose.

In his autobiography, Simon described how at the age of 22 he had written, "without any management experience," a textbook to train city managers. The work required mere culling and organizing of the literature. "Only intelligence and literary skill were required, not experience." Then, at age 25 and with "minimal management experience," Simon wrote *Administrative Behavior* (1948), considered a pillar of organization science (Gavetti et al., 2007); it was built upon by others who worked in the Carnegie tradition, including March and Simon (1958) and Richard Cyert and March (1963). Even if it was not based on Simon's experience, however, *Administrative Behavior* was of course based on experience—Barnard's. Furthermore, for Simon, *Administrative Behavior* did not entail a mere culling of the literature as he had done at age 22, but intense study of *The Functions* (Simon, 1991: 86). In his Nobel acceptance speech in 1978, Simon stated that despite his numerous references to Barnard's book, he had failed to express the impact that Barnard's work had on his thinking (Simon, 1979: 500). Moreover, Simon did far more than read and re-read the book. He organized at least two formal study groups, and perhaps many more informal ones, to interpret and explicate it in the company of scholars and managers. In this way, following Barnard's view, Simon subjected the book to the test of experience.

In 1939, Simon convened one such seminar with colleagues at the University of California, Berkeley. He noted that one senior faculty member "shocked" him by saying he had not read the book because it was "too hard" (Simon, 1995: 1023). In 1942, Simon organized an evening seminar to study the book with federal agency administrators in Chicago. "Aided by the insights gained from Barnard, I soon realized that a little administrative experience goes a long way. Life in organizations is not very different from life elsewhere" (Simon, 1991: 73). With regard to "bounded rationality" as a condition that differentiated organization studies from economics, Simon wrote that

by the age of 25, I had already had ample experiences in life to understand the limits of the economists' framework of maximizing subjective expected utility as applied to actual human behavior. The scantiness of my experiences with organizations posed no particular limit to my development of an alternative approach to decision making.

Rewriting the rational economic decision as an organizationally bounded rational decision could "be easily achieved with only a bookish knowledge" (Simon, 1991: 73).

Simon's casual reference to "only a bookish knowledge" hides the depth of Barnard's contribution and Simon's process of probing it. When Simon expressed surprise that his book, based on "inference rather than empirical experience," was "a realistic account of many organizational phenomena" (Simon, 1991: 87–88), he did a disservice to Barnard and his ability to capture experience. He also did a disservice to his own process of fitting Barnard with his experience, however little, and of listening to managers fit him into their experience via the seminars.

In April of 1945, according to Wolf (1995b), Simon approached Barnard "cold" with a draft of *Administrative Behavior*. He praised Barnard's "very stimulating writing in administrative theory" and said he could think of no one whose criticisms he would value more highly. This initiated an eighteen-month exchange of letters and culminated in Barnard's writing the book's preface. The two men's common project to build a management science lent a congenial tone but also glossed over the gulf between them. They debated many points but above all, the boundaries of the new management science. In essence, Simon worked to facilitate rationalization so that he and others could rapidly build the field, while Barnard made the rationalization process the focus; that is, building the management science was the occasion to study the rationalization entailed in building *any* science.

This dispute shows most clearly in two documents: Barnard's detailed critique of Simon's book, where Barnard expresses his frustration with what he found to be Simon's inconsistent and uncritically examined uses of the term "rationality," and Barnard's exposition of his applied-social-science epistemology. In the latter document, Barnard explained that scientific fields set borders around themselves and create artificial constructs for their intellectual convenience and to solidify their autonomy. Barnard envisioned an applied social science that explained this process per se instead of subordinating itself to its workings.

In his autobiography, Simon put his finger on the difference between himself and Barnard, although he did not speak in such personal terms. The key insight of *Administrative Behavior* is that behavior is determined by

the irrational and nonrational elements that bound the area of rationality. The area of rationality is the area of adaptability to these nonrational elements. Two persons, *given the same possible alternatives, the same values, the same knowledge*, can rationally reach only the same decision. Hence, administrative theory must be concerned with the limits of rationality, and the manner in which organization affects these limits for the person making a decision. The theory must determine . . . how institutionalized decisions can be made to conform to values developed within a broader organization structure. The theory must be a critique of the effect (judged from the point of view of the whole organization) of the organizational structure upon the decisions of its component part and its individual members. (Simon, 1991: 87–88; emphasis added)

This view posited a common understanding of "rationality" ("given the same values, the same knowledge") and the empirical existence of an "area of rationality." Simon's science departed from this premise; but Barnard's would explain how it was achieved, especially how it entailed *interplay between rational and nonrational processes.*

Barnard held that rational and nonrational behavior could not be separated and that, if a single one prevailed, it was nonrational behavior. Moreover, he could not accept the straightforward use of the term "rationality": It did not describe an empirical phenomenon but was an *attribution made by persons*, including scientists. Thus its use applied to subjective, intersubjective, and so-called nonrational processes that an applied social science had to explain.

BARNARD'S APPLIED-SOCIAL-SCIENCE EPISTEMOLOGY

Although Barnard read extensively in many fields, especially the social sciences, he failed to find a theory that explained his experience adequately. In *The Functions*, Barnard theorized his experience based on taking responsibility both as an individual in a new experimental condition of executive/leader and as a scientist presenting his findings. The book was well received and led to further collaboration with Lawrence Henderson and Harvard. More important, over time, Barnard appreciated how much he learned and how much his powers had increased by writing *The Functions*. He also systematically reflected on another experimental condition: the method entailed in writing *The Functions*. That is, he formalized the theoretical and methodological framework of a new social science in which such research was exemplary (Wolf, 1995a).

Barnard never published this document; nor is there any evidence that he kept working on it as such. He drafted it in 1940 and sent it to Lawrence Henderson, with whom he continued corresponding until Henderson's death in 1942. Wolf alluded to but did not elaborate on the document's significance; but it is of crucial importance because in it, Barnard integrates his executive and social-scientific processes.

The point merits emphasis: Simon and Barnard differ fundamentally as to the object of analysis and how to know it empirically. Barnard regards organization not as an objectively existing phenomenon but as "a construction of the human mind applied to concrete events." He explained this idea most extensively in an unpublished, undated document that appears to be a discarded draft of the introduction to *The Functions* (CIBP, Book 8: 1-3288–10). Unless otherwise indicated, the quotations in the next several paragraphs are from this draft.

These ideas correspond perfectly to Follett's idea of the state. Barnard wrote, "No one ever saw, felt, heard, smelled or otherwise experienced an organization. All that can be experienced is some raw events from which we infer the organization." The idea that organization is a "mental construct" may be difficult to accept. For management, "organization" has a convenient utility, much as the "electro-magnetic field" does for the electrical engineer. But any serious inquiry cannot take the construct for granted. Constructs, in general, "react upon the quantity and quality of cooperative acts." When persons impute organization, "a system of cooperation," this recognition "changes the character of their subsequent cooperative behavior, and they endeavor to preserve what they may call an organization as if it were a thing or instrumentality of itself." The construct supposes "interrelatedness or interdependence of innumerable activities of wide space and time." Initially, it is merely convenient to suppose such existence. Then, the existence is "habitually incorporated in every day speech." Thus the "interrelatedness or interdependence underlying the construct" is ascribed to the construct itself; that is, "the cart is placed before the horse." In this way, Barnard theorized, "we say that men act in certain ways because of the State, that they are controlled by the corporation, that the great organization does this and that. This is not correct." We "do not act in certain ways because of [the State, organization, or other collective entity], but (1) because the actual direct interconnection or interdependence of these acts with those of others constitutes [this entity]; and (2) because within limits the acts are modified by the belief in the existence of something called [this entity] as a sort of Mystical Thing." Authority works similarly.

It is a construct based upon observation of the uniformity of dependence of some kinds of acts upon some other particular kinds of acts. The kinds of acts upon which others generally are dependent are those which interlock the acts of organization as a whole purposefully and which relate to coordination over the whole area of operations and through a longer period of time. The discrimination of such kinds of acts is a matter of evaluation, the ascription of greater importance to some acts of cooperation than to others.

Barnard called these discriminatory, evaluative acts the "subjective aspect of authority." Thus he explained "the problem of democracy" and other systems of governance: They relate to

> an agglomeration of interrelated acts of minute organizations and of individuals and to the constructs which so affect men's minds as to maintain or destroy the interconnections of such acts. The maintenance of cooperation on a large scale depends upon the preservation of conditions which permit these unit organizations to function and upon a concordance or orientation of their activities in particular directions.

In what Wolf entitled Barnard's "Notes on the Nature of Decision" (henceforth "The Notes"), Barnard explored what he called the "nonlogical" bases of knowledge, which an applied social science had to comprehend. Although Simon thought that he differed with Barnard mostly on the matter of whether intuition can be formalized (Simon, 1995), the more satisfactory explanation was Barnard's: the difference stemmed from Simon's own nonlogical process (i.e., per habitual practice in professional science requiring a separation from "lay" and experiential knowledge) and thus ignorance of the nonlogical basis of organization. The next section closely follows Barnard's argument in this regard.

Detailed Presentation of "The Notes"

Barnard divided the text into twelve parts. This analysis incorporates Wolf's formerly missing part 12. The explication takes the parts in numerical order (all from Wolf, 1995a).

Barnard stated his purpose in Note I: to show that "appropriate behavior . . . requires intuitions and intellectually held fictions which definitely conflict with scientific facts and conclusions" and that any applied social science had to take this into account. With this statement, Barnard distinguished between economics and management: economics cannot explain itself socially, but management can. On the other hand, "management of affairs" had generated "a body of extensive common experience." Thus "the social factors in the behavior of individuals" remained uninvestigated.

The coincidence of collective organization and individual decision-making had yet to be explored. "False attitudes" concerning "reason, the rational, logic, intelligence and the nature of language" prevented serious study. Psychology had advanced by studying "organic structure, adaptation, conditioning, responses, and habituation, imitation and the behaviour of masses, institutions and customs, organizations and societies, ecology and interdependence," but "understanding of the nature of behaviour still called 'rational'" had not. "Respect for the importance of what is 'not reason' has certainly increased, but its respectability has not."

Barnard enumerated the typical expressions of fragmentation—rational and nonrational, logical and illogical, reasoning and unreasoning. These attach to values privileging "reason" and "a subjective psychology abstracted from the interactions and interdependencies of living and acting" that "dominate our efforts to understand the behaviour of men in society."

He used different language to escape from the dichotomy and grasp "the nature of the interrelations of knowledge and action." He focused on decisive behavior rather than rational behavior. Somewhat confusingly, within the category of decisive behavior, he distinguished between responsive and decisive acts. (This, presumably, is the kind of problem Barnard would have fixed in a revision.) Responsive acts do not involve "any process of deliberation or conscious choice." Decisive acts occur "in conjunction with a decision," which involves "a conscious choosing between two or more alternatives, at least one of which is regarded by the actor as a means to an end-in-view." Decisive behavior conforms to conditions that "are socially instituted or established" or that relate to "social equipment" such as "conventions, institutions, norms, beliefs, attitudes, prescriptions, and social knowledge." More important, the social equipment follows from the physiological need for decision, "mere action for its own sake." Barnard held that the social equipment arises from the requirements of the decisive processes rather than the reverse. At the same time, however, this equipment also complicates decisive behavior. It "necessarily involves inconsistencies and conflicts of knowledge and concept." Therefore, a "secondary requirement" in the adaptation of societies is "to neutralize or make innocuous the inconsistencies and conflicts." An "elaborate secondary structure of conventions, habits, and attitudes" evolves. Thus "intelligent behaviour" is "characteristically non-logical behaviour."

Barnard then provided a superstructure that makes nonlogical processes appear logical, "a scientifically-founded epistemology of the social sciences." This epistemology had to include an understanding of how individuals make imputations about "the character of knowledge" where concrete events are concerned. That is, actors have "conceptions of knowledge" that they impute to so-called empirical phenomena, and applied social science had to comprehend this very process. For example, calling a science "social" is not an empirical description but an imputation. "A merely descriptive statement about social action is perhaps generally impossible except in strictly physical terms or at most in physical and biological terms that eliminate the social aspects. That which makes it social probably involves the fact of aim, intention, purpose and appropriateness."

This new epistemology thus involved "an inescapable interaction between knowledge and action of a kind or degree not present" in natural science. "[F]rom the standpoint of a scientific epistemology of social science, and from that of the scientific study of social action, the interrelation between knowledge and action has specifically to be taken into account." Also, adding more complexity, the theory had to include decisive behavior "as a function of all the factors of the situation," of which "the ego is merely one."

In Note II, Barnard acknowledged his key sources, particularly the sociologist Vilfredo Pareto's "non-logical action." Barnard accepted Pareto's idea that nonlogical action has survival value. Reconciling "conflicting conceptions," nonlogical processes facilitate decision-making. He noted his disagreements with rational-actor theory in economics and with Dewey's pragmatism. Above all, he cited his experience, in which he had observed "conflicts of practical and scientific generalizations" and "conflicts of fact at different levels of discourse." For example, he said, "factual" statements correspond to "conflicts at different levels of authority in organizations and in different degrees of specialization," so "those at higher levels of executive work must speak and understand alternatively in several levels of discourse." Facts differ "according to the viewpoint or interest from which they are approached." Above all, "uniformity of discourse" does not develop over time and the differences persist. Barnard speculated that "some protective method of preventing interference" was involved. He hypothesized "barrier techniques" or "conventions and conventional attitudes which prevent the use of 'arbitrary' concepts beyond the area in which they are useful"; and "techniques of translation or transformation" that prevent "'impracticable' spread of fictions into sectors of behaviour in which they would be ineffective or abortive." In turn, this "imposes a need for 'theories' harmonizing inconsistent fictions," which "become derivations and rationalizations."

Finally, he referenced *The Functions* and particularly his reflections after writing the book. He had observed an "implicit" proposition "that the structure and operation of organizations were largely determined by the requirements of the processes both of organized decisions and of the decisions of individuals." Thus decisions, "a central topic in the entire undertaking," necessitated further study. This conclusion parallels Barnard's experience in 1936 when, after agreeing to publish his commencement speech, he realized that he had used the term "organization" without understanding what he meant by it.

In Note III, Barnard clarified that *The Functions* treated organizational decisions rather than individual decisions. But since most organizational decisions "involve many subsidiary decisions of individuals acting organizationally," an exposition of individual decision-making was a necessary preliminary step. Barnard delineated seven stages in decision-making: (1) "the apprehension and acceptance of the end-in-view"; (2) "the organization of the situation"; (3) "the discrimination of the factors of the situation"; (4) "the discrimination of alternatives"; (5) "the integration of alternatives and end"; (6) "the translation of the strategic factors into terms of acts"; and (7) "the fixing of choice."

He then underscored the nonlogical nature of each stage and of the process as a whole. For example, he stated that the process as a whole "depends on a sense of teleology, i.e. a sense, a feeling, a conviction, that the end-in-view determines the means." Inevitably, stages were resolved "intuitively," through "responsive, habitual, inculcated, prescribed, inspired, conditioned, originating in the sentiments, and not conscious" processes. In particular, for individual decision-making, an end, "if it is to become an end-in-view, must be presented to a condition of desire in the individual." Desire, "a sentimental or non-logical factor," was the necessary condition of decision. And, if absent, desire could be inculcated—typically through nonlogical processes.

In Note IV, Barnard showed how nonlogical factors dominate individual decision-making at stage 1. Ends may be presented subjectively, by individuals to themselves, and/or objectively, by others. In all cases, he said, nonlogical factors prevailed. At stage 1, nonlogical factors already dominated. The "ends for decisive action are, to a very large extent, not only socially presented" but also "socially accumulated." That is, "what to do, what may be done . . . requires a collection of ideas of possible objectives. Such collections depend on discovery, invention and experience. The possibilities of discoveries, invention and experience by isolated individuals appear extremely limited and this is indicated by the slow development of peoples from barbarism." Absent "considerable collections of possible ends," behavior "will be almost entirely responsive" or nonlogical.

In Note V, Barnard showed how nonlogical processes dominated stages 2–7. The end, a nonlogical factor, "serves as a basis for organizing intelligibly the situation in which the decider finds himself." The objective situation is meaningless "except from some 'point of view.'" This point of view then discerns "attention to objects, elements and factors of the area of concentration; a vaguely discriminated area of attention; and a background which has a more or less unconscious effect on the organism and the formation of judgment." Barnard concluded, "The mere recital of these elements of the process will indicate that it is essentially intuitive." The same reasoning applied to stage 3. Most strategic factors "are selected on the basis of habit." Stage 4, discrimination between alternatives, often involves "evaluation of contingencies," with "experimenting, research, calculation and formulating probabilities, etc." These processes entail "intermediate decisive behaviour . . . requiring one or many subsidiary decisions." Unless this complicated course is taken, "discrimination between alternatives is non-logical or intuitive" and governed by habit. Barnard invoked the condition of bounded rationality: "When new ends in new situations are to be accomplished, the selection of alternatives . . . in most cases, will proceed intuitively in the ordinary sense of the word (not in the more comprehensive sense) . . . most decisions are made under conditions of limited time or under pressure or when there are not and practically cannot be made available even restricted and rough data permitting logical processes." It is worth stopping here to underline how much Barnard's thinking differs from Simon's: Barnard addressed this "more comprehensive sense" of boundedness in nonlogical processes that enabled the condition imputed—nonlogically—as "organization," whereas Simon imputed empirical existence to organization and disregarded the processes that explain his very imputation.

In stage 5, the integration of alternatives and end, "the present situation is imaginatively projected into a conception of the future situation," so the process is "intuitive." Stage 7—"the decision 'to do or not to do'"—is "an intuitive and emotional process. The emotion required for positive decision is expressed best in 'courage', and for negative decision in 'wariness', 'fear', 'diffidence' or 'wisdom.'" Barnard presented a catch-22 whereby his argument prevailed either way. Even if the "entire process" has been as rational and "logico-experimental as possible," then the decision-maker "is aware of the limited and abstract character of the elements which worked and the existence of incalculable unknowns. The courage to process assumption or assumptions is necessary." And, if "the entire process has proceeded on the minimum of logical operations, the decision is as intuitional as possible except that there is awareness of alternatives, of the end-in-view, and of the act decided on as a means to an end. Perhaps here the word is 'nerve' rather than 'courage.'"

Note VI discusses outcomes. Outcomes actually affect decision processes because "until the point of action is reached the decider does not know what his decision is." Until the physiological state of "immediate readiness" is reached, the decider is "often unable to sense the intuitive elements of the situation." The imminent moment enables the decider to integrate these intuitive elements.

Note VII is an internal summary about halfway through the text. Barnard explained that Notes III–VI derived from his experience and his inductions from experience. He emphasized that stages 2 and 5 involve "non-logical, irrational, or intuitive" processes. Since logical processes "involve subsidiary chains" of decisive behavior, "ultimately all decisions rest upon non-logical, or intuitive processes." He summarized the key elements of decision: "apprehension and acceptance of the end as an end-in-view," a situation "organized through this end," and the discernment of strategic factors in the situation. Choosing, one integrates "present and projected situations through the means taken to be available." Integration, belonging to organic knowledge, involves nonlogical processes (see below).

Decision-makers are not aware of these processes or stages. "The process is usually nonintellectual except in the restricted sense of consciousness of some alternatives, of the end-in-view and of the choice made." But intelligent behavior requires completion of each stage. The capacity to resolve each phase "depends on the end, the situation and . . . the equipment of the organism as a whole." Barnard noted a tendency to "treat capacities or faculties of individuals as independent of the other elements of the situation." However, "a capacity or ability has no meaning except in terms of that to which it relates." Furthermore, "the interaction between the environment and the organism varies the conditions"; and individual "equipment" is "of first importance." For decisive processes, this equipment—"in a broad sense . . . its experience"—is "social, and embodies a great variety of social tools for decision."

In Note VIII, Barnard warned of the misleading nature of his presentation due to its "analytical character," which made the processes appear logical. Verbal statements are "necessarily logical." Even when related to nonlogical processes, "the formal character of verbalization tends to be imputed to the things described." Differentiating between decisive action and scientific processes helped explain this point.

Barnard rejected the application of the term "rational" to decision-making. He admitted, though, that the term applied if it meant "properly grounded" in a "particular system of logic or reasoning or of scientific method or practice." In this case, differences of opinion as to the term's meaning stem from the differences in these systems of reasoning. But an "entirely different order of confusion" arises when the word describes action or behavior. In this context, typical uses of "rational" are: (1) "action based on thought"; (2) "action based on valid thought"; (3) "action which is justifiable by thought independently, i.e., what would be done if rational processes underlay it even though in fact the action was responsive"; (4) "action which is effective or successful"; and (5) "action which leads to valid, properly grounded, sound assertions, conclusions, statements and judgments."

In each case, the application has a nonlogical basis. In the first two meanings, "the criteria relate to the subjective processes imputed to the behavior." The first, a "vague and uncritical" use, "appears . . . to be implicit and sometimes explicit in much economic theory." The second use "assumes 'thought' to underlie action, but has no regard for the quality of the thought." Barnard noted that his entire discussion had "perhaps made it clear that at least a difficult question of degree of 'thought' would be involved in a precise use of 'rational' as applied to the processes of decision." In the third example, "there is either an historically logical basis for the action (it may have been imitated or prescribed or be habitual where the original instance was based on reasoning) or the action can be justified as a correct process under the known circumstances from the logical point of view." One imputes rationality to an act "when it appears . . . to be one that could be justified by him as rational." For example, Dewey "defines rational as an appropriate use of a means to an end. Yet it is obvious that most responsive, and therefore non-rational, acts are precisely that." The fourth case presents "an appropriate use of means to an end as determined after the fact" when "the selection of means was responsive, or accidental." Most judgments of rational action are based on the effectiveness of action, but "even purely responsive acts are effective." Also, many ineffective acts are rational if based on a "logico-experimental" process. The fifth confounds the effect of action and the processes leading to action.

Barnard then discussed the circumstances of decision-making. In most situations, "there is insufficient basis for rational decision" because of unknowns. "Definitions, postulates and assumptions" restrict the unknowns in "thought," and conclusions conform to these limits.

Decision, on the contrary, involves . . . actors and data that are known; factors that are recognized, requiring assumptions as to relevant data; factors recognized but as to which no assumption can be made; and elements of the situation which are not recognized and therefore cannot be comprehended as factors. The effectiveness of decisive action as means to an end will depend on all the elements, recognized or not; and in all situations, and as respects all decisions, unrecognized factors are inescapable. Whether they are important or not is often only inferred from achievement or failure. Hence, in most situations of decisive action, it can be said that there is insufficient basis for rational decision, since unreasonable assumptions are required, and insufficiency of assumptions is unavoidable. When a problem of action is consciously apprehended, however, it is generally impossible to avoid decision, even if it be only to take no action.

Yet the term "rational," applied to decisions of action,

implies the use of a criterion, appropriate to the testing of the validity of statement, for a quite different category in which not validity of statement but effectiveness of change is the final criterion. In other words, the rules of appropriate decisions are of a different order from the rules of valid thought.

Barnard then argued for the rejection of cause-and-effect logic in both science and decisive action but admitted the practical impossibility of doing so. "Experience convinces us of the convenience—even the necessity" of this device. In science, the "artifice" of cause-and-effect reasoning is that of isolation; in action, it is that of concentration. In science, "cause" refers to "abstract relationships" rather than concrete events. Even in "the simplest of systems" with a few mutually dependent variables, "resort to mathematical expression" is required and "verbal logics" do not suffice. In "the field of decision," concentration of attention, rather than "logical isolation," is required. "The boundaries of the area of concentration cannot be defined because the situation as a whole is largely 'felt,' i.e., is below the level of abstraction, not consciously apprehended." In the area of concentration, one discriminates among "potentially alternative factors of change, one of which will be selected as a potential 'cause' of a desired effect." This is selected "not with a view to statement but with a view to effective action."

In decision processes, as contrasted with "valid thinking," the "critical difference" stems from the tolerance or intolerance of contradiction. In decision, "contradiction is not only permitted but sometimes even required." In valid thinking, "contradiction is never admitted." The appropriateness of a decision "is not a matter of consistency but of adaptation to a complex concrete situation, most of which is not susceptible to verbal statement. If verbalization is involved, then "a selection or forcing of facts to fit the limitations of the system of language" occurs. In decisive processes, "inconsistency and contradiction in terms of verbal logic are inevitable." This is because "the items of public and private knowledge involved in, and of particular knowledge evolved during" decision stages are "necessarily incomplete components of the process." The decision-maker and the observer of decision-making are aware of this "material" as "isolated abstractions or of groups of abstractions conceptually interconnected." Deciders and observers "tend to regard these elements as complete and not realize that they are set in a matrix of interactions, emotions and attitudes, and that their direct connections are with this subconscious material. Known and verbalizable factors interact with factors that are unknown and/or unverbalizable." Also, if an accepted end-in-view is accompanied by desire, "the immediate physiological object of the processes is resolution of uncertainty, not attainment of the end." The objective is not the end-in-view but the decision. Decision processes entail "something analogous to a momentum or a driving tension which requires not the attainment of the consciously received end, but relief or restoral of the 'normal' sense of equilibrium." Resolution of a stage is an imputation based on this physiologically restorative function. In sum: using the term "rational" to describe decision and its processes in concrete situations is erroneous.

In Note IX, Barnard restated his purpose, to show the "'logics' of decisive behavior." He distinguished "enquiry" as a particular case of decisive behavior. Knowledge is a product of enquiry. It has value independent of the way it is attained. "But some of the process of construction is exceedingly convenient . . . especially as respects the material, the quality of the data." Knowledge is "made by directed operations." These operations are not well understood per se or in relation to the uses of knowledge. In particular, the process of validating or "appraising reliability for further use . . . is mistaken to constitute the complete process of investigation itself." Thus one might assume that the architect's plans constitute the process of construction. "The scaffolding and tools of construction are omitted from the plans . . . [as are] the processes of labour—responsive and decisive behaviour—which are covered in the term labour, in the case of a building, and investigation, research and experiment, in the case of enquiry." But knowledge too depends on constructive processes, which involve "the same use of false and conflicting assumptions" as are found in ordinary decision-making. In "the working processes of decisive action in science," the final criteria are "convenience, appropriateness, and probabilities." Here Barnard explained Simon's impending appropriation of his own work.

In Note X, Barnard explained the importance and functions of decisive behavior. It distinguishes men from other species and sets conditions and processes of social action. Social institutions and practices are "aids to discrimination permitting deliberate choice." They also condition responsive behavior; and when repeated habitually, decisive behavior becomes responsive behavior.

This point merits emphasis because it shows the tenuous nature of the responsive-decisive distinction. Furthermore, many decisions aim to promote responsive behavior. Decisive behavior thus "radically changes" the character of responsive behavior. Barnard made decisive behavior "a central fact of social action." Even if "responsive capacities underlie all decisive behavior . . . and the larger proportion of all acts of most men are responsive," the "differential factor of human societies nevertheless lies in decisive behaviour." Decisive behavior is "the intellectual element in behaviour" because it associates means and ends. Institutions, conventions, and customs "facilitate the process of decision." Impressed by "the extent of decisive behaviour and the fitness of the social environment to it," Barnard posited decisive behavior as "itself a fundamental biological need." In this way, "the power of decisive behaviour on the formation of social institutions does not depend on its supposed superior efficiency of adaptation to the external environment, but on the internal constitution of men." Decision then becomes a "primary need"—"action for its own sake"—like other physiological needs.

Decisions enable further decisions. Acts of decision "enlarge the experience of individuals." More important, they add to the "aggregate of the widened experiences of members of societies." In conscious choice, one entertains at least two alternatives, and "thus much wider experience" is secured.

In Note XI, Barnard explained the interaction between individuals and "external elements" in decision-making. Each individual has a unique anatomy and physiology that affect decision-making. Each also "possesses a number of special senses on which decision is more consciously dependent." "Upon and through these properties" the organism interacts with environments. Its activities "impress" effects that "alter the organism" and make its behavior different from what it would have been otherwise. The aggregate of these effects constitutes the organism's "experience." Experience enables or disables the organism in its relations with elements in the social environment. Physical limitations, such as sensory disabilities, may occur. But the senses may be artificially extended, too, "by devices, instruments, and co-operation." Experience is the crucial factor that enables relating decisive processes and "social materials." It is acquired unconsciously and consciously. Conscious experience or "personal knowledge" entails awareness of what one does, perceives, and feels. "Reception" or "formal knowledge" involves "comprehension of oral or written communication, together with thought in verbal terms, of intellectual knowledge." Experience acquired without consciousness is "organic knowledge." As stated earlier, Barnard believed that most learning transpires subconsciously. The "fundamental knowledge for both responsive and decisive behaviour is organic knowledge." Individuals differ greatly in their personal knowledge and their ability to transform their experience into knowledge.

Experience permits "conscious recognition" of "conditions as previously experienced," recollection of what was experienced and done, and projection of experience. Imagination and conception belong to the latter category. "The contrasts or comparisons which are permitted by experience" in these four forms "permit distinguishing particular aspects that are similar in different situations and those which are different in similar situations. This analysis and discrimination permits the combination or synthesis of aspects or elements in new forms by imagination, and in relations between elements or aspects of conceptions. Finally, experience permits language, by which facts or descriptions and feelings may be intercommunicated."

Identifying memory solely with conscious faculties is a "pernicious error" that impedes understanding of decision making. It assumes that we forget what we experience unconsciously "and that we do not imagine or conceive what we are not aware of imagining or conceiving." Yet functions associated with "a high level of consciousness" go on sub- or unconsciously. Thus Barnard posited "organic recall, recognition, imagination and conception," referring to "states or activities of the body which may be inferred from behaviour though not consciously verbalized." The point is that this behaviour is "adapted to the situation" (responsive). That is, "decision does not occur without most of its processes lying permanently below the level of consciousness." Thus "'intuitive' may . . . be defined as organic, but not conscious, recognition, recall, imagination and conception."

To execute decisive processes, many "requisites" must be acquired "directly by personal active experience or by inculcation by example and verbally." If the requisites are few, then the possibilities for decisive behaviour are limited "to a few occasions or types of situations." If the requisites are many, "the possibilities of decision are expanded to many occasions and many types of situations." Whether the possibilities are exploited depends "on the ends which are presented and the intensity of the desire—the will—to attain them." Barnard enumerated "forms of experience" belonging to the organism: characteristic physiological reactions, muscular behavior, emotional dispositions, attitudes, organic knowledge and sensory capacities, and intellectual knowledge and sensibilities. He stressed that experience itself alters these forms physiologically. In particular, it affects the intuitive processes. "The entire organism is involved" in decisive and responsive behavior. This explains why decision-making is easier under "customary conditions" and harder under unusual conditions.

Several of these forms of experience relate logical and nonlogical, or responsive and decisive, behavior. Everyday observation shows how individuals act in ways that "take into account concrete objects, events and movements that were never 'observed' in any ordinary meaning, that cannot be explained by the actor and that are not understood by him." This proves the ubiquity of organic knowledge. In countless situations, the first and second decision stages depend on organic knowledge used intuitively. Generally, when one associates effective behavior with "experience," this refers to organic knowledge. In diagnosis, for example, "the effective 'sensing' of abnormalities" comes from one's organic knowledge. Psychology and sociology have not sufficiently advanced to help managers or politicians diagnostically, yet "the sense of formal or structural similarity of conditions which phenomenally are quite dissimilar" is a fundamental capacity. Organic knowledge enables "behavioral recognition" of "'types' of situation, and differences of types" without precise description.

In concluding Note XI, Barnard discussed how forms of experience interact within the organism. He planned to consider "the social materials of experience" and how "processes of experience" interact with these materials. "Social knowledge" alters personal and organic knowledge; different organic knowledge affects one's use of "social materials."

In Note XII, Barnard attributed propensities for decisive behavior to individuals and circumstances while stressing that social institutions are "materials" that facilitate decision. "The capacity of the individual to make decisions . . . depends upon the materials, facilities or equipment provided by or in society." Barnard concluded Note XII, and the text as a whole, by itemizing these "social elements." They included "institutions," "prescriptions," "norms," "social attitudes," "knowledge" and—organizations. Thus, for Barnard, the organization is a tool that facilitates decisive behavior in the individual.

REINTERPRETING *THE FUNCTIONS*
ACCORDING TO "THE NOTES"

In "The Notes," Barnard explained the science for which his book was exemplary: a new epistemology that could comprehend the subjective processes of organization, which could only be known organically and be formalized accurately (i.e., consistent with experience) by the individual. At the same time, Barnard showed how the new "organic" applied social science, in contrast to professional science "abstracted from the interactions and interdependencies of living and acting," would have unprecedented explanatory power.

This was all too complicated for Simon and the Carnegie School. They focused on separating the management academy from both experience and economics in order to demarcate a new scientific field, just as Barnard theorized. But as Chapter 4 showed, the elite MBA, particularly the elite EMBA, helped create a new institution—the executive-scholar. This individual, integrating scholarship and personal responsibility at a high level exceeding even William Rainey Harper's founding vision for university-based adult education, could well exemplify and build on Barnard's ideas. Part III explores the possibilities of integrating this individual into the management academy and realizing new knowledge-creating possibilities as a result.

PART III

Building on Follett and Barnard

Part III explores ways of building on Follett and Barnard. Chapters 8 and 9 show how individual researchers and educators, working relatively independently, may do so. Chapter 8 results from a close, long-term collaboration with an executive who organizes his practice consistent with the management science theorized and exemplified by Follett and Barnard. In particular, it focuses on the function of developing responsibility in others, the subject that Barnard said his book had neglected.

Chapter 9 focuses on the manager and the development of personal responsibility. Describing the author's experiments with Master's-level teaching and written in the first person, it probes the subjective and intersubjective microprocesses of dynamic relating. It offers both a research and a pedagogical contribution by formalizing the self-reflexive processes and the personal experience entailed in dynamic relating. Ironically, although Follett and Barnard recorded their experiences in writing, they did not write about experiencing their experiences. The closest example is Barnard's description of the executive processes (1968 [1938]: 215–84). But Barnard, theorizing, wrote in the third person and avoided an explicitly introspective process. Chapter 9 thus also proposes teaching and research methods such as autobiography and iterative writing. On the nonlogical level, it aims to relax professional science's stigma against use of the first person.

Chapter 10 takes up this and other attitudes that constrain management science. In essence, Chapter 10 draws on Follett and Barnard to analyze the prospects for using their work to build management science today. It proposes research initiatives that individuals could undertake independently, as well as institutional reforms, particularly the development of the institution of the executive-scholar.

CHAPTER 8

Integrating Research and Responsibility

Collaborating with an Executive

WITH MAX PÉRIÉ

☽

This chapter, a collaboration between a senior executive, Max Périé, and myself, interprets executive work through the lens of Follett and Barnard. The executive establishes a moral code for his organization, subordinates himself to it, and uses himself to develop responsibility in others. In this way, he builds a self-governing whole of which he is also an integral member. The executive works to secure the essential contribution: that organizational members take personal responsibility for the whole. The chapter thus sheds important light on what Barnard said were practices "almost impossible" to observe and what Follett said could not be done by anyone for anyone.

INTRODUCTION TO THE COLLABORATION

Max Périé (henceforth "the executive") and I ("the author") began collaborating in 2007. The executive, who had enrolled in an Executive MBA program and was the director of accounting for an international company, registered for a course taught by the author. The program encouraged dialogue between theory and practice, and students wrote papers based on their professional experience.

The executive enrolled in the EMBA program in unique circumstances. His company had rewarded him financially for improvements he made to the organization, in particular, the efficiency and quality of financial reporting, such as the year-end closing of the account books. The executive attributed his success to a number of methods, particularly his use of groupware; but he had not systematically investigated or documented them. He also suspected that his process entailed more complexity than he could easily state. Thus, like Barnard, he used the Executive MBA (EMBA) program to rationalize his executive processes. He had also considered forming a consulting company to offer these services, a prospect that raised the stakes for him to formalize his method. He set up a website to further this endeavor.

The author's EMBA course, a survey of human resource management (HRM), distinguished between professional HRM and general management. Focusing on the latter, the course drew extensively from Barnard. The executive found Barnard's work on nonlogical processes and their formalization particularly interesting. Likewise, the author found original-research value in the executive's approach, which resonated with her research on Follett and Barnard. The executive provided extensive documentation of his managerial practices, such as internal memoranda, progress reports, and problem reports. He also provided academic papers, with similarly detailed attachments, from two students who had interned in his office.

The collaboration gained momentum when the executive invited the author to learn about his methods firsthand by attending his team's annual kickoff event. She did so and spent an additional day meeting individually with the executive's team members and observing how they organized themselves electronically. She sat in on a team meeting, also organized electronically, between the executive and his supervisory team. She set up confidential lines of communication with two team members who expressed interest in the research. At her request, they wrote about their own experiences in the organization. The author also interviewed the two former interns.

From the growing database of documents, the author created a formal case study, which she used in a Master's-level course on the human aspects of technology implementation. The case took on further life when the executive and one of his supervisors agreed to present their versions of the experience in person and to engage in a dialogue with students.

After the executive expressed an interest in professional research, he and the author decided to use their data as the basis for a jointly written academic paper. In essence, it conceptualized Management Information Systems (MIS) as an integrative executive practice supported by information systems. The paper was rejected for publication, but it drew the author's attention to gaps in the field and provided inspiration for writing this book. It also generated more data and insights. Most important, the paper led to systematic synthesis between theory and data as the author began interpreting the executive's process in light of her research on Barnard and Follett. She used their theories to generate new requests for data from the executive and to reinterpret previously furnished data in this light. She and the executive compared theory and data to test how theory captured experience and how the data elucidated, and could better elucidate, theory.

Following the approach presented in the previous three chapters, the executive takes not only a formal position but also has a personal relation to responsibility. He explained: "Our salary comes in return for fulfilling a function that one has in the enterprise. It's management's job to clarify and insist on this fact." Responsibility is subjective and invisible.

I can't measure productivity in a factory sense. I look for personal investment. Personal investment depends on a feeling of being part of building the institution, being one of the builders whether it's the master, the mason or the apprentice; but the point is being part of this team. And to be part of the team does not consist of assembling everyone and showing them the three or four people who are building the cathedral because then everyone else would only be spectators. Each person has to bring his stone to the cathedral.

The executive concerns himself with how individuals feel part of the whole and contribute accordingly. Thus, as Barnard noted, "[i]t is practically impossible to observe effective executive behavior directly" (Wolf & Iino, 1986: 112–22).

This chapter enables new insight based on close relations between research and action enabled via the EMBA program, which integrates high-level scholarship and high-level management. The collaboration that led to this chapter grew out of such a program. The co-authors agreed on a joint purpose, to build knowledge of management consistent with Follett's and Barnard's science. The collaboration improves on Barnard's "Jekyll and Hyde" method of splitting himself in two, which he found impossible for most people and highly demanding on himself (Wolf, 1973: 13). This particular collaboration makes the scholar into an interpreter of the practitioner. That is, the scholar formalizes the executive's organic experience (see Chapter 7) in terms acceptable to the scientific community without compromising that experience from the executive's point of view. The executive takes responsibility for the faithfulness of the interpretation. In this construct, the scholar brings a theoretical lens through which to interpret the executive's unformalized experience. However, while this division of labor prevails, the joint purpose is to build a science of management (see Chapter 10).

This collaboration benefits as well from a trusted relation between the author and one of the executive's team members who expressed an interest in the research. The team member provides a third view, which neither Barnard nor Follett captured. While all of the team members agreed to be interviewed about their experience with the executive's methods, this individual further agreed to write a report and to participate in a classroom session. The manager left the room when his subordinate spoke, which facilitated candor and detail in his team member's responses to the students' questions. The team member also expressed appreciation for the opportunity to discuss her experience in a classroom setting and to contribute to original research in the field.

THE EXECUTIVE'S MORAL CODE

Confirming Barnard's insistence on the executive's need to establish a moral code, the executive repeatedly introduced or summarized data in the form of maxims; also, the data he provided often included such sayings. Thus, organically and habitually, the executive demonstrated the function of articulating and inculcating a moral code. For example:

— "The neglected little problem of today will become tomorrow's huge catastrophe."

— "It's better to plug the hole in the boat even if your feet are a little wet than to try to save the boat by emptying it of water constantly."

— "If your time costs 3 and mine costs 10, don't hesitate to disturb me for a few minutes if it saves you an hour because it's in the company's best interest."

Using collaborative technologies such as Lotus Notes (see below), the executive worked to operationalize these ideas in his organization. He did so as well in our research collaboration: he did not respond to queries without putting them into a database and imposing a structure on them, such as main theme and subtheme.

On a more general level, the executive's moral code distinguished between two types of human relations, contractual and personal. He stated that he regards his relationship to the company and to his team as both contractual *and* personal. He explained:

In administrative work, I don't think we have rigid quantitative criteria such as in factories. I thus prefer to work with the personal implication of people in their mission. It's a kind of choice to sublimate oneself to enjoy one's work. This occurs through the awakening inside each one of us, of a sense of enjoyment in doing daily tasks, not because the action is satisfying, but because it helps us fulfill a role, mission, strategy that is satisfying . . . The premise is not to consider everyone acting in his or her own self-interest but rather doing things in such a way that they act for the group towards an end that takes them beyond themselves. We like to feel useful for the organization. But for that to happen, we need to be treated not like children but like adults.

However, "competition inside and outside of the organization makes it easy to feel afraid and to not feel responsible—e.g., my boss/the hierarchy is responsible, not me." Executive responsibility must secure the most minimal contributions, "to assure that professional commitments and routine tasks are completed." Beyond that, members should be able to articulate the department's mission "not only generally but also in detail—detailed, but not exhaustive. Exhaustivity belongs to each one of us because each person can improve the management's planning. It is thus a common responsibility that is brought about and enabled."

On the other hand, when individuals refuse to accept minimum responsibility, implicitly or explicitly, "they impose an authoritarian structure." The executive, to fulfill his own responsibility, must order them to take responsibility, which is paradoxical. As Barnard pointed out, this secures minimal and routine but not optimal and creative contributions. The executive noted this and asked himself:

Does my administrative process extend formal power at the expense of informal power and reduce the individual sphere? I had to convince myself that it was, on the contrary, a tool of liberation to the extent that it made routine actions secure and thus gave each person the possibility of more freedom and ability to use himself or herself more imaginatively.

How did he convince himself of this? Ultimately "a principle backs up the management," and management self-affirms: "An executive will never modify fully and definitely the individual and group mood of the administrative team he is in charge of; hence it's his own everyday attitude that he has to assume and strongly believe in to inspire respect." In this way, the executive illustrates what Barnard called the subordination to self-created moral codes.

THE EXECUTIVE'S METHODS

The executive joined the organization at a time of significant change in the internal and external environments. Locally, he confronted problems with the timely and accurate closing of the accounts and the implementation of a new enterprise resource planning (ERP) system.

In 2002, the executive assumed leadership of a twenty-five-to-thirty-person team in the accounting department of a textile and apparel company that faced new competition from China and India. The company began transitioning from a national company with a few overseas offices to an international company with manufacturing, sales, and administrative offices worldwide. In these conditions, then, the executive developed a new moral code for the accounting organization. Regardless of local differences, it had to produce comparable numbers and use methods that would lead to comparable numbers, for analysis and planning on an international scale and for the long term. In other words, the executive articulated the moral code in keeping with the company's growth. He added more complexity and responsibility to accounting's previous function of aggregating numbers it knew to be comparable.

The executive is also a certified public accountant. This point bears emphasis because it helps explain his status inside and outside the organization. As noted in Part I, accounting is the most professionalized of the corporate-technical specialties, having established a community that certifies itself and which, through this independent status, legitimizes the firm as it relates to external regulatory, judicial, and public bodies. This status helps protect accountants against internal pressures such as profit maximization. Accountants' personal standing in their professional community is at stake when they authorize results. Also, accountants work with the company's most privileged information before most others see it, if they ever see it.

The executive joined the company from the outside. He immediately encountered delays and complications with the year-end financial close. He found underlying habits and routines that led to the problems. For example, he learned that his predecessor had run the department in a way that was "simultaneously lax and authoritative": he established "no vision or planning" but "reigned through verbal sanction." He focused on "individual relations with each accountant" such that each one "reported only to him" and "acted in the interest of their own small job." His staff gave him "predigested" information "to protect themselves from him." The moral code was: "Keep your head down or you'll get hit." It also was "do as you have always done." The situation was aggravated by no training budget and low turnover.

The executive probed these practices and attitudes further. A typical response was, "I did my assignment and so I can close my area." Even when an accountant's assignment overlapped with that of other accountants, he or she did not bother to see if the other accountants had completed their tasks. Also, when one accountant's completion of a task enabled another accountant to close his, the latter often did not know that he could now proceed. Another typical response was, "I don't need any planning because I know what I have to do." The executive replied, "YOU HAVE TO DO THIS, now you are part of a team; and the management and the others need to know if an action that you must perform has been done or not. This has an impact on the total process." He called this "administration by decree" or "dogmatic intervention," the sheer assertion of power.

Summarizing the situation, he said he faced a "coercive environment in which compliance with law was more important than trying to fix or adapt it." The executive not only disagreed with this attitude but also he thought it undermined the company's new strategy and business conditions.

Furthermore, and consistent with Follett and Barnard, the executive envisioned an organization that transcended routine, with the capability to build itself in ever-changing conditions. He did not call this creative experience, though, but a "learning organization." In Barnard's sense, he aimed to secure greater contributions from members. To this end, he automated as much of the accounting routine as possible so the organization could focus on more creative work. This action conformed to his reasoning about his own position; for example, he said that if a machine could do what he did, then he could not justify his salary. "It's a vision that I permanently keep trying to share: Our mission, codes of conduct, personal investment (shown in the language one uses, the attachments and data one gives), answers that go beyond the simple question asked . . . I see it as building a real institution."

The executive began by organizing *himself*. He tracked tasks he owed others and that others owed him. He utilized a specific tool, Lotus Notes, known for its organic capabilities. As one Notes expert stated, "The border between Notes as a product and Notes applications is not as clear as in 'conventional' application platforms . . . Complexity and modifiability make Notes different from most other programs" (Karsten, 1995: 7). Thus Wanda Orlikowski (2000) took advantage of the interpretability of Notes to study the "social construction" of technology. That is, Notes facilitated bridging from technical into social aspects of organization because the technology is more of a capability than a thing. The sociology-of-technology literature shows that although technical advances support collaboration, nontechnical and human factors constrain it. Indeed the executive pointed out that Notes itself was built through a close collaboration between designers and users: programmers built it to report bugs individually, resolve them collaboratively, and report solutions and resolutions. But the two functions separated as information technology (IT) departments institutionalized and took charge of design. As Follett would say, this broke the "vital relation" between design and use. With his privileged access to corporate data and his mastery of electronic-collaboration technology (proven in his previous managerial position), the executive did not experience such a rupture. In fact, he took his methods of self-organization to a larger scale.

Experiencing the Moral Code and the Methods:
A Subordinate's Point of View

This section presents a team member's point of view on the executive's methods. We quote it extensively because it shows how the executive functioned personally and because it captures a team member's experience of working with him, including the effects on herself and others.

The author asked the team member, a supervisor, to prepare a timeline of milestone events within the organization and to describe each event's significance. Her account began with the executive's arrival in 2002:

We did not know it yet, but this man was going to renovate and give a new élan to our service. Up until that time, each one of us was accustomed to working at our own desk, not always sharing information with the colleagues sitting near us, to such an extent that sometimes we did the same thing twice. Also, we wasted a fair amount of time looking for information from preceding years. Sometimes, this took a long time. We didn't really have work procedures, or the procedures were often in the person's head. You couldn't transfer tasks from one person to the other, because nothing was formalized . . . Each person kept his own information close to the vest, on his own computer, and had complete control over it. Sharing was perfected to the art of one's careful choice. You felt useful because you had power over information.

I worked this way for many years, about twenty, and I experienced all the advantages and disadvantages of it, without really thinking much about it for the entire period. Anyhow, I didn't know any other way and I got used to it. To be completely frank, it didn't seem "abnormal" to me.

His methods of organizing himself, of delegating, and of assigning and administering responsibility were initially very surprising and even destabilizing. But ultimately, sticking to this concept, the results are beneficial.

I began to understand that management could proceed in another way with customized tools. One can easily organize, control, affix, confirm the work of individuals. What's necessary is to well know and understand one's environment and to fix a goal. I also realized that "hierarchical power" by means of private control of information is completely outdated. (When he said this, it surprised me, but it gave me food for thought and I eventually had to admit its obviousness.)

Communication and information-sharing are always helpful even if it's not always easy to disclose one's information or one's work . . . Every day, you send out information to a certain public. We expose ourselves to criticism or even reprimands if we are even just a bit deficient in our information. In exposing ourselves we take the risk of being judged either on the form or content, which can also expose weaknesses in our process. This shouldn't be an obstacle but rather a step in making progress. An error can be excused one time, but if we want to be credible, we have to stop the mistake from occurring again. So in this case, I think we gain the confidence of those with whom we interact who also appreciate improvements in the rendering of information. (These methods are not always transparent to the outside but they do provide internal security.)

All this brings me to Lotus Notes because this tool allowed us to apply everything I've said above . . . Max [the executive] began to use this tool to document all the tasks that each one of us had to do, by when. Initially, I did not understand what he was doing and above all, why he stored all the information in that way. I had never seen this type of tool and I wondered how it could work . . . Afterwards I realized that through this tool it was possible to document all the completed work, to plan, and furthermore to manage everyone so that each task would be done, or would be progressing toward completion.

Today, I use some Lotus databases to manage and track daily, monthly, quarterly, and yearly actions in my own service. I track actions with other co-workers. I can follow up to see if the work has been done or at what stage it is. I can send reminders. This way of working is not just one-way. I can also receive actions from others.

I should say that this way of working does not happen overnight. You have to force yourself, but after a while, it becomes automatic—if we're willing to put up with it.

The "new" idea entailed a saying—"one person, one task, one date"—and more important, the personal relations that convert this saying into a habitual practice. Merely entering these data helped to inculcate responsibility. It also made the relation of responsibility public. Everyone knew what each individual and the team as a whole had done and what task(s) they still had to do. This entailed a new vocabulary for the organization: the "to do," or action item; the "interlocutors" who coordinate to complete the "to do"; and the "countdown" or timeframe that structures the coordination (that is, "D-day," thus "D–3" if the task had to be done three days before the close). These new words joined with new practices—and eventually, new habits and attitudes. Thus the "to do" is not just jargon. As organizational members repeat it and link it to coordinated action with consequences for the whole, the term gathers physiological effects precisely as Barnard described. The executive emphasized that the accountants began to use this vocabulary in general conversation, not just when engaged in purely technical tasks such as entering "to do"s. To him, this proved that he and his co-workers were "building a true institution" in Barnard's organic sense whereby the relationship to action is "interested, intimate, habitual."

Methods of Social Organization

As noted earlier, the executive wanted to build the organization to do more than routine tasks. On precisely this level, however, he had mandated a certain minimal use of Lotus Notes by his staff. Over time, however, he noticed that some engaged the tool more creatively than others. He hired an intern to look into this further by studying how each individual used the tool in his or her own way. The study distinguished a range of uses. To some extent, the nature of the job explained the different uses of the tool. But some individuals, on their own initiative, took advantage of the more creative aspects of Notes. In effect, Notes itself provided the occasion for making more creative contributions.

The executive said that this analysis showed him that not everyone accepted his method and idea of co-creating the organization. He took this into account in his planning—not by ordering the less receptive ones to do more, or resenting that they did not want to do more, but by formally recognizing and stating that certain positions simply did not require more advanced technology and creative contributions. According to the executive, this policy freed individuals from the burden or potential burden of feeling obligated to follow others and also created a protected category whose value was not lowered just because it used the technology minimally. He also used this policy on a personal level, to come to terms with the fact that his vision would not always be shared and did not need to be.

With this [baseline plus optional] approach, each accountant could rely on a part of his knowledge and make it work in the IT environment with which he was most at ease. The idea was to not confront everyone simultaneously with the totality of a new IT environment or take a "big bang" approach to new technology, especially if the person didn't really need it for his position. I had to avoid destabilizing and instead approach it as capitalizing on his know-how. This capitalization is very important because it puts the coworker in an open position, more prone to listen and maybe accept, eventually, in the long term, a bigger part of this administrative process.

In this way, the executive put a premium on what the employees did know, not just what they did not know, and how they could best contribute to the whole. An employee who did not want or need to use advanced tools, but who felt constant pressure to do so, would not make his or her best contribution. The executive included himself in these dynamics: recognizing that his own extensive use of and high regard for Lotus Notes could divide his team, he took preemptive action by creating the protected job category. Another way of putting this, following Follett, is that he saw his part in the whole and adjusted his action accordingly. He also used his analysis of the situation to limit his assertion of authority and to prevent himself "from generating stress for people who wanted calm and quiet in their workplace."

The design function of Lotus Notes did not limit what individuals could create. However, the executive did not have a training budget, so by necessity he was the system trainer. If a team member wanted to learn how to use Notes's design capabilities, he had to learn from the executive. The executive considered that this added an educational dimension to his practice, which invoked dynamics of reciprocity more than professional contractual relations. For example, he wondered if those he tutored might reciprocate his deviation from a strictly formal role by more creatively reinterpreting their own roles. At the very least, his own practice injected a more experimental feeling into the organization. The executive said he was impressed by what some employees left at the door when entering the workplace.

Imagination is what characterizes and differentiates one person from another. We use it a great deal outside of work and not enough inside of it. For example, I have a musician in my department. He plays in an orchestra that performs locally, and he is responsible for publicity. But in my department, he has one of the simplest roles.

Through his administrative methods, the executive extended his reach and even institutionalized some functions that Barnard classified as belonging exclusively to the executive. He did this by strengthening the formal organization, to which he added a new management level of four supervisors between himself and the accountants. At the same time, he addressed Barnard's challenge of inculcating personal responsibility. This was a significant change for the organization as he had first encountered it.

Delegating Personal Responsibility

The executive offered new supervisorial responsibility to four individuals in the organization. As noted earlier, the previous director had no layer between himself and the individual accountants, so this was a major change. One of these individuals, the consolidation supervisor (CS), described the experience as "unsettling." She explained that the installation of a new enterprise resource planning system was the pretext for this change. The executive lent organization to the implementation, which was causing chaos. He linked specific tasks of the ERP installation to each of the four new supervisors. "Each point was assigned and each person was responsible for following them, and he followed how they followed them." The CS said this was "something completely new for me, because we were not accustomed to working like that."

[I] felt completely disoriented and was afraid of answering his questions . . . I felt guilty if I did not resolve this or that problem, because it was I who was in charge of and responsible for it. And when he had status meetings, I had to explain the outcome of my actions. It is not always flattering to announce before a group that the point has not satisfactorily advanced or the solution hasn't been found. To avoid that, you have to do your absolute best. It's this pressure, I think, that obliges us to go beyond our own limits. In facing your responsibilities, you really learn. You figure out the best thing to do and you capitalize on what you achieve. Gradually I got used to this way of working and I acquired a taste for it. Each new step was a kind of victory over myself and gave me the desire to go further.

Under the previous accounting director, the CS had been a consolidation assistant, and the director had done the lion's share of the work. Under the new executive, the CS took more responsibility for consolidation.

[The executive] reassured me and helped me find the answers to my questions, even when they had to do with the basic organization of the work, since the old methods were no longer appropriate. He pointed me in certain directions and I adapted the solutions in my own way. He let me be the master of the game, correcting me if I was at risk of making a mistake. I could count on him if we were not always in agreement on what solution to take. Each person put in his own view. We were always able to move forward. Sometimes, when we disagreed, I remember that he let me go ahead even knowing that I was doing the wrong thing. I then realized my mistake and changed my opinion. He was right and let me realize (on my own) my own mistakes. This, also, helped me learn. I was no longer responsible to a boss who gave orders but to a person who helped me understand my mistakes. This type of management was completely new to me. I have to say that I appreciate it because it's helped me advance. Feeling confident gives you an even greater sense of responsibility . . . I think that if [the executive] had not had confidence in me, I would still be the consolidation assistant under a responsible person.

The CS concluded,

If your boss is confident in you, you owe it to him to make him right. You absolutely must succeed in order not to deceive him and in order to be proud of yourself . . . Today, I work with people on my team in the same way, conveying what I know to them and trying to give them their own sense of this responsibility.

This passage captures the subjective aspects of the CS's appropriation of personal responsibility, in particular, the dynamics whereby responsibility is not only given to the individual; more important, it must be *taken* by the individual ("He let me be the master of the game").

Logical Paths to Nonlogical Wholemaking: The Executive Assistant

The executive accepted the limits of formal organization, but he also wanted to integrate informal organization into his administrative practice. He engaged an employee whose function often crosses the informal-formal borderline: the executive assistant. The informal aspects of this job may include seemingly trivial tasks such as making coffee and planning parties. But executive assistants often execute vital functions such as protecting or gatekeeping for the executive and maintaining the office's formal and informal status, with morale implications for the entire organization. In this case, as the executive pointed out, the executive assistant's "lack of involvement in career competitions" facilitates this function. She is not an accountant and she does not aspire to become one.

The executive's analysis of how he and his assistant form a team shows how he integrates formal and informal organization and logical and nonlogical aspects.

The assistant is the single person who is most greatly in contact with the executive; and—major advantage—she has no other career interest that can be antagonistic with him. This enables her to have a relationship with him that can be a human relation, putting values—not just "technical" values—first for both him and for her. She is not an extension of my power but really a power entirely separate with whom I share the same vision. Without this, she would not have the group's confidence. Her power is connected to the fact that she understands the human changes in our organization—she listens, and people confide in her. She reflects the director's humanity. And, if he listens to her, she brings him back to earth, like Icarus.

He analyzed her position's nonlogical elements. Her discretion "permits her to keep a certain distance with regard to what she hears. It is primary in that she does not enter into daily conflicts in the organization, she holds herself back from this, and that's in the interest of the organization per se." She gains the director's confidence because of her "seriousness and trustworthiness in managing detail." Because of this, he avoids becoming overwhelmed by details and can devote himself to the larger goals of the organization.

He especially valued his assistant's particular and personal knowledge "of the historical experience of the enterprise." He wrote, "I appreciate her years of experience in the organization," especially her "knowledge of internal pre-existing powers." In this way, with her advice, he could do "the easier thing, which is to give technical instructions." Administratively, "she looks for ways to help me save time. She identifies matters that she can take care of, substituting herself for me in that she represents part of my power. She organizes meetings in my place, without my asking; but she knows my priorities and compares them to her analysis of the 'atmosphere of the department'."

He also emphasized the assistant's nonlogical knowledge of nonlogical phenomena: "At an instant, she has a sense of the temperature in the teams." He underlined, "This point is most important. Today's little problem becomes tomorrow's huge catastrophe. Applying this to people management, anything that the assistant feels is very important with regard to 'today's little problems' is also important to me." Divided among his ambition, the pressure of his own hierarchies, and the few privileged relations that he has with certain members of his team, the executive can lose his sense of the general atmosphere of his organization or neglect its more discreet members.

The assistant intermediates between the formal and the informal, serving not only as a literal go-between in passing messages from individuals to the executive but also bridging the social distance that some individuals feel in the hierarchy. Also, passing messages through her can help neutralize strong emotional content that might create misunderstandings or ill will. Transmitted through the assistant, the communication is easier for the director to say and for the employee to hear. "The first two times, the employee can feel that there is a difficulty and he can resolve it without a conflict being exposed openly. The employee saves face and the director does not have to assert formal control. But, the third time, the director can't hide anymore and must confront the person himself." In other words, the executive uses the communication channel to accommodate nonlogical and logical content and processes.

With the assistant's help, the executive assigned formal responsibility in a way that takes account of its informal dimensions. He asked her to track the status of "to do"s. He considers that this assignment includes using her personal discretion; it is up to her how to do it, and he does not always know what she hears or whether she conveys it to him completely. Likewise, the executive permits his assistant to know, and to keep to herself, "if a task is overdue, if a person has problems that he or she doesn't want to admit to the formal hierarchy, or if a person is putting ill will into his or her work." As another example, the executive told his assistant that a team member had suffered a death in the family "so that she [could] take this into account in her relations with him. And of course, I told her in confidence." The executive and the assistant leave undiscussed what "take into account" means. In another case, when the assistant learned that a team member was contemplating divorce, the executive and the assistant discussed the matter. "Considering the pressure that I put on this person in particular, she considered it important to tell me this so that we could figure out the best way to work together so that this person could get through this matter and this period of private life."

The executive also instituted an annual kickoff meeting in the early fall. The first year was "a failure" because it was run as "a monologue . . . by managers." But year by year, this situation improved. After the first kickoff, he asked his executive assistant to gather feedback from the day's experience. Individuals reported that they appreciated hearing from "the other person" in distribution or in production. They appreciated the meal that was provided. They also reported enjoying "a feeling of belonging to something greater than them[selves]." Concerning his own experience, the executive said, "People want first to feel their environment and then decide to participate or not in its goal. We might call it a shift from group feeling to institution readiness."

As stated above, the executive brought a new mood to the department. This element of organization is difficult to capture and impossible to control. But it captures exactly what Barnard meant by the nonlogical aspects of organization. The executive said he addressed this matter explicitly by bringing interns into the organization. He regarded them as "creative motors" and "learning sponges" because of the "learning desire" and "ambition" they brought to their work. He also said that the interns had a more independent point of view. The executive had a strict policy of not hiring former interns so accountants did not feel that their jobs were threatened by them.

We desperately needed young blood; the accountants were deeply caught up in their daily work and unable to modelize [in Lotus] their own environment. Also, they were very proud of themselves. The interns were not subordinates of permanent employees. Rather, they helped develop Lotus databases so the "old ones" could access the data and learn how to develop databases.

The interns made models of routines for the people in charge of those operations without concern for taking credit or control of them. The executive also thought that the interns thus allowed the accountants to preserve their professional pride. Instead of having to make excuses for not learning or using the system, they had practical resources that did not threaten their confidence or their position.

Recent Communications

In early 2010, the company hired a new CEO. The executive used the occasion to link the ongoing integration of his team to the change in top leadership. He explained, "I wanted to take advantage of this event to make an impression with this message. I am going to reinforce it now, and again and again, until the team's level meets the expectations." I had asked the executive if he ever wrote out his philosophy and shared it with his team. He answered that he felt his management philosophy showed in everything he did. Yet, in light of the case facts, this message to his team about the new CEO merits citation:

Here are the topics from today's meeting concerning the change in top management: Let's keep them in mind.

Externally, accounting's level is OK but we're at the "barely there" [level] in a few areas.

The general feeling at headquarters is that expectations will be raised for everyone: We're in the big time.

We need to get used to higher quality in the following ways: Respect meeting times, and if a task needs to get done for the meeting, it's done. Our new management expects us to work at this level. Be ready, because we don't know what's happening at headquarters.

Our role is to provide meaningful and good numbers. Our system allows us to step up on this. In my opinion, the keys are:

— Planning our actions and blocking out time in our agendas for planning

— Following up on action items

— Meeting deadlines

— Innovation and imagination to raise productivity and quality without incurring more costs

— PICK UP THE PHONE TO BE CLOSER TO THE SUBSIDIARIES AND OUR CONTACTS to clarify questions and give the right answers.

— Always get a confirmation of received mail before thinking that the matter has been sent to the other person.

— Don't say that a task is unresolved because it's someone else's fault. FIND CREATIVE SOLUTIONS OR RESOLVE THE PROBLEM AND TELL EVERYONE IT'S SOLVED BEFORE PEOPLE ASK ABOUT THE STATUS.

— Don't ask others a question whose answer takes very little time to find yourself.

As for the rest, no problem, our organization has already met a higher standard and the way will be shorter for us. But let's be sure of ourselves.

Throughout this research collaboration, the executive insisted that he was building an organization that could adapt in dynamic conditions. Thus, following Follett, he posits a "so-far integrated" organization always building more capacity to build itself.

After writing this chapter, I sent it to the executive for his review, and in particular so that he might comment on what was missing or underemphasized. Here is his reply:

I would emphasize three aspects which all are related to the time dimension which is crucial in my job and seems to me missing (or at least not enough taken in account) in the management articles that I read.

First, concerning the relation with the individuals who report to me: the author quoted "élan" as one of them. After reading that, everything seemed brighter. But, in the meantime, people's lives change. Our team is affected by a crisis in one person's life. The equilibrium can be so fragile. Also, when people get more involved in the organization, they ask for more rewards. Do they get what they were expecting? Not always; a manager cannot fully answer [every]one's dreams or expectations. I face the person at the end of the day. Just like that, the habits of day-to-day operations need a new start all over again.

Second, concerning the relation between the author and myself: it is an association lasting now over three years with a great deal of mutual respect: one sees what the other can bring to one's quest. We kept up the link without expecting immediate reward. Researchers have to produce articles during the year without having time to get deep into a new analysis which will take them far from the original highways of their field. The transfer of my experience has taken time. For example, I do not have the words to describe the integrated behavior which generates day-to-day decisions, which is the purpose of our "association." These decision processes are not taught and are not well described by theory. Hence it is a "one step forward, one step back" iteration that we have had together, and still have, in exploring new ways of studying management and organization.

Lastly, time is a swell, like the sea at the seaside—nice and calm but also dangerous and surreptitiously destroying a "stable" situation. As managers, we have a momentum to maintain, we have to always show the vision to the team. And this way, we generate an unstable situation. Research has to take this dynamic situation into account: the wording "all things being equal" does not fit this field of research: time, the passage of time, external impacts on one's individual behavior, [and] other stakeholders inside and outside the company affect the equilibrium that is the manager's responsibility to maintain and that is key to fulfilling his mission.

From my point of view, it is important to get researchers to think about how to cover these three aspects. External analysis without being "part of it" [provides] a too simplistic view. The practical constraint of research deadlines is also simplistic. A long-term collaboration between a researcher and a manager seems pretty rewarding. It can help managers and their peers by showing how their dynamic problems have been put into words—which we do not know how to do.

And, we all know that to put events in words is already a big step forward [in building] theories and find[ing] solutions. Barnard did a great thing there.

This chapter has shown how an executive's practices may be understood as putting the ideas of Follett and Barnard into action today. Their theories help him explain what he is doing, and his example makes the theory more understandable. However, because it is filtered through the executive co-author, the chapter does not present personal experience directly. Chapter 9 takes up this challenge.

CHAPTER 9

Integrating Education, Research, and Responsibility

Experimenting with Master's-Level Teaching

☽

Chapter 8 examined the executive function of inculcating personal responsibility in others. This chapter broadens the focus. It examines the managerial level and the development of personal responsibility in oneself as well as in others. Because it is based on a personal experiment and my own experience in classroom teaching, I have written it in the first person. I understand the student-teacher relation in formal education as the analogue of Barnard's dynamically relating executive-leader in formal organization. In this way, I offer a scientific contribution that formalizes the subjective and intersubjective microprocesses of dynamic relating. According to Follett and Barnard, the self-governing relation is the crux of all dynamic relating; the rest is "merely" a matter of scale. Reading Follett and Barnard will not lead to an understanding of this phenomenon; it must be experienced and learned organically. This chapter departs from this idea and method.

Follett interpreted the student-teacher relation as a particular form of dynamic relating. The teacher serves the student by "increas[ing] his freedom—his free range of activity and thought and his power of control." Teachers can only teach what they have learned themselves. "As the teacher has all his life been trying to integrate his own knowledge and experience, past and present, to organize them into an effective whole for the controlling of his life, so that is his duty to his student—to teach him how to transmute experience into power." In a "joint search for meanings," teacher and student make "an unbroken continuity between the life and understandings and aspirations of the teacher and the life and understandings and aspirations of the student" (Fox & Urwick, 1973: 304). This idea may sound vague; but in this case, the circumstances permitted me to experiment with it: I was asked to teach a course on narrative, a method of accounting for one's life experience (Linde, 1993), in a Master's program on entrepreneurship.

Preparing the course while immersed in reading Barnard and Follett, I considered how to translate their ideas into meaningful classroom lessons—for example, Follett's (1924) instruction to keep relating to the emerging situation. The improvisational nature of this instruction is discussed below. This chapter also takes up a secondary process, writing about one's own experience. Just before drafting this chapter, I had completed Chapter 7 on Barnard's social science, a process that facilitated my interpretation of Barnard's organic epistemology through my teaching experience, and vice versa. In particular, I had written about my experience of the microprocesses of the epistemology.

In Follett's science (Chapter 5), one conceives of an emerging totality with which one relates reciprocally. This is of course an imputation and a concept, so it entails the mind acting on itself. But the process has objective consequences when shared imputations are experienced as external phenomena acting on the individual. Organization is powerful objectively as one experiences it "acting back" on oneself, and even more so as one acts further on the acting back in one's ongoing relating. Thus, by integrating his work on both "The Notes" and *The Functions*, Barnard consciously observed that his physiology and habits changed organically and responsively—that is, unconsciously—as others imputed authority to him and as he accepted this imputation, which he then experienced as a physical burden coming from an outside entity. In this way, responsibility was not a thing or an externality but a relation, or "a relating" per Follett, like Barnard's description of organization itself ("a construction of the human mind applied to concrete events"). Barnard evidently experienced the "social power" of shared imputations—a simultaneous distinction and dissolution of duality because phenomena act on the self and are made by the self at one and the same time.

This microprocess is the key to dynamic relating. In my case, I believe it played out in the students' imputation of leadership to me and my relation to this imputation. I speak in Barnard's terms, in a context whereby a group sees itself as a whole and its members concur, consciously and/or unconsciously, that its formal leader merits the further attribution of informal leadership; that is: (1) she knows what she is doing; (2) she knows she cannot do what she must do without this imputation, which is in their hands; and (3) the people cannot be fooled (Barnard, 1968 [1938]: 281–82). The formal course evaluation confirmed this understanding:

all of the students gave the highest possible rating on a question about the teacher's dedication to learning. In short, following Barnard, I experienced the leadership imputation from the students and used the resulting organic experience of authority to delegate back to the students the responsibility that they had delegated to me. That is, they accepted my leadership, including the recognition that they were the source of authority, and they accepted the transfer of responsibility back to them, which they experienced as an exercise of their own personal agency. I experienced this as a freeing process; and I believe they did likewise.

There were other aspects of the teaching experience, outside my control, that encouraged dynamic relating. I was a visiting professor with little reputation preceding me. With an employment contract consisting of a four-day intensive seminar, I had few expectations. Indeed, my nearing retirement lent a culminating quality to the experience: if I was ever going to have a chance to understand dynamic relating in teaching, this was *it*.

Writing the syllabus six months before the start date, I had already imposed an organization on the course, which I called "Varieties of Narrative Entrepreneurship." The idea was to relate narrative theories and methods to entrepreneurship. Of course, narrative means many things and has various applications. Having been told that about twenty students would register, I assembled case studies that I had used before to show the relevance of narrative to venturing. These included storytelling to pitch a business idea and using genre analysis to decide what story to tell (O'Connor, 2002; 2004). I also wanted to convey a bigger idea that integrated narrative and entrepreneurship.

In the course description, I advanced the thesis that the simultaneous exercise of viewpoints of author, character, and reader enhances opportunity creation and exploitation. I organized narrative and entrepreneurship under a common moral code uniting entrepreneurship's pursuit of opportunity and narrative's ability to accommodate scope and depth (O'Connor, 2008). That is, one may consider a given narrative as a microcosm, a self-contained world where actors are acted upon and act. An expanded narrative includes the circumstances of the author's writing; a more expanded narrative recounts the reader's personal encounter, and the circumstances of that encounter, with the expanded narrative. Follett described this as a process of creating "enlarged circumferences" (Fox & Urwick, 1973: 325). In my research, I called it "embedded narrative" (O'Connor, 2000).

This view enhances entrepreneurial practice because it opens more opportunities for relating. Narrative moves from a literary/analytical to a developmental and exploratory activity. At one and the same time, it takes the student introspectively into his "own bent" and extrospectively into "the common life" and reflection on "how he can best make his contribution to the common life" (Fox & Urwick, 1973: 324).

In documents I sent to the university in advance, I described the course's purpose: to expand relational capacity and accommodate simultaneously the viewpoints of the narrator, the protagonist, and the reader, under the shared value of opportunity discovery and creation. To cultivate this view, I asked students to write their autobiographies, emphasizing the relationship between their professional projects and their life stories.

In addition, I organized the class on the principle of iteration. Students were to submit their autobiographies a month before class, present them orally in class, and redraft them as a final paper. Informally, the students would rework their autobiographies after hearing those of others. The iterative process would lead to substantive changes in the "same" viewpoint and "same" content in a short period of time. It would also make these changes, in themselves and others, apparent.

I anticipated that, because of the seminar's condensed format, the iterative process would heighten attention to the malleability of viewpoint and content in the personal sense (the definition of the first person in autobiography)) and in the practical or strategic sense (the definition of goals and milestones). The exercise was intended to make the two orientations relate more closely. It was also intended to collapse the duality between past and future: the seemingly closed "past" story could alter the open future story, and vice versa.

These viewpoint and content changes also heightened the students' and my own attention to the allocation of responsibility to themselves, others, and circumstances. In this way, the exercise helped relax the grip of logical processes in the classroom generally and with regard to a common practice in business programs particularly: students opt for a practical degree but use school to avoid or defer decision; and the experience of prolonging only adds more stress.

In their autobiographies, the students expressed concern about how to make the right career decision and avoid making the wrong decision. They seemed to feel overwhelmed. In choosing a literary passage that had made a strong impression on them, most selected one that focused on an uninitiated character's difficulty integrating into an oppressive world.

Follett's essay on the student-teacher relation captures many of the complex but key ideas and methods that I tried to incorporate into the course: "We tend to control our lives in proportion as we are able to organize our experience, for experience as mere happenings is of little use to us. Scattered bits, kaleidoscopic bits, have no force. The driving power of an organized experience is perhaps what the student needs most to learn." The teacher's function, then, "is to train the student to watch for meanings, to organize meanings, perhaps to create new meanings, and all with the aim of increasing his ability to live not only harmoniously but effectively with his fellows." The student should "also bear in mind his own part in creating the situation which he, as all of us, so often attributes to 'life,' that is, to a force wholly outside ourselves. The understanding of this truth tends greatly to enrich and to dignify our lives—the realization of our creative function, and that . . . through the acts of our everyday lives, the realization of our responsibility in a universe which is being created anew at every instant" (Fox & Urwick, 1973: 311–312).

Although eighteen people registered for the class, I received only seven autobiographies before the start of class. Gradually I realized this meant that only seven people would show up, but I did not think about the practical implications of the much smaller class size. The turning point occurred on the first day, when I came face to face with these seven people. After some preliminary remarks and an icebreaker in which students interviewed and introduced each other in pairs, I began delivering the morning lecture as planned.

I had distributed the six pages of lecture notes for day one in advance. The notes covered a lot of territory—interdisciplinary work in narrative and various ways that management and organization studies, and the entrepreneurship field particularly, had appropriated it. Without imposing Barnard's method of concentration (Chapter 7), I could lecture on these topics forever; therefore, when distributing the notes, I had asked students to select topics that particularly interested them for elaboration. But if they had indeed read the notes, the students did not express any such interests.

Hoping to stimulate discussion, I began going through the notes chronologically. This did not help. Within about ten minutes, I felt ridiculous. There was a mismatch between the formality that I had anticipated and thus imposed, or felt that I had to impose, and this unanticipated small-group situation. I also felt the deadening effects of my monologue on myself. I wondered how to get the students engaged.

At the mid-morning break, the students and I happened to walk together to the cafeteria, sit down at the same table, and talk through the entire break. The previous evening, a colleague had told me that teachers and students did not interact at breaks or lunch, so I was surprised by this. I cannot recall what we discussed during the break, but I picked up on the students' interest in my background. The quality of their listening and curiosity made an impression on me. I worried that they were putting me on a pedestal.

After the break, as I had not yet formally introduced myself to the students, I thought I could use the opportunity to go beyond introductions and get into the course content. This idea coincided with a comment made in the student introductions as well as with my impressions from the break. A student had said that he took the course because he found my autobiography interesting. The autobiography featured how I dealt with the problem of integrating business and the humanities, and more personally, of finding an institution or structured circumstance into which I could fit my unstructured desire. The students had expressed similar concerns in their autobiographies. I decided to narrate my autobiography in such a way as to explore integration as a universal dilemma and to demonstrate the power of narrative in this respect. More generally, I hoped to stimulate student interest by combining a personally engaging story with teaching to draw them in despite themselves and get them to take some initiative.

Revisiting the experience six months later, I would add another interpretation, following Barnard's discussion of how executives secure contributions from individuals in formal organization. Student interest, participation, and co-creating (taking personal responsibility for their individual experience and for the classroom experience generally) represent a sequence of higher-order contributions. I had asked for contributions at the outset, but the students were either not inclined or not ready to provide them. Another way to put this, emphasizing elements over which I had control: I had not done my part to win their contributions. Telling my own story was a crucial first step in this regard.

Since there were so few students, I could take my time, look each student in the eye, and feel that I was talking to particular individuals rather than to a "class." They appeared to be listening attentively. But when the lunch break began, one student approached me to say that he felt lost. He could not follow the points about narrative analysis and entrepreneurial opportunity. I reasoned that I had not integrated the story content with the narrative practices I hoped to demonstrate. The events were interesting, like most life stories, but the personal details were distracting and in fact detracted from the teachings on narrative. I then confided in the student. I told him that, wanting to take advantage of the fewer numbers and customize the course, I was changing plans but had not yet decided on a new plan. I revealed that I was not a prepared teacher and risked compromising my professionalism. Or/and, I showed that I gave higher priority to the students and the learning opportunity than to convenience or pride.

At the end of the day, my candor came back to haunt me. A student said, "There is no organization in this class." I had a Jekyll-and-Hyde reaction: lacking organization, I was not a good teacher. On the other hand, I told myself, if I was dynamically relating, then I had the best organization possible and had to persevere.

In response to the student who felt lost, I had decided to spend the lunch hour reworking my talk to demonstrate the relationship between narrative and entrepreneurial competencies. Since we had shared the morning break together, I told the students why I was not joining them for lunch. Three or four volunteered to bring me a sandwich. I think they appreciated my seriousness. Most of them had overheard the conversation between the student and me—the criticism, my thanks, and my promise to help.

Preparing new teaching notes, I thought back on the students' autobiographies: they had fallen into one of two extremes, either focusing very clearly on the short term or covering a long chronology but losing focus and clarity. My problem was to show them how to expand their view without compromising on specifics. I took a case-study approach and selected the Barnardian dilemma of individualism versus collectivism, the case of Barnard himself, and my personal relation to this dilemma and case.

It was not a move I felt uncomfortable with, because I have long spoken publicly of my project to integrate business and the humanities and specifically to achieve a tenured position in a business school with my humanities Ph.D. (O'Connor et al., 1995). To develop the plot, I singled out a few milestone events along the way. Detailing each one, I juxtaposed what I knew then versus what I learned later and what I realized spontaneously while telling the narrative in real time. I thus brought out narrative's attribute of non-closure and how narrative choice affects the retrospective and prospective perception of opportunity. The presentation also helped balance the academic bias toward logical processes and content by integrating personal responsibility, as noted earlier. To demonstrate these rather complex points, I reproduce my narrative in the next section.

AUTOBIOGRAPHICAL NARRATIVE

Having done graduate work in literature and in business, in separate programs, I sought a professional position that took advantage of both in equal measure, and not only in terms of content but also in terms of status. That is, I wished not to be looked down upon but to be seen as a resource because of my humanities degree. (At that time, the joke about taxi-driving humanities Ph.D.'s. was a cliché.) For several years, I worked in what I felt to be an unsatisfactory integration of business and the humanities: so-called management communication programs (MCPs), which teach public speaking and "business writing." Getting this work was relatively easy, even at the top-ranked business school that hired me. MCPs, especially in high-status MBA programs, help socialize students, particularly foreign students. This is crucial for classroom performance; some professors weigh participation as heavily as 50 percent. Students whose educational backgrounds emphasize passive learning not only experience discomfort but also are academically and socially penalized.

This popular concept of humanities-business integration held me back from more creative interpretations, but it also provided valuable professional experience. It helped me overcome the inferiority that I often felt in status-conscious environments, especially elite academic and business circles. I did not realize it then, but having a top-ranked business school on my résumé would help me establish credibility elsewhere for the rest of my career. At the time, though, I grew increasingly impatient, even angry, with the MCP's disconnect between artifice and substance. That is, I was hired to help students with their "business communication." This meant public speaking understood as a technique honed through videotaping, playback, and feedback. This context-free approach did not come close to engaging what I understood, or vaguely understood, as the power of the humanities—not that I knew what this meant in a business-school context; but I knew that the MCP, which I increasingly regarded as a finishing school for MBAs, was not it.

At the urging of a colleague, I began attending professional conferences and discovered the organizational culture movement, which took up semiotics, metaphor, and narrative, among other literary concepts. It was a Eureka moment: my literature background was useful in organization studies! Also, the "linguistic turn" and postmodernism had hit the prestigious Academy of Management, particularly its avant-garde Organization Theory division. They found my Ph.D. in literature "cool." Seriously, I thrived on the respect of those who appreciated my training in literary theory and analysis. I positioned myself as a "qualitative researcher," and respectable journals published my research. I did not, however, reach my professional goal of landing a tenure-track job but remained a lowly lecturer. I learned, again after the fact, that qualitative research was considered inferior and peripheral by the mainstream academy. For the most part, only tenured professors engaged in it. So if I really was integrating, it was at the least legitimate ring of the circle. What I thought was a solution only unveiled another layer of the problem. I remained at the periphery, not the center. This raised a new question: What was the center, and what did being there entail?

At one of my first invitations to present a paper at what I perceived as a serious academic seminar, an economics professor whom I respected criticized my research for emphasizing textual over contextual analysis (O'Connor, 1996). I had to agree with him: just like the MCP, I was mechanically "applying" close-reading techniques from my humanities training for a different discipline and situation. I vowed to integrate text and context, words and action. Since I had been analyzing classical management texts, I began by reading their authors' biographies. These led me to references on the circumstances in which they wrote. There were so many that I began taking a suitcase instead of a backpack to the library.

Researching the life and times of Elton Mayo, I came upon a perplexing finding. Elton Mayo was called a humanist by organization scholars. But the Mayo I observed was the antithesis of humanism because of his separateness. More important, I was baffled that scholars called him a humanist in the first place and that this reputation endured in the literature. This led me to wonder more about the field itself and the kind of field in which this would occur. I connected one data point to another until I had the Harvard-based research for Chapter 4.

For three years, this quest took me further into the history of business schools and management thought. I also achieved an important professional milestone: my paper on Harvard Business School's mutual institutionalization with foundations and corporate CEOs won Best Paper at the Academy of Management and was published in a top-tier journal as well as in a compendium of leading research in organization studies (O'Connor, 1999a; O'Connor 1999b; Clegg, 2002). I received a job offer for a position with tenure, which I declined for personal reasons. But I was finally getting some purchase on the meaning of integrating business and the humanities and on finding or making a place for myself in the field of management and organization. I told colleagues that although the first person did not appear in the paper, it was the most personal thing I had ever written because it helped me explain my experience to myself.

Many doors opened for me, and they are still opening. This power acted back on me just as Follett and Barnard stated. Understanding that I had made a contribution just by following a natural intellectual process, I stopped orienting myself according to the idea of center or periphery and followed the momentum of the ideas. The object was not to fit into the field but to understand the obstacles to my doing so. In Barnard's terms, this would produce new knowledge about the field because of the original relation—intimate, interested, and habitual—that I brought to the research.

INTEGRATING FOLLETT AND BARNARD

Concluding my narrative, I took the students into real time: my research on Follett and Barnard, and for this book. After all, these two protagonists had provided the foundations supporting everything I was doing, through their examples and their theory backed by their life experience. I told the students about Barnard's dilemma of individualism and collectivism. I explained that, for him, this was a philosophical and practical problem, as well as a personal and arguably universal one.

We studied the passage from his 1934 commencement address, in which he spoke of his youthful individualism and shock upon joining the telephone organization. Each student took one paragraph at a time and read it aloud. I filled the students in on his intellectual biography. They seemed interested and wanted to know more. They asked why they had never heard of Barnard. This led me to say more about this book and my continuing trajectory.

This discussion took us to the end of the first day, Tuesday. Students turned in their second pre-assignment, in which I had asked them to quote and discuss a literary passage of their choice "that has made a strong and lasting impression" on them. I also asked for feedback on the day. One student said that he felt there had been too much monologue and not enough interaction. Several others nodded. I agreed.

That night, I read the assignments they had submitted. They had chosen some beautiful passages, most of which were new to me, and discussed them insightfully. I resolved to set aside class time on Friday so the students could share the fruits of this exercise with one another. The next day, Wednesday, I began by asking the class to form two groups and develop a wish-list for the course. After forty-five minutes of discussion, they had identified about a dozen topics. During the first break, I put the topics into four categories: learning about contexts; finding and creating opportunities; using conflict creatively; and storytelling with impact. I responded substantively to each point, with examples from my autobiography and from my research on Barnard and Follett. Then I asked the students to iterate the wish-lists one more time. I used the same approach to address their remaining concerns.

At the end of the day, wrapping up, I gave the students their opportunity: the next day, each person would have an hour to use as he or she wished. I suggested that they relate a narrative that had personal interest for them. I proposed to devote Friday, the final day, to the literary passages, with each student again having one hour. Beyond that, I did not give further instruction except to one student who said he could not decide what to present. He had chosen a topic but did not think it would interest the others. I told him that what mattered was that the topic interested *him*. He nodded and said he would not worry further.

The next two days took on a momentum of their own. Until then, I could not recall ever teaching without feeling that I was responsible for everything, or almost everything. This experience was the opposite. The students did the heavy lifting, or what I have typically experienced as that. Each speaker had the floor, or took charge of it, or was given charge of it. In the discussion, the floor belonged to everyone. With the exception of the student who had been worried about his topic—whose narrative left me suspecting that he had changed his mind from the day before, a hunch that he confirmed—my impression was that presenters spoke candidly about what was on their minds and the others listened and commented in kind. Most of the students commented on one another's presentations.

I believe that my own comments worked analytically like a close reading and organically like advice grounded in personal experience. For example, as one student related his autobiography, it came across to me as a series of unrelated fragments. Also, each fragment ended with the statement that he had abandoned that path because he "did not like it." The narrative also showed that this student was academically accomplished, with an outstanding education and recommendations. After each one of his internships, he had received a job offer. His tuition was paid by a government scholarship that funded future leaders.

When no one in class commented on this recurring pattern in the narrative, I told the student that I missed the idea of a thread or organizing principle in the autobiography. I told him that he would be good at anything he chose to do and that inevitably he would run into unpleasantness on any path. This did not mean he had chosen the wrong path but that on any path he would face tests that he could meet in various ways.

Barnard's dismantling of the rationality criterion and particularly his dismantling of the idea of correct decision (see Chapter 7) applies perfectly in this case. The appropriateness criterion says that effective action has to do with unforeseeable acts that happen after one makes a decision. The point was not to tell the student what to do, but to provide the alternative logic of appropriateness that applies to the realm of action, as opposed to science and logic.

Each exchange was of course personal; but I did not sense much awkwardness in the room. Because all of the students were working in a second language, however, they had some obvious difficulty putting words to experiences and feelings. In retrospect, I imagine that for a few students the class was disorienting, to say the least. I respected them for participating in the experiment.

For the literary passages on Friday, I sat back and enjoyed the ride. Each presenter distributed a copy of his text, read it aloud, and discussed it. Most of the students asked questions about the choice of text and what impressed the presenter about it. Naturally, some answers were more revealing than others. The exercise was particularly rich for me because I was familiar with their autobiographies (which remained confidential between each student and me).

I will give one example. One student came from a country whose regimentation and collectivism he condemned. For his literary work, he chose a video clip from the film "The Shawshank Redemption." In it, inmates sit together at mealtime, discussing music, harmonica-playing, and hope. They debate whether, in prison, hope is necessary or fatal. The student mentioned that he watched the film often. I asked how often. He said about twenty times a month, but only certain scenes. He used the film to strengthen his resolve to stay outside the regimentation of his home culture. From his autobiography, I recalled that he had received what he considered to be an important part of his education abroad, in a culture very different from his own. He expressed appreciation for the entrepreneurial economic life of his host country. He was also concerned about his family and his obligation to make a life for himself and for them in his home country. He also observed that his host country presented legal and social barriers to integrating foreigners. I told him that he might have to consider himself as having more than one home in the course of his life.

At the beginning of this chapter, I described how the leadership of the class went from the students to me, and from me back to the students. Ultimately, the course was led by everyone, by all of us as peer educators. This was summed up by the student who brought the most life experience to the class. In fact, upon reading his autobiography, I feared I had nothing to teach him. He was professionally accomplished, having started a few companies; and he was running two when he registered for the seminar. For his Thursday narrative, he told the class he would present a life experience that taught him something and that he hoped would benefit them. When he finished, only a few students commented or asked questions. It was the end of the day and we were tired, but I think the quiet had to do with the closure of his narrative and narration. I asked him if we might be of any help or use to him. He answered that every person in the class had given something to him. (He later told a program administrator that it was the most valuable course he had ever taken.)

In his narrative, he talked about one of his first work experiences. Most of the time he had sat at his desk doing the minimum amount of work he thought necessary. He also said that he despised the company's business, which was advertising. He remarked that he never learned the names of some of the people with whom he worked routinely. He was asked to leave within a few months. In his last conversation there, his employer advised him to stop wasting his life and grow up—to take seriously his choice about what to do, to choose what he wanted to do, and do it. The student had taken the advice; and this showed in his curriculum vitae as well as in his manner of listening and commenting intently on each student's narrative. In Barnard's sense, I believe that the discussions made an impression on him, and that he *let* them make an impression upon him.

The literary passage exercise worked in the opposite way from the autobiography: it asked students to react to a text and then explain their reaction in light of their biographies. Specifically, I had asked students to select a passage that had made "a strong and lasting impression," that is, a physical reaction to something that resonates. Subsequent reflection and discussion bring out more facets of the dynamic between the prompt and what it provokes.

I noticed that as students exchanged points of view and asked the presenter for further interpretation, the conversation took on greater intensity. There was something more important, deeper, to be said. For example, one student selected the passage from *The Catcher in the Rye* in which the narrator, Holden Caulfield, discusses his deceased brother. At first, the student mentioned the writing and Salinger's deft transition from discussing a baseball glove to talking about the brother's personality. Then he emphasized how moving the excerpt was. There was more conversation. Finally he said something that I felt to be much more intimate: the passage explained Holden's breaking all the windows in the garage and his parents' sending him to psychoanalysis. Salinger's text reads: "It was a very stupid thing to do, I'll admit, but I hardly didn't even know I was doing it, and you [the reader] didn't know Allie." The passage does not explain Holden's action but puts it in a circumference that includes his love and his loss. The student said that the passage helped him understand that we only see others on the surface and have no idea of the depth that lies beneath.

In relating my autobiography to the students, I said that I had failed to reach my formal goal and considered myself a professional failure. Yet I was standing at the front of the room, teaching graduate students in a respected institution. I was a formal and informal leader. And as stated earlier, I believe I earned their respect and that their actions and the formal evaluation demonstrated this. The paradox in itself communicated something important.

Later, after I told a colleague about this, he said he did not accept my calling myself a failure. He said that word was too strong. But, as I insisted, it is literally true. In retrospect, I think that my perhaps overly dramatic example gave the students pause to reflect on the imputations that one assigns to failure not as a past deed but as an ongoing work in progress or even "accomplishment."

ONE STUDENT'S FINAL PAPER

To convey the impact of this course on the students, particularly regarding personal responsibility, I close this chapter with the example of one individual and his final paper. In his first draft, he indicated an intense interest—he called it an "obsession"—with computer technologies. He also showed an interest in business. Instead of entering a technical program, he chose to study business administration because it was less narrow. While in school, he joined the university's information technology group. He thrived there, spending more time on IT projects than on class assignments. Eventually he reached a limit: "I could not profit, as I had reached the same level of knowledge as my leader." He started a one-person Web consulting business. The first draft of his narrative ended with a statement about enjoying the work and especially the work-school balance.

When presenting the narrative orally in class, he said he had hesitated to start a company because of the risks entailed. His friends in banking had said they could find positions for him in their firms, and he implied that these positions were more secure than a startup. During the discussion, I pointed out that he was assuming that working for a bank entailed little or no risk. At the time, the full magnitude of the financial crisis that began in 2008 was beginning to be felt, so the comment made an impression.

In the final version of his narrative, he made several changes. He shifted his emphasis from the work-school balance to the project to build a business from a one-person to a larger company. Also, he identified a strategic opportunity that would increase the scope of the business. (To include his narrative in this book, he deleted the confidential details.) Finally, he integrated, and continues to integrate, the many social structures that support his business idea. For example, as he notes below, I encouraged him to keep the good will of his friends in banking and consult with them about raising capital, providing beta test sites, and building a clientele.

The narrative exercise helps desire take form, if "only" in language. This student's autobiography had already illustrated this point. Starting informally at a young age, first through self-teaching and then more concretely in part-time employment and in his side business, he pursued his strong interest in computers. What would be the next and larger expression of his desire? It would be full time. It would involve others. It would take institutional form: a formal organization in Barnard's terms—with a purpose sufficiently strong, and with executive leaders sufficiently strong, to win the confidence of investors, partners, and prospective customers and build from there. Writing the narrative helped the student to think in this more expansive way. Specifically, he refers to an exercise in which he explored "upcoming mega trends in business, society, economy, and technology." The student does not provide his analysis, but it was obviously fruitful. It is also exactly what Follett meant by "enlarged circumferences" for weaving the "individual bent" and "the common life."

An Entrepreneurial Narrative

The following is the full text of the autobiography of the student discussed above.

Context: In the first draft of my autobiography and during my narrative presentation in class, I pointed out my strong, enduring interest in computer science, especially Internet technologies. Over the past ten years, I taught myself how to create graphics and program websites. I also taught myself several programming languages and am proud to say that I know more about this than several of my friends who have taken advanced courses in information technology. I also have excellent work experience, at the Institute of Information Management at [my university], where I worked on the Web development team. I learned much about databases, server architectures, and IBM platforms. The manager gradually delegated more advanced projects to me and eventually trusted me with the most challenging ones. I also began to understand the importance of organizing projects. The project management methods I use now in all my Web projects come from my experience at the Institute. A clear project timeline is crucial because projects usually take longer than expected. I believe this has to do with the complexity of such projects as well as the special requests that emerge over time.

There is another event which encouraged me to become an entrepreneur. My ex-girlfriend's father is the owner and founder of an IT company with about thirty employees. He told me that 100 percent commitment, trust in oneself—through the bad times—and a broad social network are the three essential requirements for business success. Although he had a tough life at the beginning, he eventually became very successful. His inspiration and the way he lived his life encouraged me to take this path.

Presently, I have enough work to operate on a steady scale, with one big project every month. The Internet has huge potential. With more than 1.6 billion people online, no company can allow itself to step back from this opportunity. An online store may be a good solution for some, but not for others. I like the diversity of the work. It ranges from giving advice, like a consultant, to providing all the services that go with building and maintaining a Web presence. By setting up websites, I get in touch with people and businesses with which I am quite unfamiliar. The different perspectives are exciting and I learn much from every project. Educating the customer about how new technology can create new business, and tailoring a Web presence to his or her particular needs, is personally satisfying. The idea of adding value and expanding my horizons is vital to me. I like the creative side of my job, resulting in individual, unique websites that make an impression on people and stick in their memories. This is an extraordinary way to express myself. My websites are being viewed by thousands of people and I love the positive feedback I get from people I work for, friends as well as people I did not know before. In addition, I like being self-employed: nobody tells me what to do or when to do it. This independence is very important to me.

Of course, I have to make money. But the market size is immense, and this opportunity is not going away soon and will only get bigger. Moreover, companies have to update their Web presence every few years. I do compete with big professional Web agencies, but people like a direct, personal contact and are also willing to pay a premium as soon as they understand the value I can create for them through high-quality applications. I enjoy sharing my knowledge with interested people who are not always familiar with the latest technology. I give workshops to inform customers about the new capabilities that will be most beneficial to them. This work is also satisfying, especially when people say that the lectures are insightful and helpful, which they often do.

Emerging Events: During our class, on Wednesday, you asked us to give a short narrative about our business opportunity the following day. That evening, I traveled home by train (a forty-five-minute trip) and thought about what I could present. I was confused at first, because I had never taken a long-term view, but had focused solely on the opportunity that I had already envisioned. It was only from your general comments on our first assignment that I noticed that I had stopped my narrative at the present time and did not provide any long-term outlook. I asked myself what would be my capacity to act and make a difference in the future. Could I find a real business opportunity that would be new? Or would I end up creating websites my whole life? I thought that in the long run creating websites might become boring. I thought about my abilities and the coming megatrends in business, economy, society, and technology.

At first this was hard, and I stared at the blank page. But eventually I came up with several fascinating IT ideas and almost forgot to get off the train at my station. [Author's comment: These ideas have been deleted for confidentiality.] The following day, I presented my existing business opportunity (creating websites) and outlined some of the ideas I came up with the evening before. You enforced my belief that I should stick to IT, because even if I was now a professional, I had started and stayed on this path because I love these modern technologies. I took your advice and decided that I would finish my Master's in banking and finance. However, I also put more attention on developing the business opportunity and on my desire to be an entrepreneur. I also profited much from the insights that [another student] gave us in his presentation on the startup company he wrote his Master's thesis about.

From the excerpts of Chester Barnard's texts we read during class, I realized that I would not be able to develop my business idea without the help of other people. Barnard speaks about collectivism, organizations, and social interrelationships. He also talks about individualism and how he thought in his early years that this would be the source for making progress but altered his view after working in an organization.

Fortunately, one week earlier, I had arranged to go to a bar in the evening of the last day of our course (Friday) with Felix, a colleague from the Institute. I initially did not intend to approach him with my business idea, but then I thought that it would be wise to do so.

I told him about the course you had been giving and that it was the best course I had ever taken at the university. I introduced my business idea to him and explained that this endeavor could be seen as an emerging narrative, which would be embedded in a larger context. He was very excited about my concept; and he liked my enthusiasm and commitment to realizing the idea. Furthermore, Felix told me that his father was the founder and CEO of a technology company with over 250 employees and that it was also his own intention to become an entrepreneur one day but that he had not yet come up with a feasible idea. It became clear that he could be my business partner.

The next day, Felix called his father, who is not very familiar with IT, and explained the concept. His father became our business angel and generously gave us an initial capital of over €50,000 (around $63,000). We are carefully investing the capital. In the meantime we are also working to raise more capital.

A friend of mine who works in venture capital told me that investors usually get very nervous and want to see progress every few months. In our case, we can take the necessary time to develop the software for a stable release. This gives us a first-mover advantage as well as several months to develop know-how and programming advances.

During the course, you said that sometimes we have to start going and proceed until we are finished or cannot go any further and the time comes to start again with another idea. We made this one of our maxims, and we meet every Thursday to keep driving our idea. In addition, I set up a secure online collaboration platform where we share documents and important information about rival ideas. It is a valuable tool because we can access it from any computer with Internet access.

We have written a business plan by employing a template Felix received in a course on IT startups. We use it as a guideline for ourselves as well as to raise capital. We are also working with a lawyer, a relative of Felix's, to get legal advice. We introduced our business idea to him and asked for his feedback. He was very excited and encouraged us to proceed.

We both think that it is very important to communicate with other people and hear their opinions. However, we must also protect our idea. On the technical side (mostly my job), we have made contacts with IT professionals in India through Felix's father. We are considering outsourcing some of the software development. The costs of developing such software in a European country are relatively high compared to outsourcing. However, we have to consider that the quality of externally developed software could be much lower and may need additional work to improve it.

In addition, I have studied the relevant technological issues that could hinder the project. We have also prioritized the features to be implemented in the first versus later releases. We have developed a marketing plan to get the word out and create a positive impression. We have evaluated the initial market potential and calculated several potential growth scenarios. After all this planning, the most important thing we have learned is to have solid software from the beginning because negative word-of-mouth could destroy the business. We also decided that we should focus on the EU market. If we are successful there, then we will expand.

We are looking into potential partners. Felix and his family have a broad social network and know many people in corporate marketing and IT departments.

Outlook: After the exams next week, we will visit Felix's father in Germany and discuss the next steps which have to be taken. Felix originally intended to do an internship in the summer, but now we will both devote ourselves to this opportunity.

It is interesting that Felix asked his mentor, a former Goldman Sachs analyst currently working at a large bank, whether it would be bad for his career record to have "wasted" time with an unsuccessful business idea. She replied that entrepreneurial effort would be regarded as positive because only a few people would be courageous enough to take the effort.

We are very ambitious, and our goal is to develop the software by September 2010. We know that it will be a very hard job and that major problems could arise during development. From experience, I well know that IT projects are very hard to plan and almost always take much longer than initially expected. We have identified the difficulties that could arise and added some time to our estimate. Although we have received the capital without any obligation, it is our (or at least my personal) responsibility to put in 100 percent effort to succeed. Not only will we create value for ourselves, but also our investor-partners will profit from the business. Also, customers profit from simplified and faster processes and other functions that help them do business. I am looking forward to exciting, adventurous, and work-intensive months.

Your course clearly opened my eyes to new possibilities that I could not have imagined before. I had always really enjoyed IT, but I was too narrowly focused on creating websites. You showed us that essentially our whole life is a story and that we can take the necessary actions as authors to influence it in the direction we want. Also during the course, I recaptured a vital interest in literature. For years I thought that literature would be a waste of time or an amusing distraction. I experienced that I can learn much from literature and that it is superior to any theory I have ever studied because it allows more complex structures.

Reflection on the course: At the beginning of the course, I thought that I had made a mistake by taking this class because we were so few, and you gave me the impression that the course was not very well organized. I definitely prefer to act, learn, and work in a structured, clear way with predefined objectives. However, drawing from my life experience, I decided not to rely on my first judgment and therefore came back to your class on the second day. Looking back, I am glad to have not missed the opportunity to be a student in your course, which would have been one of the biggest mistakes I have ever made (though of course I would never have known that) because it was the best course I have ever taken.

I support this with three arguments. First and most important, through your sharing of your own life experience and the paths you have chosen (and not chosen), I gained knowledge that is very helpful for my own life. I learned that I can "write" my own life by creating an individual identity. In contrast, all the other courses I have taken have tried to teach me some theory or knowledge that will become unimportant as time goes on.

Second, through your intellectual ability to redesign the course (during the course!), you took the responsibility and managed to address the individual needs of all students. This is very unusual for teachers, in my opinion, because they usually do not care much about the students and just want to "distribute" the contents of their lectures. You gave me guidance on my business opportunity and encouraged me to keep going.

Third, you were able to create an inspiring, unique, and very personal atmosphere that created a lot of trust among the participants. I learned from you but also from every other member of the class; and interestingly, this did not end after the course was over. I will never forget the course, the advice and vital discussions, and the people who were in it.

The class described in this chapter is not a typical offering. But its core idea and method could easily be used in any course and in the life planning of which adult business education is a part. In essence, through narrative exercises, students interpret their formal education as an opportunity in their ongoing trajectory of developing themselves and making their way in life.

Business school students already write essays and present letters of recommendation as part of the admissions process. They discuss their career trajectories, their proven experience in responsible positions, and how they plan to use their business degree. However, the essays are for the most part ignored once students are admitted. The experience of this course suggests that autobiographical and opportunity-defining narratives could contribute much to integrating personal responsibility and formal education. The exercise could be used in individual courses as well as orientations, mid-term retreats, and final papers or exams. Narrative approaches accommodate the introspective and intersubjective processes of self-government. In management education and science, these processes must no longer remain eccentric and stigmatized. In fact, they must be as fully integrated as possible without violating privacy or doing harm. Chapter 10 takes up this challenge.

Conclusion and Solution

Integrating the Knowledge Traditions and Building a Science of Management

♉
.

In this chapter, I use Follett and Barnard to evaluate the prospects for a science of management, which understands integration per se and particularly the processes by which it creates new value(s) in dynamic conditions. This science posits the creative construct of a "whole," such as a city (Follett) or organization (Barnard), beginning with one individual, following the examples of Follett and Barnard. The elements—citizens, members—relate to the whole as interdependent parts and as autonomous or "sovereign" (Follett) entities. In both respects and at the same time, the elements find and/or create value(s) in these relations or "relatings" (Follett). As more elements relate more closely, they and the whole realize greater value(s).

Management science is distinguished from all other sciences by its concept of a superstructure in which science itself is understood as one of many autonomy-seeking entities relating interdependently with other institutions. In addition, this science's reach extends to the subjective processes by which individuals, such as scientists, cooperate to endow constructs, such as disciplines, with value(s). This scope and depth take management science far beyond the present boundaries of institutionalized science.

Follett theorized that, in dynamic conditions, institutions pursue autonomy amid interdependence. Barnard explained that they do so by creating artificial boundaries and convenient fictions. Follett showed that relating itself is dynamic: institutions lean either to excess centrifugal relating and become esoteric or to excess centripetal relating and become subsumed by another entity. Also, conditions may favor institutions' moving closer to or away from one another. However, in integrative logic, separating is a way of relating. This point is particularly salient in the research university, which assembled institutions that developed independently of one another for centuries.

Follett and Barnard wrote in conditions when science was freeing itself from the confines of amateurs and collegians. It gained autonomy, even dominance. If the Ph.D. measures position in the knowledge order, then science overturned the classical order in less than a half-century. But this remarkable accomplishment is taken for granted today. In fact, the college and the theological seminary had a stranglehold on higher education for centuries. Opening the new era, William Rainey Harper declared that the college ruined as many minds as it cultivated. What was at stake for Harper was not the battle between the college and science, but that between a smaller and a larger mind and between restrained and unrestrained conditions for developing the mind. Like Follett and Barnard, he understood that science must advance by creating continuously freeing conditions for the growth of knowledge. However, he did not develop a science to understand how the institution of science could do this. Follett's and Barnard's management science explains that professional science grew by emphasizing autonomy. It broke with other institutions and exaggerated its differences with them.

Part I described how the research university brought together four knowledge traditions: classical paideia/humanitas as institutionalized in the college; science as institutionalized in the amateur; occupational training as institutionalized in the guild; and the School of Opportunity (SOO) as institutionalized in the individual. To co-assemble, however, is not to integrate. Integration means relating in ways that create new value and values. The university did this only partially. Basic and applied science related reciprocally and gained more separate and combined value. Basic science became more valuable as it was applied; and applications brought new problems for basic science to solve. Occupations elevated their status to professions by relating to basic science. The tool of formal organization took applied science to the further "application" of going to market and routinizing the process of doing so.

However, while the synergy between basic and applied science and the new whole created value, the opposite occurred in the paideia/humanitas and SOO traditions. The former was associated with the old in general and with a declining social order in particular. It also was seen as retarding the new through its values of preservation and passive transmission. In seeking autonomy from the traditional order, the integrating research university exaggerated that order's deficiencies. It devalued the paideia/humanitas tradition by subordinating it to the research and graduate school as pre-professional education. It established

an elite order oriented around the natural and physical sciences, esoteric methods, and the logic of discovery. Prestigious thought schools
and five-star journals organized accordingly. The high order needed a
low order. The SOO, embodied in University Extension, took this rank
because it opened to the general public and organized on their terms.
Extension also served entry-level jobs and the positions far down on
the basic–applied science food chain, such as those perceived as merely
administering organizational routines.

Professional science generally, and the business school in the research
university specifically, have achieved the necessary status in the academy
and in industry to create new knowledge by integrating the four traditions, in particular, integrating paideia/humanitas and the SOO into the
knowledge institutions. The business school has laid the groundwork
for doing this by using the logic of these two devalued traditions for
admissions and membership purposes. However, it has not used them
scientifically, for new knowledge creation. That is, the business school
recognizes individuals for proven responsibility in formal organization
specifically. In some cases, such as during the postwar economic recovery, it has weighed responsibility as much as, if not more than, formal
education.

The responsibility requirement is manifest in regular MBA programs
through the requirement that applicants have "management experience"
and present letters of recommendation to that effect. The Executive
MBA program introduces an even higher standard: individuals continue
to execute responsibility in their organizations while pursuing an advanced degree for two years. That is, following Barnard, individuals are
in the experimental condition of integrating personal responsibility in
formal organization and in scholarship per a high standard. They pursue
knowledge for governance at the new level afforded by the EMBA; they
exercise personal responsibility in the formal organization and in the
research university simultaneously. This is an institutional innovation
that enables the systematic pursuit of knowledge per the prototypes of
Follett and Barnard.

The executive-scholar bridges the gap between the formal institutions
that exclude organic knowledge and the individual who generates it. *The
institution of the executive-scholar* will contribute to knowledge institutions to the extent that it, too, becomes an autonomous and interdependent institution. At this time, it remains a fledgling institution requiring
more formal and informal organization. Informally, academics, executives, and society at large must cultivate the value that prizes knowledge
of management. They must also appreciate the solid foundations and
fledgling status of management knowledge. This book cultivates that

value and codifies that knowledge, but it is only one step. Formally, individuals must organize themselves individually and collectively with the purpose of building a science of management.

Following the example of this book, individual researchers, working independently, have the opportunity to build a science of management. However, for this research to proceed, others must recognize its value. Reputation based on publications in top-ranked journals is the currency of academe. This status ripples out into industry, whose specialists enjoy status through their ties to ranked universities. This dynamic could further a science of management. That is, university governing bodies have placed journals such as *Administrative Science Quarterly*, the *Academy of Management Journal*, and others in the top ranks. Like the business school and management academy generally, these publications derive their academic weight from connections to the academic disciplines. Yet because of their status, these journals could be the medium for launching and driving a discipline of management if the editorial boards were so inclined. This idea essentially proposes a top-down strategy based on the academic-leadership status of a select few journals, institutions, and individuals. It places confidence in the status quo and looks to academic leaders to function as leaders in the broader sense, per Follett's and Barnard's examples.

Equally important is the content of the articles published in these journals. There is widespread ignorance of Follett and Barnard, and this book only begins to reintroduce them. Matters of text availability and interpretation are not trivial. Many of Follett's most important writings remain unpublished or out of print. The same holds for Barnard. Both authors merit critical editions with thick contextualization, including historical, institutional, and biographical data, of their complete works. Follett's biography is done, but Barnard's is not. Because of the difficulty of Barnard's writing, because he understood his project as building a new discipline and new language supporting it, his texts in particular merit close reading and analysis by numerous scholars whose interpretations will bring out the scope and depth of his thought.

This is to say nothing of the prospects for utilizing the work of Follett and Barnard in management.Chapters 8 and 9 are highly exploratory attempts at best. The field needs studies that depart from the premises of Follett and Barnard on the definition of management, and studies that use their integrative method, linking self-governing, society-building, and science. More difficult to describe, but also necessary, are studies that draw from their intellectual, moral, and aesthetic sensibilities and from the ideas and work of readers inculcated in these sensibilities.

Further studies following directly on this book's argument would be helpful, particularly Barnard's discussion of the organization of knowledge (Wolf, 1995a). Barnard finds an opportunity to study management not only as a new field but also as a case study of the reorganization of knowledge that corrects for an overemphasis on specialist logics. In particular, the knowledge-action epistemology demands basic interpretation—it is a most difficult text—as well as attention to potential applications (see Wolf, 1995a; and Chapter 7 in this volume).

ORGANIZED INITIATIVES

The executive-scholar represents a new institution that remains virtually untapped for new knowledge creation. Like Follett and Barnard, EMBAs and working MBAs engage in individually self-directed, but institutionally undirected, experiments that integrate scholarship and responsibility. A promising path for building a discipline of management would integrate the executive-scholar and the manager-academic. Managers and executives enter MBA programs with agendas for their own and their organizations' development. How they integrate their school and work experiences is unknown. How they use their scholarship in governing themselves and in executing their responsibilities in formal organization is also unknown—a subject for course papers perhaps, but not for scholarly journals. Chapter 8 has presented one experiment in this regard. A science of management would develop more value in this relation. Specifically, academics, EMBA students, and alumni would organize under the joint purpose to build a discipline of management. In this endeavor, academics would consciously organize as co-builders of the new discipline. This new community and institution would have real stakes in and would take formal responsibility for management knowledge.Executives without formal ties to the management academy might enter into this collaboration as well.

Two upcoming occasions present opportunities for small-scale but structured organization: the seventy-fifth anniversary of Barnard's classic work in 2013 and the hundredth anniversary of Follett's in 2018. Manager-academics, executive-scholars, and executives could collaborate to write articles for a special issue of a top-tier management journal and/or to mount a special forum at the Academy of Management annual meeting. These efforts could lead to more structured and enduring collaboration and, over the long term, to entirely new institutions—the executive-scholar, the manager-academic, and management science.

IN CLOSING

Some attitudes and values bear significantly on the prospects for a science of management: that society is more given than made and more imposed upon us than created by us; that society cannot advance socially as it has materially; and that static conditions are preferable to dynamic conditions. Thus we meet "the morality that underlies enduring cooperation" (Barnard, 1968 [1938]: 284).

The first idea relates to the burden of personal responsibility. Follett's and Barnard's science makes the individual the locus of multiple responsibilities: for consciously creating new knowledge about value(s) creation; for governing oneself to do so, particularly by upholding the invisible values that are the source of this knowledge (for example, Barnard's credo and his subordination to it); and for contributing to the institutionalization of this knowledge by formalizing it in writing and submitting it to test. Few individuals will embrace all of this responsibility, the mere statement of which may be unsettling. However, for Follett and Barnard, management scientists and professionals are obligated to do so.

The second idea stems from the elite heritage and legacy of paideia/humanitas. Knowledge for governance was associated with an exclusive society that had interests in the status quo and used knowledge institutions, such as the college, to preserve it. To some extent, the association of class and knowledge still prevails; and the idea of a science of and for society may be met with cynicism. Here, Follett's insistence on interdependence merits emphasis, as does Barnard's observation that power is delegated upward. That is, entities do not accumulate and hold power independently; rather, their power derives from the quality of their relating to other entities with which they are interdependent and that in fact grant them "their" power. Management scientists and professionals recognize this basic principle: as entities separate from others and as others separate from them, these entities lose their ability to relate and ultimately, "their" power. Therefore, if cynicism about management science exists, then management science must factor this response into its own relating. After all, the management academy has spent the past half-century emphasizing its relationship to professional science, which itself has spent the past century solidifying its autonomy from "laymen" and experiential knowledge. So the counterbalancing move, towards integration and interdependency, is in order not just for management but also science.

Finally, concerning the third point, the idea of maintaining or pursuing a static order may have to do with a need for reliability and for minimizing stress. The concept of cooperation based on routine certainly has more intuitive resonance and common-sense appeal than that of cooperation based on constant disruption. However, this point also relates to the previous argument about personal responsibility. A static society enables one to identify and blame "the powers that be" for "the" status quo. Management science does not permit this. Instead, it would collapse the duality between the member and the society of which he is a part.

Modifying these ideas and values does not entail a change in attitude or perception but a change in relating oriented to human creativity in two different but complementary ways: recognizing objectively existing dynamic and interdependent conditions; and subjectively interpreting oneself as integral to these conditions. In this way, Follett's and Barnard's science follows the classical ideal to develop "as perfect and complete a human being as may be" (Ben-Rees, 1982: 23, citing Livingstone, 1945); but it modifies this ideal for the dynamic individual, institution (science, university, profession), and society. That is, classical paideia/humanitas served a narrow slice of humankind because its societies had slavery and excluded slaves and women from institutions associated with freedom (for example, "liberal studies," from "liber," meaning "free," as in the education of a free person and the education to make the person free). The research university, by linking basic science, applied science, and occupational training, effectively institutionalized individual opportunity. The downside, though, was that this knowledge-, wealth-, and status-creating institution would seem to do for us only what we can do for ourselves: to create the value(s) by which we cooperate to create more value(s). Follett and Barnard, and their science, would know this invisible and circular process the only way it can be known—intimately, interestedly, and habitually. Depending on how we relate to them, "they" will take us anywhere from a few steps to a very great distance.

Appendix

Form:	Classical college
Model:	Oxford and Cambridge
U.S. exemplar:	Harvard College
Purpose:	Initiation into governance
Proof:	Bachelor of Arts degree
Ownership:	Clergy and aristocracy
Core content:	Moral philosophy; sacred texts of Western civilization
Sources of content:	Theological doctrine; Latin and Greek
Methods:	Values inculcation; recitation; memorization
Relations:	Paternalistic
Values:	Preservation, transmission
Legitimacy crisis:	Cannot create new knowledge, wealth, status

TABLE 2. THE VOCATIONAL KNOWLEDGE TRADITION

Form:	Apprenticeship, proprietary school (Twentieth century: professional school)
Model:	Any combination of formal education and practice-- for example, the clinic
U.S. exemplar:	Harvard Law School
Purpose:	Authorize membership in an occupational community (Twentieth-century: membership in a professional community)
Proof:	Certificate; license to practice (Twentieth century: graduate degree)
Ownership:	The guild; the master (Twentieth century: university + professional community)
Core content:	Skills, technique (Twentieth century: basic and applied science)
Sources of content:	Masters (Twentieth century: professional scientists)
Method:	Learning by doing (Twentieth century: apply basic science to cases)
Relations:	Master-apprentice (Twentieth century: professor-student)
Value:	Know-how (Twentieth century: formal education)
Legitimacy basis:	Must show synergy with basic science

TABLE 3. THE SCIENTIFIC KNOWLEDGE TRADITION

Form:	Scientific school (Twentieth century: graduate division)
Model:	German university
U.S. exemplar:	University of Chicago
Purpose:	Create new knowledge
Proof:	Ph.D. (original thesis)
Ownership:	Amateur (Twentieth century: professional)
Core content:	Principles; theory
Sources of content:	Academic disciplines and thought schools
Methods:	Experimentation; discussion (the seminar)
Relations:	Community of scholars
Value:	Discovery (Twentieth century: professionalism)
Legitimacy basis:	Must show synergy with applied science

TABLE 4. THE SCHOOL OF OPPORTUNITY KNOWLEDGE TRADITION

Forms:	Learning clubs and societies; mentors; autodidacts
Model:	Anyone known for being self-educated
U.S. exemplars:	Anne Hutchinson's in-home Bible studies; Benjamin Franklin's Junto (Twentieth century: University Extension)
Purpose:	Learning by and for oneself
Proof:	No formal proof
Ownership:	No formal ownership
Core content:	Various
Sources of content:	Various
Methods:	Self-initiative and -application
Relations:	Peer
Value:	Do-it-yourself
Legitimacy crisis:	Considered inferior to formal education

TABLE 5. THE FOUR BUSINESS SCHOOL MODELS

The Collegiate School of Business (CSB)

Ideal type:	The Wharton School of Finance and Economy (1881)
Purpose:	Reform the classical college (see Table 1) and the gentleman
Content:	Applied social science/social reform and accounting
Sources:	Political economists and professionalizing accountants
Home:	The classical college
Tradition:	Classical (see Table 1)
Crisis:	Schism between political economists and accountants

The Vocational School of Business (VSB)

Ideal type:	NYU School of Commerce, Accounts, and Finance (1900)
Purpose:	Upgrade occupations to professions
Content:	Technical specialist
Sources:	Technical specialists
Home:	University Extension
Tradition:	Vocational (see Table 2)
Crisis:	Schism between academic and technical specialists

The Professional School of Business (PSB)

Ideal type:	Harvard Business School (founded 1908; achieved autonomy 1924)
Purpose:	Upgrade business school into professional school; make business a basic and applied science; remake the gentleman into the executive-statesman
Content:	Human relations; decision-making (cases)
Sources:	Cases; Harvard Law School (exemplar)
Home:	Professional (graduate) school
Tradition:	Classical and vocational (Tables 1 and 2)
Crisis:	Schism between HBS and the professionalizing academy

The Graduate School of Business (GSB)

Ideal type:	Carnegie Graduate School of Industrial Administration (GSIA) (1948)
Purpose:	Integrate the PSB with the mainstream academy; make the manager into a decision scientist
Content:	Scientific foundations outsourced from the academic disciplines
Sources:	The behavioral sciences and the quantitative sciences
Home:	The disciplines (graduate division of research university)
Tradition:	Scientific (Table 3)
Crisis:	Implies but cannot produce a science of management

References

Abbreviations used in the in-text references:

B	Box number (for archival references)
CIBP	Chester I. Barnard Papers, Private Collection of William B. Wolf
GLBP	George Leland Bach Papers
GSBA	Graduate School of Business Administration, University of Chicago
F	Folder number (for archival references)
HPJP	Henry Pratt Judson Papers (Judson Administration Papers)
RMHP	Robert M. Hutchins Papers (Hutchins Administration Papers)
SC-SUL	Special Collections, Stanford University Libraries
SCRC-UCL	Special Collections Research Center, University of Chicago Libraries
UEP	University Extension Papers, Special Collections Research Center, University of Chicago Libraries
UPA	University of Pennsylvania Archives

Manuscript and Archival Collections

George Leland Bach Papers (GLBP), Department of Special Collections, Stanford University Libraries (SC-SUL)

Chester I. Barnard Papers (CIBP), Private Collection of William B. Wolf

Department of Economics Records, Special Collections Research Center, University of Chicago Libraries (SCRC-UCL)

William Rainey Harper Papers, Harper Administration Papers, Special Collections Research Center, University of Chicago Libraries

Robert M. Hutchins Papers (RMHP), Hutchins Administration Papers, Special Collections Research Center, University of Chicago Libraries

Graduate School of Business Papers, Special Collections Research Center, University of Chicago Libraries

Henry Pratt Judson Papers (HPJP), Judson Administration Papers, Special Collections Research Center, University of Chicago Libraries

Leon Carroll Marshall Papers, Special Collections Research Center, University of Chicago Libraries

School of Commerce and Administration Papers, Special Collections Research Center, University of Chicago Libraries

School of Social Service Administration Records, Special Collections Research Center, University of Chicago Libraries

University Extension Papers (UEP), Special Collections Research Center, University of Chicago Libraries

General References

Aaronson, S. 1992. "Serving America's Business? Graduate Business Schools and American Business, 1945–60." *Business History* 34 (1): 160–82.

Abbott, A. 1999. *Department and Discipline: Chicago Sociology at One Hundred*. Chicago: University of Chicago Press.

Allmendinger, D. 1975. *Paupers and Scholars: The Transformation of Student Life in Nineteenth-Century New England*. New York: St. Martin's Press.

Artz, F. 1966. *The Development of Technical Education in France, 1500–1850*. Cambridge, MA: MIT Press.

Ashby, E. 1958. *Technology and the Academics: An Essay on Universities and the Scientific Revolution*. London: MacMillan.

Augier, M., and J. March. 2007. "The Pursuit of Relevance in Management Education." *California Management Review* 49 (3): 129–46.

Augier, M., J. March, and B. Sullivan. 2005. "Notes on the Evolution of a Research Community: Organization Studies in Anglophone North America, 1945–2000." *Organization Science* 16: 85–95.

Bailyn, B. 1986. "Foundations." In B. Bailyn, D. Fleming, O. Handlin, and S. Thernstrom, eds., *Glimpses of the Harvard Past*, pp. 1–18. Cambridge, MA: Harvard University Press.

———. 1960. *Education in the Forming of American Society*. New York: Vintage.

Bailyn, B., D. Fleming, O. Handlin, and S. Thernstrom, eds. *Glimpses of the Harvard Past*. Cambridge, MA: Harvard University Press.

Baldridge, J. 1971. *Power and Conflict in the University: Research in the Sociology of Complex Organizations*. New York: John Wiley.

Baltzell, E. 1979. *Puritan Boston and Quaker Philadelphia: Two Protestant Ethics and the Spirit of Class Authority and Leadership*. New York: Free Press.

Bannister, R. 1987. *Sociology and Scientism: The American Quest for Objectivity, 1880–1940*. Chapel Hill: University of North Carolina Press.

Barnard, C. 1968 [1938]. *The Functions of the Executive*. 2nd ed. Cambridge, MA: Harvard University Press.

———. 1958. "Elementary Conditions of Business Morals." *California Management Review* 1 (1): 1–13.

———. 1957. "A National Science Policy." *Scientific American* 197 (5): 45–49.

Barnard, C. 1948. *Organization and Management*. Cambridge, MA: Harvard University Press.

Bates, R. 1965. *Scientific Societies in the United States*. Cambridge, MA: MIT Press.

Ben-Rees, D. 1982. *Preparation for Crisis: Adult Education 1945–80*. Ormskirk, Lancashire, UK: G. W. & A. Hesketh.

Bennett, C. 1937. *History of Manual and Industrial Education, 1870 to 1917*. Peoria, IL: Manual Arts Press.

Bennis, W., and J. O'Toole. 2005. How Business Schools Lost Their Way. *Harvard Business Review* 83 (5): 96–104.

Bensel, R. 2000. *The Political Economy of American Industrialization, 1877–1900*. New York: Cambridge University Press.

Berk, G. 1994. *Alternative Tracks: The Constitution of American Industrial Order, 1865–1917*. Baltimore: Johns Hopkins University Press.

Biles, G., and A. Bolton. 1994. "Chester I. Barnard: President of the USO, 1942–1945." *International Journal of Public Administration* 17 (6): 1107–25.

Blair, K. 1980. *The Clubwoman as Feminist: True Womanhood Defined, 1868–1914*. New York: Holmes and Meier.

Bliss, W. 1898. *The Encyclopedia of Social Reform*. New York: Funk and Wagnalls.

Bliss, W., and R. Binder. 1908. *The New Encyclopedia of Social Reform*. New York: Funk and Wagnalls.

Boroff, D. 1961. *Campus U.S.A.: Portraits of American Colleges in Action*. New York: Harper & Bros.

Bowlker, K. 1912. "Address of the President." *Bulletin*, Women's Municipal League of Boston, March–April: 6–10.

———. 1909. "Address of the President." *An Account of the Women's Municipal League of Boston as Given at the First Public Meeting, January 20, 1909*, pp. 1–8. Boston: Southgate.

Breckinridge, S. 1933. *Women in the Twentieth Century: A Study of Their Political, Social, and Economic Activities*. New York: McGraw-Hill.

Brewer, J. 1942. *History of Vocational Guidance: Origins and Early Development*. New York: Harper & Bros.

Bridenbaugh, C., and J. Bridenbaugh. 1942. *Rebels and Gentlemen: Philadelphia in the Age of Franklin*. New York: Reynal & Hitchcock.

Broehl, W. 1999. *Tuck and Tucker: The Origin of the Graduate Business School*. Hanover, NH: University Press of New England.

Brubacher, J., and W. Rudy. 1997. *Higher Education in Transition: A History of American Colleges and Universities*. 4th ed. New Brunswick, NJ: Transaction.

Bryson, G. 1932a. "The Emergence of the Social Sciences from Moral Philosophy." *International Journal of Ethics* 42 (3): 304–23.

———. 1932b. "The Comparable Interests of the Old Moral Philosophy and the Modern Social Sciences." *Social Forces* 11 (1): 19–27.

Burke, C. 1982. *American Collegiate Populations: A Test of the Traditional View.* New York: New York University Press.

Cabot, E. 1909. "Report of the Department of Education." *An Account of the Women's Municipal League of Boston as Given at the First Public Meeting, January 20, 1909*, pp. 9–13. Boston: Southgate Press/T. W. Ripley Co.

Cabot, R. 1934. "Mary Parker Follett, an Appreciation." *Radcliffe Quarterly*, April: 80–82.

Calvert, M. 1967. *The Mechanical Engineer in America, 1830–1910: Professional Cultures in Conflict.* Baltimore: Johns Hopkins University Press.

Capon, N. 1996. *Planning the Development of Builders, Leaders and Managers for 21st-Century Business: Curriculum Review at Columbia Business School.* Boston: Kluwer.

Carson, M. 1990. *Settlement Folk: Social Thought and the American Settlement Movement, 1885–1930.* Chicago: University of Chicago Press.

Charlton, K. 1986. The Liberal-Vocational Debate in Early Modern England. In J. Burstyn, ed., *Preparation for Life? The Paradox of Education in the Late Twentieth Century*, pp. 1–18. Philadelphia, PA: Falmer Press.

Chernow, R. 1998. *Titan: The Life of John D. Rockefeller, Sr.* New York: Random House.

Cheyney, E. 1940. *History of the University of Pennsylvania, 1740–1940.* Philadelphia: University of Pennsylvania Press.

Chittenden, R. 1928. *History of the Sheffield Scientific School of Yale University, 1846–1922.* New Haven, CT: Yale University Press.

Church, R., and M. Sedlak. 1997. "The Antebellum College and Academy." In L. Goodchild and H. Wechsler, eds., *The History of Higher Education*, pp. 131–48. New York: Simon & Schuster.

Clark, W. 2006. *Academic Charisma and the Origins of the Research University.* Chicago: University of Chicago Press.

Cleeton, G. 1965. *The Story of Carnegie Tech, II: The Doherty Administration, 1936–1950.* Pittsburgh, PA: Carnegie Press, Carnegie Institute of Technology.

Clegg, S., ed. 2002. *Central Currents in Organization Studies I: Frameworks and Applications.* Thousand Oaks, CA: Sage.

Cleveland, Frederick. 1904. "Introduction." In C. Haskins, *Business Education and Accountancy*, pp. v–xii. New York: Harper & Bros.

Cohen, M. 2007. "*Administrative Behavior*: Laying the Foundations for Cyert and March." *Organization Science* 18 (3): 503–6.

Cordasco, F. 1973. *The Shaping of American Graduate Education: Daniel Coit Gilman and the Protean Ph.D.* Totowa, NJ: Rowman & Littlefield.

Cross, C. 1999. *Justin Smith Morrill: Father of the Land-Grant Colleges.* E. Lansing: Michigan State University Press.

Cruikshank, R. 1987. *A Delicate Experiment: The Harvard Business School, 1908–1945.* Boston, MA: Harvard University Press.

Cunningham, R. 1976. "Is History Past Politics? Herbert Baxter Adams as Precursor of the 'New History.'" *The History Teacher* 9 (2): 244–57.

Curley, J. 1957. *I'd Do It Again: A Record of All My Uproarious Years.* Englewood Cliffs, NJ: Prentice Hall.

Daft, R., and A. Lewin. 2008. "Rigor and Relevance in Organization Studies: Idea Migration and Academic Journal Evolution." *Organization Science* 19: 177–83.

Dalzell, R. 1987. *Enterprising Elite: The Boston Associates and the World They Made.* Cambridge: Harvard University Press.

Daniel, C. 1998. *MBA: The First Century.* Lewisburg, PA: Bucknell University Press.

Daniels, G. 1968. *American Science in the Age of Jackson.* New York: Columbia University Press.

Davis, A. 1984. *Spearheads for Reform: The Social Settlements and the Progressive Movement, 1890–1914.* New Brunswick, NJ: Rutgers University Press.

Donham, W. 1954. "The Case Method in College Teaching of Social Science." In P. McNair, ed., *The Case Method at the Harvard Business School*, pp. 244–55. New York: McGraw-Hill,

———. 1947. "An Experimental Course in Human Relations in Harvard College." *Journal of General Education* 2 (1): 8–16.

———. 1936. "Training for Leadership in a Democracy." *Harvard Business Review* 14 (3): 261–71.

———. 1932. *Business Looks at the Unforeseen.* New York: Whittlesey House/McGraw-Hill.

———. 1926. "Research in the Harvard Business School." *Proceedings of the Stanford Conference on Business Education*, pp. 109–20. Stanford, CA: Stanford University Press.

Drucker, P. 1995. "Introduction: Mary Parker Follett: Prophet of Management." In P. Graham, ed., *Mary Parker Follett—Prophet of Management: A Celebration of Writings from the 1920s.* Boston: Harvard Business School Press, 1-10.

Dyer, J. 1966. *Tulane: The Biography of a University, 1834–1965.* New York: Harper & Row.

Eliot, C. 1869 [1961]. "The New Education." In R. Hofstadter and W. Smith, eds., *American Higher Education: A Documentary History*, pp. 624–41. Chicago: University of Chicago.

Emmett, R. 2011. "Sharpening Tools in the Workshop: The Workshop System and the Chicago School's Success." In R. Van Horn, P. Mirowski, and T. Stapleford, eds., *Building Chicago Economics: New Perspectives on the History of America's Most Powerful Economics Program.* Cambridge, UK: Cambridge University Press.

Emmett, R., and L. Kovacek. 2008. "Was the Chicago School a Creative Community?" http://papers.ssrn.com/s013/papers.cfm?abstract_id=1710800.

Evans, S. 1993. "Women's History and Political Theory: Toward a Feminist Approach to Public Life." In N. Hewitt, and S. Lebsock, eds., *Visible Women: New Essays in American Activism*, pp. 119–40. Urbana: University of Illinois Press.

Everett, J. 1946. *Religion in Economics: A Study of John Bates Clark, Richard T. Ely, and Simon N. Patten.* Morningside Heights, NY: King's Crown Press.

Farrell, B. 1993. *Elite Families: Class and Power in Nineteenth-Century Boston*. Albany: State University of New York Press.

Farrell, M. 2001. *Collaborative Circles: Friendship Dynamics and Creative Work*. Chicago: University of Chicago Press.

Fayol, H. 1962 [1916]. *Administration Industrielle et Générale*. Paris: Dunod.

Feldheim, M. 2004. "Mary Parker Follett: Lost and Found—Again, and Again, and Again." *International Journal of Organization Theory and Behavior* 7 (3): 341–62.

Flexner, A. 1910. *Medical Education in the United States and Canada; a Report to the Carnegie Foundation for the Advancement of Teaching*. New York: Carnegie Foundation for the Advancement of Teaching.

Follett, M. 1924. *Creative Experience*. New York: Longmans, Green.

———. 1918. *The New State: Group Organization the Solution of Popular Government*. New York: Longmans, Green.

———. 1915. "The Boston Placement Bureau." *Bulletin*, Women's Municipal League of Boston, May: 14–28.

———. 1914a. "The Boston Placement Bureau." *Bulletin*, Women's Municipal League of Boston, March–April: 22–29.

———. 1914b. "Midnight Oil in the Schools." *Boston Evening Transcript*, April 1: 20.

———. 1913a. *Evening Centers—Aims and Duties of Managers and Leaders Therein*. Boston: City of Boston Printing Department.

———. 1913b. "Evening Recreation Centers." *The Playground*, January: 384–400.

———. 1913c. "Committee on Extended Use of School Buildings." *Bulletin*, Women's Municipal League of Boston, May: 8–13.

———. 1913d. "The Aims of Adult Recreation." *The Playground*, October: 261–68.

———. 1912a. "Report of the East Boston Centre." *Bulletin*, Women's Municipal League of Boston, May: 5–12.

———. 1912b. "The Placement Bureau." *Bulletin*, Women's Municipal League of Boston, December: 7–18.

———. 1911. "Report of Committee on Extended Use of School Buildings." *Bulletin*, Women's Municipal League of Boston, March: 18–20.

———. 1909. "Report on Schoolhouses as Social Centres." *An Account of the Women's Municipal League of Boston as Given at the First Public Meeting, January 20, 1909*, pp. 14–16. Boston: Southgate.

———. 1896. *The Speaker of the House of Representatives*. New York: Longmans, Green.

Fox, Daniel. 1967. *Discovery of Abundance: Simon N. Patten and the Transformation of Social Theory*. Ithaca, NY: Published for the American Historical Association by Cornell University Press.

Fox, E., and L. Urwick, eds. 1973. *Dynamic Administration: The Collected Papers of Mary Parker Follett*. New York: Hippocrene.

Franklin, F. 1910. *The Life of Daniel Coit Gilman*. New York: Dodd, Mead.

Furner, M. 1975. *Advocacy and Objectivity: A Crisis in the Professionalization of American Social Science, 1865–1905.* Lexington, KY: University Press of Kentucky.

Gale, R. 1999. *The Divided Self of William James.* New York: Cambridge University Press.

Gambrell, M. 1937. *Ministerial Training in Eighteenth-Century New England.* New York: Columbia University Press.

Gavetti, G., D. Levinthal, and W. Ocasio. 2007. "Neo-Carnegie: The Carnegie School's Past, Present, and Reconstructing for the Future." *Organization Science* 18, 3: 523–36.

Geiger, R. 2000. The Crisis of the Old Order: Colleges in the 1890s. In R. Geiger, ed., *The American College in the Nineteenth Century*, pp. 264–76. Nashville, TN: Vanderbilt University Press.

———. 1986. *To Advance Knowledge: The Growth of American Research Universities, 1900–1940.* New York: Oxford University Press.

Geiger, R., with J. Bubolz. 2000. College as It Was in the Mid-Nineteenth Century. In R. Geiger, ed., *The American College in the Nineteenth Century*, pp. 80–91. Nashville, TN: Vanderbilt University Press.

Gide, C., and C. Rist. 1948. *A History of Economic Doctrines from the Time of the Physiocrats to the Present Day.* Trans. Ernest Row. Boston: D. C. Heath.

Gillmor, C. 2004. *Fred Terman at Stanford: Building a Discipline, a University, and Silicon Valley.* Stanford, CA: Stanford University Press.

Gitlow, A. 1995. *New York University's Stern School of Business: A Centennial Retrospective.* New York: New York University Press.

Gleeson, R. 1997. "Stalemate at Stanford, 1945–1958: The Long Prelude to the New Look at Stanford." *Selections* 13 (3): 6–23.

Gleeson, R., and S. Schlossman. 1995. "George Leland Bach and the Rebirth of Graduate Management Education in the United States, 1945–1975." *Selections* 11 (3): 8–38.

———. 1992. "The Many Faces of the New Look: The University of Virginia, Carnegie Tech, and the Reform of American Management Education in the Postwar Era." *Selections* 8 (3): 9–27.

Gleeson, R., S. Schlossman, and D. Allen, D. 1993. "Uncertain Ventures: The Origins of Graduate Management Education at Harvard and Stanford, 1908–1939." *Selections* 9 (3): 9–32.

Gordon, R., and J. Howell. 1959. *Higher Education for Business.* New York: Columbia University Press.

Gorrell, D. 1988. *The Age of Social Responsibility: The Social Gospel in the Progressive Era, 1900–1920.* Macon, GA: Mercer University Press.

Graham, P. 1995. *Mary Parker Follett—Prophet of Management: A Celebration of Writings from the 1920s.* Boston, MA: Harvard Business School Press.

Greek, C. 1992. *Religious Roots of American Sociology.* New York: Garland.

Guralnick, S. 1975. *Science and the Ante-Bellum American College.* Philadelphia, PA: American Philosophical Society.

Hagstrom, W. 1965. *The Scientific Community.* New York: Basic Books.

Hall, P. 2000. "Noah Porter Writ Large? Reflections on the Modernization of

American Higher Education and Its Critics, 1866–1916. In R. Geiger, ed., *The American College in the Nineteenth Century,* pp. 196–220.

Hapgood, H. 1906. College Men in Business. *Annals of the American Academy of Political and Social Science* 28 (1): 58–69.

Handlin, O. 1973. *The Uprooted: The Epic Story of the Great Migrations That Made the American People.* Boston: Little, Brown.

Hart, A. 1918 [1903]. *Actual Government.* 4th ed. New York: Longmans, Green.

———. 1896. "Introduction." In M. Follett, *The Speaker of the House of Representatives,* pp. xi–xvi. New York: Longmans, Green.

———. 1888. "Preparation for Citizenship at Harvard College." *Education* 8: 630–38.

Hartz, L. 1948. *Economic Policy and Democratic Thought: Pennsylvania, 1776–1860.* Cambridge, MA: Harvard University Press.

Haskins, C. 1904. *Business Education and Accountancy.* New York: Harper & Bros.

Hatchuel, A. 2009. "A Foundationalist Perspective for Management Research: A European Trend and Experience." *Management Decision* 47 (9): 1458–75.

———. 2005. "Towards an Epistemology of Collective Action: Management Research as a Responsive and Actionable Discipline." *European Management Review* 2: 36–47.

———. 2000. "Quel horizon pour les sciences de gestion? Vers une théorie de l'action collective." In A. David, A. Hatchuel, and R. Laufer, eds., *Les Nouvelles Fondations des Sciences de Gestion: Eléments d'Epistémologie de la Recherche en Management,* pp. 7–43. Paris: Librairie Vuibert.

Hawkins, H. 1992. *Banding Together: The Rise of National Associations in American Higher Education, 1887–1950.* Baltimore: Johns Hopkins University Press.

———. 1979. "University Identity: The Teaching and Research Functions." In A. Oleson and J. Voss, eds. *The Organization of Knowledge in Modern America, 1860–1920,* pp. 285–312. Baltimore: Johns Hopkins University Press.

Hawley, R. 1912. "Director's Report." *Bulletin,* Women's Municipal League of Boston, May: 13–24.

Haynes, B., and H. Jackson. 1935. *A History of Business Education in the United States.* Cincinnati, OH: South-Western Publishing.

Hefferlin, J. 1969. *Dynamics of Academic Reform.* San Francisco: Jossey-Bass.

Herbst, J. 1982. "Diversification in American Higher Education." In K. Jarausch, ed., *The Transformation of Higher Learning, 1860–1930:* 196–206. Stuttgart: Klett-Cotta.

———. 1962. "Liberal Education and the Graduate Schools: An Historical View of College Reform." *Journal of Education Quarterly* 11 (4): 244–58.

Higham, J. 1979. "The Matrix of Specialization." In A. Oleson and J. Voss, J., eds., *The Organization of Knowledge in Modern America, 1860–1920,* pp. 3–18. Baltimore: Johns Hopkins University Press.

Hocking, E. 1916. "The Holt-Freudian Ethics and the Ethics of Royce." *Philosophical Review* 25: 479–506.

Hofstadter, R. 1955. *The Age of Reform: From Bryan to F.D.R.* New York: Vintage.

Hofstadter, R., and Hardy, D. 1952. *The Development and Scope of Higher Education in the United States.* New York: Columbia University Press.

Hofstadter, R., and W. Metzger. 1955. *The Development of Academic Freedom in the United States.* New York: Columbia University Press.

Hofstadter, R., and W. Smith. 1961. *American Higher Education: A Documentary History.* Chicago: University of Chicago Press.

Holt, E. 1915. *The Freudian Wish and Its Place in Ethics.* New York: Henry Holt.

Hoskin, K. 2006. "Management as Product of the European Knowledge Tradition: A Modern Form of Ancient Paideia?" In P. Gagliardi and B. Czarniawska, eds., *Management Education and the Humanities,* pp. 159–73. Cheltenham, U.K.: Edward Elgar.

Hotchkiss, W. 1941. *Northwestern University School of Commerce: The Pioneer Decade.* Chicago: Northwestern University.

———. 1913. "The Northwestern University School of Commerce." *Journal of Political Economy* 21: 196–208.

Jaeger, W. 1963a [1944]. *Paideia: The Ideals of Greek Culture.* Vol. III: *The Conflict of Cultural Ideals in the Age of Plato.* Trans. G. Highet. New York: Oxford University Press.

———. 1963b [1943]. *Paideia: The Ideals of Greek Culture.* Vol. II: *In Search of the Divine Centre.* Trans. G. Highet. New York: Oxford University Press.

———. 1962 [1939]. *Paideia: The Ideals of Greek Culture.* Vol. I: *Archaic Greece, the Mind of Athens.* Trans. G. Highet. New York: Oxford University Press.

Jaher, F. 1982. *The Urban Establishment: Upper Strata in Boston.* Urbana: University of Illinois Press.

James, E. 1910. *The Origin of the Land Grant Act of 1862.* Urbana: University of Illinois.

James, H. 1930. *Charles W. Eliot: President of Harvard University, 1869–1909.* Vol. 1. Boston: Houghton Mifflin.

Johnson, W. 1978. *Schooled Lawyers: A Study in the Clash of Professional Cultures.* New York: New York University Press.

Kanigel, R. 1997. *Frederick Winslow Taylor and the Enigma of Efficiency.* New York: Viking.

Kanter, R. 1995. "Preface." In P. Graham, ed., *Mary Parker Follett—Prophet of Management: A Celebration of Writings from the 1920s,* pp. xiii–xix. Boston: Harvard Business School Press.

Karsten, H. 1995. "'It's Like Everyone Working around the Same Desk': Organisational Readings of Lotus Notes." *Scandinavian Journal of Information Systems* 7 (1): 3–32.

Kaufman, M. 1976. *American Medical Education: The Formative Years, 1765–1910.* Westport, CT: Greenwood Press.

Kett, J. 1994. *The Pursuit of Knowledge under Difficulties: From Self-Improvement to Adult Education in America, 1750–1990.* Stanford, CA: Stanford University Press.

———. 1968. *The Formation of the American Medical Profession: The Role of Institutions, 1780–1860.* New Haven, CT: Yale University Press.

Khurana, R. 2007. *From Higher Aims to Hired Hands: The Social Transformation of American Business Schools and the Unfulfilled Promise of Management as a Profession.* Princeton, NJ: Princeton University Press.

Kimball, B. 1996. *Orators and Philosophers: A History of the Idea of Liberal Education.* New York: College Entrance Examination Board.

Klausner, S., and V. Lidz, eds. 1986. *The Nationalization of the Social Sciences.* Philadelphia: University of Pennsylvania Press.

Kohler, R. 1996. "The Ph.D. Machine: Building on the Collegiate Base." In R. Numbers and C. Rosenberg, eds., *The Scientific Enterprise in America: Readings from Isis,* pp. 98–122. Chicago: University of Chicago Press.

Kohlstedt, S. 1976. *The Formation of the American Scientific Community: The American Association for the Advancement of Science, 1848–60.* Urbana: University of Illinois Press.

Lane, W. 1912. "Education and Work: A Twilight Zone." *The Survey* 29 (5): 225–28.

LaPiana, W. 1994. *Logic and Experience: The Origin of Modern American Legal Education.* New York: Oxford University Press.

Lee, M. 2010. "The Role of the YMCA in the Origins of U.S. Nonprofit Management Education." *Nonprofit Management and Leadership* 20 (3): 277–93.

Leslie, W. 1992. *Gentlemen and Scholars: College and Community in the "Age of the University," 1865–1917.* University Park: Pennsylvania State University Press.

Levine, D. 1986. *The American College and the Culture of Aspiration, 1915–1940.* Ithaca, NY: Cornell University Press.

Linde, C. 1993. *Life Stories: The Creation of Coherence.* New York: Oxford University Press.

Locke, R. 1984. *The End of Practical Man: Entrepreneurship and Higher Education in Germany, France and Great Britain, 1880–1940.* Greenwich, CT: JAI Press.

Lockwood, J. 1938. "Early University Education in Accountancy." *Accounting Review* 13 (2): 131–144.

Lyon, L. 1921. "The Corporation School and Its Place in a Scheme of Business Education." *Journal of Political Economy* 29: 721–45.

Mann, C. 1918. *A Study of Engineering Education.* Boston: Merrymount Press.

March, J. 2008. *Explorations in Organizations.* Part V: 413–53. Stanford, CA: Stanford University Press.

March, J., and H. Simon. 1958. *Organizations.* New York: Wiley.

Marshall, L. 1928. *The Collegiate School of Business: Its Status at the Close of the First Quarter of the Twentieth Century.* Chicago: University of Chicago Press.

———. 1913. "The College of Commerce and Administration of the University of Chicago." *Journal of Political Economy* 21 (2): 97–110.

Martin, T. 1987. *The Sound of Our Own Voices: Women's Study Clubs, 1860–1910.* Boston: Beacon Press.

Massie, J. 1965. "Management Theory." In J. March, ed., *Handbook of Organizations*, pp. 387–422.Chicago: Rand McNally.

Mayo, E. 1933. *The Human Problems of an Industrial Civilization*. New York: Macmillan.

———. 1924. "The Basis of Industrial Psychology." *Bulletin of the Taylor Society* 9: 249–59.

McCrea, R. 1913. "The Work of the Wharton School of Finance and Commerce." *Journal of Political Economy* 21 (2): 111–16.

McGivern, J. 1960. *First Hundred Years of Engineering Education in the United States, 1807–1907*. Spokane, WA: Gonzaga University Press.

McGrane, R. 1963. *The University of Cincinnati: A Success Story in Urban Higher Education*. New York: Harper & Row.

McGrath, E. 1959a. *Liberal Education in the Professions*. New York: Bureau of Publications, Teachers College, Columbia University.

———. 1959b. *The Graduate School and the Decline of Liberal Education*. New York: Bureau of Publications, Teachers College, Columbia University.

———. 1936. "The Control of Higher Education in America." *The Educational Record* 18 (2): 259–72.

McGrath, R. 2007. "No Longer a Stepchild: How the Management Field Can Come into Its Own." *Academy of Management Journal* 50 (6): 1365–78.

McMahon, A., and S. Morris. 1977. *Technology in Industrial America: The Committee on Science and the Arts of the Franklin Institute, 1824–1900*. Wilmington, DE: Scholarly Resources.

Metcalf, H., and L. Urwick, eds. 1940. *Dynamic Administration: The Collected Papers of Mary Parker Follett*. New York: Harper & Bros.

Meyer, D. 1972. *The Instructed Conscience: The Shaping of the American National Ethic*. Philadelphia: University of Pennsylvania Press.

Mintzberg, H. 2004. *Managers Not MBAs: A Hard Look at the Soft Practice of Managing and Management Development*. San Francisco: Berrett-Koehler.

Moore, K. 2008. *Disrupting Science: Social Movements, American Scientists, and the Politics of the Military, 1945–1975*. Princeton, NJ: Princeton University Press.

Morgan, J. 1969. "The Development of Sociology and the Social Gospel in America." *Sociological Analysis* 30 (1): 42–53.

Morison, S. 1930. *The Development of Harvard University since the Inauguration of President Eliot, 1869–1929*. Cambridge, MA: Harvard University Press.

Muncy, R. 1991. *Creating a Female Dominion in American Reform, 1890–1935*. New York: Oxford University Press.

Nelson, D., and S. Campbell. 1972. "Taylorism versus Welfare Work in American Industry: H. L. Gantt and the Bancrofts." *Business History Review* 46 (1): 1–16.

New York University. 1956. *The New York University Self-Study*. New York: New York University Press.

New York University. 1900. "Outline of Studies." New York University School of Commerce, Accounts and Finance, 1900-1901.

Nohria, N. 1995. "Mary Parker Follett's View on Power, the Giving of Orders, and Authority: An Alternative to Hierarchy or a Utopian Ideology?" In P. Graham, ed., *Mary Parker Follett—Prophet of Management: A Celebration of Writings from the 1920s*, pp. 154–62. Boston: Harvard Business School Press.

Oberschall, A. 1972. The Institutionalization of American Sociology. In A. Oberschall, ed., *The Establishment of Empirical Sociology: Studies in Continuity, Discontinuity, and Institutionalization*, pp. 187–251. New York: Harper & Row.

O'Connor, E. 2008. "Explorations in Organizations through Literature: An Introductory Essay." In J. March, ed., *Explorations in Organizations*, pp. 413–33. Stanford, CA: Stanford University Press.

———. 2004. "Storytelling to Be Real: Narrative, Legitimacy Building, and Venturing." In D. Hjorth and C. Steyaert, eds., *Narrative and Discursive Approaches to Entrepreneurship*, pp. 105–24.London: Edward Elgar.

———. 2002. "Storied Business: Typology, Intertextuality, and Traffic in Entrepreneurial Narrative." *Journal of Business Communication* 39 (1): 36–54.

———. 2000. "The Embedded Narrative as a Construct for Studying Change." *Journal of Applied Behavioral Science* 36 (2): 174–92.

———. 1999a. "The Politics of Management Thought: A Case Study of the Harvard Business School and the Human Relations School." *Academy of Management Review* 24 (1): 117–31.

———. 1999b. "Minding the Workers: The Meaning of 'Human' and 'Human Relations' in Elton Mayo." *Organization* 6 (2): 223–46.

———. 1996. "Lines of Authority: Readings of Foundational Texts on the Profession of Management." *Journal of Management History* 2 (3): 26-49.

———. 1995. "Undisciplining Organizational Studies: A Conversation across Domains, Methodologies and Beliefs." With M.J. Hatch, H. White, and M. Zald. *Journal of Management Inquiry* 4 (2): 26-49.

O'Connor, M. 1994. *Origins of Academic Economics in the United States.* New York: Columbia University Press.

O'Connor, T. 1984. *Bibles, Brahmins, and Bosses: A Short History of Boston.* Boston: Trustees of the Public Library of the City of Boston.

Orlikowski, W. 2000. "Using Technology and Constituting Structures: A Practice Lens for Studying Technology in Organizations." *Organization Science* 11 (4): 404–28.

Parker, G. 1973. *Mind Cure in New England: From the Civil War to World War I.* Hanover, NH: University Press of New England.

Patton, C. 1940. *The Battle for Municipal Reform: Mobilization and Attack, 1875 to 1900.* Washington, D.C.: American Council on Public Affairs.

Person, H. 1913. "The Amos Tuck School of Dartmouth College." *Journal of Political Economy* 21 (2): 117–26.

Peterson, G. 1964. *The New England College in the Age of the University.* Amherst, MA: Amherst College Press.

Pfeffer, J., and C. Fong. 2004. "The Business School 'Business': Some Lessons from the U.S. Experience." *Journal of Management Studies* 41 (8): 1501–20.

Pfeffer, J., and C. Fong. 2002. "The End of Business Schools? Less Success Than Meets the Eye." *Academy of Management Learning and Education* 1 (1): 78–95.

Phillips, C. 1964. *Experience with Undergraduate Business Program*. New Orleans: Tulane University School of Business Administration.

Pollard, J. 1952. *History of Ohio State University: The Story of Its First Seventy-Five Years, 1873–1948*. Columbus: Ohio State University Press.

Portman, D. 1978. *The Universities and the Public: A History of Higher Adult Education in the United States*. Chicago: Nelson-Hall.

Potts, D. 1965. "Social Ethics at Harvard, 1881–1931: A Study in Academic Activism." In P. Buck, ed., *Social Sciences at Harvard, 1860–1920: From Inculcation to the Open Mind*, pp. 91–128. Cambridge, MA: Harvard University Press.

Ramsey, B. 1993. *Submitting to Freedom: The Religious Vision of William James*. New York: Oxford University Press.

Rawles, W. 1921. "Corporation Training Schools for College Men." *Journal of Political Economy* 29: 697–709.

Reeves, F., C. Thompson, A. Klein, and J. Russell. 1933. *University Extension Services*. Chicago: University of Chicago Press.

Reid, K. 1981. *From Character Building to Social Treatment: The History of the Use of Groups in Social Work*. Westport, CT: Greenwood Press.

Rezneck, S. 1968. *Education for a Technological Society: A Sesquicentennial History of Rensselaer Polytechnic Institute*. Troy, NY: Rensselaer Polytechnic Institute.

Rogers, H. 1912. "The Placement Bureau." *Bulletin*, Women's Municipal League of Boston, December: 18–37.

Roosevelt, T. 1896. "Review of The Speaker of the House of Representatives." *American Historical Review* 2: 176–78.

Ross, D. 1991. *The Origins of American Social Science*. New York: Cambridge University Press.

———. 1979. "The Development of the Social Sciences." In A. Oleson and J. Voss, eds., *The Organization of Knowledge in Modern America, 1860–1920*, pp. 107–38. Baltimore: Johns Hopkins University Press.

Rothstein, W. 1987. *American Medical Schools and the Practice of Medicine: A History*. New York: Oxford University Press.

Rudolph, F. 1981. *Curriculum: A History of the American Undergraduate Course of Study since 1636*. San Francisco: Jossey-Bass.

Ruml, F. 1928. "The Formative Period of Higher Commercial Education in American Universities." In L. Marshall, ed., *The Collegiate School of Business: Its Status at the Close of the First Quarter of the Twentieth Century*, pp. 45–65. Chicago: University of Chicago Press.

Ryan, W. 1939. *Studies in Early Graduate Education: The Johns Hopkins, Clark University, The University of Chicago*. New York: Carnegie Foundation for the Advancement of Teaching.

Sack, S. 1963. *History of Higher Education in Pennsylvania*. Harrisburg: Pennsylvania Historical and Museum Commission.

Sass, S. 1982. *The Pragmatic Imagination: A History of the Wharton School, 1881–1981*. Philadelphia: University of Pennsylvania Press.

Schafer, A. 2000. *American Progressives and German Social Reform, 1875–1920: Social Ethics, Moral Control, and the Regulatory State in a Transatlantic Context*. Stuttgart: F. Steiner Verlag.

Schlesinger, A. 1933. *The Rise of the City, 1878–1898*. New York: Macmillan.

Schlossman, S., and M. Sedlak. 1988. *The Age of Reform in American Management Education*. Los Angeles: Graduate Management Admissions Council.

———. 1985. "The Age of Autonomy in American Management Education." *Selections* 1 (3): 16–26.

Schlossman, S., M. Sedlak, and H. Wechsler. 1998. "The 'New Look:' The Ford Foundation and the Revolution in Business Education." *Selections* 14 (3): 8–29.

———. 1989a. "Conflict, Consensus, and the Modernization of Graduate Business Education: The Case of the University of Washington, 1945–1980. Part I: The Emergence of Reform Sentiment, 1945–1963." *Selections* 5: 1–11.

———. 1989b. "Conflict, Consensus, and the Modernization of Graduate Business Education: The Case of the University of Washington, 1945–1980. Part II: Stabilizing Reform and Maintaining Consensus, 1963–1980." *Selections* 6: 1–10.

Schneewind, J. 1977. *Sidgwick's Ethics and Victorian Moral Philosophy*. Oxford, UK: Oxford University Press.

Schultz, B. 2004. *Henry Sidgwick: Eye of the Universe, an Intellectual Biography*. Cambridge, UK: Cambridge University Press.

Scott, A. 1984. *Making the Invisible Woman Visible*. Urbana: University of Illinois Press.

Scott, D. 1978. *From Office to Profession: The New England Ministry, 1750–1850*. Philadelphia: University of Pennsylvania Press.

Scott, J. 1991. *Natural Allies: Women's Associations in American History*. Urbana: University of Illinois Press.

Scott, W. 1913. "Training for Business at the University of Wisconsin." *Journal of Political Economy* 21 (2): 127–35.

Sedlak, M., and S. Schlossman. 1991. "The Case Method and Business Education at Northwestern University, 1906–1971." *Selections* 7 (3): 14–38.

Sedlak, M., and H. Williamson. 1983. *The Evolution of Management Education: A History of the Northwestern University J. L. Kellogg Graduate School of Management, 1908–1983*. Urbana: University of Illinois Press.

Selden, W. 1960. *Accreditation: A Struggle over Standards in Higher Education*. New York: Harper & Bros.

Seybolt, R. 1971. *The Evening School in Colonial America*. New York: Arno Press.

Sharer, W. 2004. *Vote and Voice: Women's Organizations and Political Literacy, 1915–1930*. Carbondale: Southern Illinois University Press.

Shils, E. 1981. *Tradition*. Chicago: University of Chicago Press.

———. 1978. "The Order of Learning in the United States from 1865 to 1920: The Ascendancy of the Universities." *Minerva* 16 (1): 159–95.

Simon, H. 1995. "Foreword: Papers in Honor of Chester I. Barnard." *International Journal of Public Administration* 17 (6): 1021–31.

———. 1991. *Models of My Life*. New York: Basic Books.

———. 1979. "Rational Decision Making in Business Organizations." *American Economic Review* 69 (4): 493–513.

———. 1947. *Administrative Behavior: A Study of Decision-Making Processes in Administrative Organization*. New York: Macmillan.

———. 1946. "The Proverbs of Administration." *Public Administration Review* 6 (1): 53–67.

Simon, L. 1998. *Genuine Reality: A Life of William James*. New York: Harcourt Brace.

Sinclair, B. 1974. *Philadelphia's Philosopher Mechanics: A History of the Franklin Institute*. Baltimore: Johns Hopkins University Press.

Sklar, K. 1995. *Florence Kelley and the Nation's Work: The Rise of Women's Political Culture, 1830–1900*. New Haven, CT: Yale University Press.

———. 1993. "The Historical Foundations of Women's Power in the Creation of the American Welfare State, 1830–1930." In S. Koven and S. Michel, eds., *Mothers of a New World: Maternalist Politics and the Origins of Welfare States*, pp. 43–93. New York: Routledge.

Skocpol, T. 1992. *Protecting Soldiers and Mothers: The Political Origins of Social Policy in the United States*. Cambridge, MA: Belknap.

Smith, J. 1950. *Royce's Social Infinite: The Community of Interpretation*. New York: Liberal Arts Press.

Snow, L. 1907. *The College Curriculum in the United States*. New York: Columbia University Press.

Snyder, E. 1985. "The Chautauqua Movement in Popular Culture: A Sociological Analysis." *Journal of American Culture* 8 (3): 79–90.

Solberg, W. 1968. *The University of Illinois, 1867–1894: An Intellectual and Cultural History*. Urbana: University of Illinois Press.

Solomon, B. 1952. "The Intellectual Background of the Immigration Restriction Movement in New England." *New England Quarterly* 25 (1): 47–59.

Starkey, K., and S. Tempest. 2009. "The Winter of Our Discontent—The Design Challenge for Business Schools." *Academy of Management Learning and Education* 8: 576–86.

Stettner, E. 1993. *Shaping Modern Liberalism: Herbert Croly and Progressive Thought*. Lawrence: University Press of Kansas.

Stevens, R. 1983. *Law School: Legal Education in America from the 1850s to the 1980s*. Chapel Hill: University of North Carolina Press.

Stewart, F. 1950. *A Half-Century of Municipal Reform: The History of the National Municipal League*. Berkeley: University of California Press.

Storr, R. 1966. *Harper's University: The Beginnings: A History of the University of Chicago*. Chicago: University of Chicago Press.

———. 1953. *The Beginnings of Graduate Education in America*. Chicago: University of Chicago Press.

Stratton, J., and L. Mannix. 2005. *Mind and Hand: The Birth of MIT*. Cambridge, MA: MIT Press.

Story, R. 1980. *The Forging of an Aristocracy: Harvard and the Boston Upper Class, 1800–1870*. Middletown, CT: Wesleyan University Press.

Tager, J. 1985a. "Massachusetts and the Age of Economic Revolution." In J. Tager, ed., *Massachusetts in the Gilded Age: Selected Essays*, pp. 3–30. Amherst: University of Massachusetts Press.

———. 1985b. "Social Change and Social Mobility: Introduction." In J. Tager, ed., *Massachusetts in the Gilded Age: Selected Essays*, pp. 125–31. Amherst: University of Massachusetts Press.

Tarbell, A. 1937. *The Story of Carnegie Tech: Being a History of Carnegie Institute of Technology from 1900 to 1935*. Pittsburgh, PA: Carnegie Institute of Technology.

Taylor, F. 1911. *The Principles of Scientific Management*. New York: Harper & Row.

Tonn, J. 2003. *Mary P. Follett: Creating Democracy, Transforming Management*. New Haven, CT: Yale University Press.

Townsend, K. 1996. *Manhood at Harvard: William James and Others*. New York: W. W. Norton.

Tucker, W. 1919. *My Generation: An Autobiographical Interpretation*. Boston: Houghton Mifflin.

Turner, J., and P. Bernard. 2000. "The German Model and the Graduate School." In R. Geiger, ed., *The American College in the Nineteenth Century*, pp. 221–41. Nashville, TN: Vanderbilt University Press.

Tyler, A. 1944. *Freedom's Ferment: Phases of American Social History to 1860*. Minneapolis: University of Minnesota Press.

United States Adjutant-General's Office. 1919. *The Personnel System of the United States Army*. Washington, DC: U.S. Adjutant General's Office.

Urwick, L., ed. 1987 [1949]. *Freedom and Co-Ordination: Lectures in Business Organisation by Mary Parker Follett*. New York: Garland.

Van de Ven, A. 2007. *Engaged Scholarship: A Guide for Organizational and Social Research*. New York: Oxford University Press.

Van Metre, T. 1954. *A History of the Graduate School of Business, Columbia University*. New York: Columbia University Press.

Veblen, T. 1965 [1918]. *The Higher Learning in America*. New York: Viking Press.

Veysey, L. 1965. *The Emergence of the American University*. Chicago: University of Chicago Press.

Walter-Busch, E. 1985. "Chester Barnard and the Human Relations Approach at Harvard Business School." *Proceedings of the Academy of Management*, pp. 139–143. Briarcliff Manor, NY: Academy of Management.

Warren, C. 1908. *History of the Harvard Law School and of Early Legal Conditions in America*. Vol. II. New York: Lewis Publishing House.

Wayland, F. 1859 [1837]. *The Elements of Political Economy*. Boston: Gould and Lincoln.

Welter, R. 1962. *Popular Education and Democratic Thought in America*. New York: Columbia University Press.

Wert, R. 1952. "The Impact of Three Nineteenth-Century Reorganizations upon Harvard University." Ph.D. dissertation, Graduate School of Education, Stanford University.

Wharton, J. 1881. "Agreement between Joseph Wharton and the Trustees of the University of Pennsylvania," June 22, 1881 (1923 reprint, Catalog No. UPP 15.3), University of Pennsylvania Archives (UPA), Philadelphia, PA.

Wheeler, D. 1943. "Addenda." In D. Worrell, *The Women's Municipal League of Boston: A History of Thirty-Five Years of Civic Endeavor*, pp. 205–6. Boston: Women's Municipal League Committees, Inc.

Wildman, J. 1926. "Early Instruction in Accounting." *Accounting Review* 1 (1): 105–7.

Williams, D. 1941. *The Andover Liberals: A Study in American Theology.* Morningside Heights, NY: King's Crown Press.

Williams, R. 1991. *The Origins of Federal Support for Higher Education: George W. Atherton and the Land-Grant College Movement.* University Park: Pennsylvania State University Press.

Wilson, R. 1968. *In Quest of Community: Social Philosophy in the United States, 1860–1920.* New York: John Wiley.

Wolf, W. 1995a. "The Significance of Decisive Behavior in Social Action: Notes on the Nature of Decision." *Journal of Management History* 1 (4): 28–88.

———. 1995b. "The Barnard-Simon Connection." *Journal of Management History* 1 (4): 88–100. N.B.: This article is missing a key document: "Chester I. Barnard, Memorandum of Detailed Observations on 'Administrative Behavior' by Professor Simon." The document, dated June 24, 1945, is held in the Simon collection, Carnegie Mellon University Archives.

———. 1974. *The Basic Barnard: An Introduction to Chester I. Barnard and His Theories of Organization and Management.* Ithaca, NY: New York State School of Industrial and Labor Relations, Cornell University.

———. 1973. *Conversations with Chester I. Barnard.* Ithaca, NY: ILR Press.

Wolf, W., and H. Iino, eds. 1986. *Philosophy for Managers: Selected Papers of Chester I. Barnard.* Ithaca, NY: ILR Press.

Woods, L. 1884. *History of the Andover Theological Seminary.* Boston: James R. Osgood.

Worrell, D. 1943. *The Women's Municipal League of Boston: A History of Thirty-Five Years of Civic Endeavor.* Boston: Women's Municipal League Committees.

Wrege, C. 1979. "Antecedents of Organizational Behavior: Dr. E. E. Southard and Mary Jarrett, the 'Mental Hygiene of Industry': 1913–1920." In *Proceedings of the Academy of Management*, pp. 17–21. Briarcliff Manor, NY: Academy of Management.

Wren, D. 2004. *The Evolution of Management Thought.* 5th ed. New York: Wiley.

Yates, W. 1992. *Lehigh University: A History of Education in Engineering, Business, and the Human Condition.* Bethlehem, PA: Lehigh University Press.

Index